COUPLE

SKILLS

COUPLE

SKILLS

Making Your Relationship Work

Matthew McKay, Ph.D., Patrick Fanning,
and Kim Paleg, Ph.D.

BARNES
&NOBLE
BOOKS
NEW YORK

Publisher's Note

This publication is designed to provide accurate and author-
itative information in regard to the subject matter covered.
It is sold with the understanding that the publisher is not
engaged in rendering psychological, financial, legal, or other
professional services. If expert assistance or counseling is
needed, the services of a competent professional should
be sought.

Contents

Introduction

Being in an intimate relationship can be one of the keenest human joys and one of the greatest sources of pain. Love begins with so much hope: the dream of one day feeling known, accepted to the core; the dream of belonging, of protecting and being safe; the dream of deep passion; the dream of a lasting bond. But hope collides with the realities of love: needs do not fit, anger divides, judgments erode the once easy acceptance, loneliness fills parallel but distant lives.

What makes intimacy work? Some say it is the strength of your dream, the strength of your commitment to love itself. Others say it's a matter of luck, the good fortune of finding that most excellent fit. Others say you must have passion or sharing or mutual interests or common values.

After exploring hundreds of relationships, we've concluded that the people who make intimacy work have certain skills. That's why we've called this book *Couples Skills*. In case after case, relationships that endure and deepen are formed by couples who know and practice basic interpersonal skills: listening, clear communication, negotiation, handling anger appropriately, and so on.

That's good news. Because you can learn a new skill by reading and practicing. It's a lot harder to change your luck or your feelings of passion or your core values.

This book will help you develop and polish the skills you need to keep love alive. In creating such a book, we've had to depart from some common approaches taken in other self-help books. This book is different in three ways.

First of all, since our goal is to teach skills, the focus of the book is on action and change rather than concepts and theory. This means that you can't just passively sit and read. You'll need to get involved: do the exercises, keep logs and journals, try new behavior, risk new responses to your partner. It will take patience and tenacity—and sometimes courage. But the dream and the hope you started with are worth the effort. Things will change—not by chance, not because you understand more or your relationship undergoes some surprise rekindling, but because you are more skillful at being a couple.

The second way that this book differs from others is that we don't expect anyone other than professional counselors to read the whole thing. Different couples need to concentrate on different skills. So each chapter stands alone. Each chapter contains everything you'll need to learn a particular relationship skill. You can pick and choose the skills that you most want to learn and leave the rest. This means that you can get started right away, without reading a lot. From the very beginning, you'll be relating differently to your partner.

To make each chapter stand alone, we have repeated some concepts or used similar exercises in two or three different chapters. And because we knew that readers would be skipping around in the book, we have provided plenty of cross-references between the chapters.

Finally, the third difference in this book is that we are not out to prove any particular theory or champion any particular school of therapy. For each skill that we wanted to teach, we picked the theory or therapeutic approach that has proven to be the most effective. For example, the chapters on schemas and distortions owe a debt to cognitive therapy. Other chapters such as the one on reciprocal reinforcement come out of a more behavioral approach to change. Some of the communication exercises go back to the days of Gestalt therapy groups. The chapters on your couple system are derived from family systems theory. Some of the negotiation chapter is inspired by findings in the fields of diplomacy and labor relations. The chapters on expectations and rules, old tapes, and defenses derive from psychodynamic theories.

Who This Book Is For

This book is for couples, married or not; heterosexual, gay, or lesbian; young or old. We have made a conscious effort to include examples of many varieties of partnership because we believe that each is a legitimate, healthy expression of human intimacy.

This book is for new lovers who are in the early, building stages of a partnership. And it's for partners of many years who want to change and improve specific aspects of their relationship.

This book is for partners who are still committed to each other, who are still willing to *work* toward a happier shared life. You'll also need the patience to sustain that effort over a period of time, since these techniques are no quick fix. The interventions you are about to make in your relationship each require a minimum of several weeks—and more often months—to take effect. To alter your emotional landscape, you'll probably need to make more than one change. And that will take even more time.

Some of the things you'll try will work, and some will be a bust—not really suited to your particular style or needs. *And so you have to be willing to fail:* to accept that something didn't work for you while nonetheless continuing to put effort into learning the next skill.

This book is *not* appropriate for couples who are dealing with a significant substance abuse problem. Since an alcohol or drug problem will negate any new skill you learn here, that problem must be addressed first.

If your partnership is currently affected by threats of violence, by battering, or any form of physical cruelty, you should seek immediate professional help. The physical safety of each partner must be assured before the book could be of value to you.

We also recommend professional help if you are currently dealing with infidelity or any other significant breach of trust in your relationship.

Working Alone/Working Together

Many of the chapters in this book are appropriate for making unilateral changes in your relationship. They will show you, step by step, how to alter your patterns of interaction. And by the nature of the couple system, when you change, your partner has to change in response. When you take some new action, there will inevitably be a reaction. Even the smallest effort you make can have a big ripple effect.

Sometimes your partner will resist the new things you try. Most people find change—even positive change—frightening. But if you are consistent, if you keep up the new behavior, chances are good that your partner will shift in a positive direction too.

While unilateral work can be effective, working together will almost always get faster results. You will both be focused on the same goal, and each of you will reinforce and support the other. You will each feel valued and cared for when you see the other trying.

How To Use This Book

Couple Skills is divided into four sections:

1. Basic Skills
2. Advanced Skills
3. Anger and Conflict
4. Understanding and Changing What Goes Wrong

We suggest that everyone read the basic skills chapters on listening, expressing feelings and scripting needs, and reciprocal reinforcement. These provide a foundation for increased openness and mutual support. With the advanced skills chapters you can start to pick and choose. If you have trouble with attacking, judgmental communications, then the chapter on clean communication is important to read. If you find yourself making assumptions about your partner's feelings and motives or magnifying your partner's flaws, the chapter on cognitive distortions can provide insight into these destructive patterns of thinking and a method for changing them. The chapters on negotiation and problem solving offer step-by-step training in conflict and problem-resolution skills.

The section on anger and conflict provides specific help with assessing and changing aversive strategies, coping with your own anger and with an angry partner, and "time out," a vital skill for stopping fights from escalating.

The last section on understanding and changing what goes wrong offers deeper insight into the mechanisms of intimacy.

The chapter on identifying schemas about your partner shows you how to recognize negative pictures that you've formed and how to trace their influence on your behavior. You'll also get help to reexamine and soften these beliefs about your partner.

The chapter on "old tapes" describes how feelings and responses from your relationship with your parents can get transferred to your partner. It gives you guidelines for recognizing the process as it occurs.

The chapter on coping with your defenses explains how avoiding, denial, and acting-out defenses help protect you from some of the inevitable pain of intimacy—but also end up costing a great deal in the coin of alienation. Defenses are addictive, so the chapter helps you develop your own "recovery" program.

The chapters on identifying and intervening in your couple system help you stop the cyclic patterns that keep you returning to the same old conflicts. You'll get a chance to map your unique system and locate the places where it is most vulnerable to change. The final chapter on expectations, rules, and acceptance will help you recognize the unconscious rules and expectations that influence your reactions to your partner. When your partner breaks your rules and fails to meet your expectations, you're likely to feel angry and alienated. Some of your expectations may conflict with those of your partner; some may be impossible to meet in this relationship. The chapter offers several ways to develop greater acceptance.

Problem Chart

The table of contents and the above summaries should give you some ideas of where to start reading. But we want to provide as many avenues into this book as possible, and some people like to see a more graphic presentation. So we prepared the following Problem Chart for those who want to see "everything at a glance."

To identify the chapters that will be most useful to you, look down the "PROBLEM" column of the chart on the next page. Then look across and note the "SKILLS" boxes marked with an "x" for that problem. These indicate which chapters offer the most effective skills to address that problem. A larger "X" indicates the chapters that you should read first.

For example, if you want to get started right away on finding out how to deal with your own anger and that of your partner, you would look down the left hand column and find "Anger, Arguing." Then you would look across to the right and see that the largest "X" directs you to the "Coping With Anger" chapter first. After reading that chapter, the smaller "x's" suggest that you might also want to read the chapters on "Coping With an Angry Partner," "Time Out," and so on.

Congratulations

Whichever way you choose to use this book, congratulations on taking this step toward developing your couple skills. Remember to do the exercises rather than just reading about them, cultivate patience, and keep trying different approaches if your first attempt doesn't work out.

Problem Chart

PROBLEM	Listening	Expressing Feelings and Scripting Needs	Reciprocal Reinforcement	Clean Communication	Identifying and Changing Cognitive Distortions	Negotiation	Problem Solving
Emotional Distance/ Lack of Intimacy	X	x	x				
Anger, Arguing				x			
Name Calling, Sniping, Belittling, Threats, Blaming		x		x			X
Unexpressed Feelings	x	X	x				
Feelings of Deprivation		X	x			x	x
Unresolved or Cyclic Patterns of Conflict						X	x
Unexpressed Needs		X		x		x	x
Conflicting Concepts of Partnership	x	x				x	x
Feelings of Unfairness, Inequity		x		x		x	x
Lack of Time/ Growing Apart		x	X				x
Misunderstanding	X	x		x	x		
Unmet Expectations		x	x			x	x
Not Feeling Heard		X		x			
Guilt			x				x
Negative Assumptions about Partner					X		
Feeling of Going in Circles							
Feeling Hurt		X					
Discouragement, Depression		x	X		x	x	x
Negativity			x		X		
Disenchantment		x	X			x	x

Assessing and Changing Aversive Strategies	Coping With Anger	Coping With an Angry Partner	Time Out	Identifying Schemas	Old Tapes	Coping With Your Defenses	Identifying Your Couple System	Intervening in Your System	Expectations, Rules, and Acceptance
x	X	x	x	x					x
x	x	x							
						x			
							x	x	
x					x		x	x	x
									X
	X								x
					x				
	x								X
x									
X		x							x
			x		x		x	x	
						x	X	x	
		x							x
					x				

Basic Skills

1

Listening

It's hard to really listen to your partner. It's easier to space out, to rehearse your reply, to filter the content for danger signs, to collect evidence for your own opinions, to pass judgment, and so on.

But listening is the most important of all the communication skills that can create and preserve intimacy. When you listen well, you understand your partner better, you stay closely in tune, you enjoy the relationship more, and you know without mind reading why your partner says and does things.

Listening is a commitment and a compliment. It is a commitment to understanding and empathy, to putting aside your own interests, needs, and prejudices long enough to see your relationship through your partner's eyes. Listening is a compliment to your partner because it says, "I care about you. I want to know what you think and feel and need."

History

Active listening is a technique originally conceived and taught to therapists by Carl Rogers (1951). The technique of identifying, assessing, and overcoming your blocks to listening was developed by McKay, Davis, and Fanning (1983). The reciprocal communication exercise in which you take turns being the speaker and the listener has been used to good effect in cognitive couples therapy by Dattilio and Padesky (1990).

Theoretical Background

There is a lot more to listening than merely being quiet while your partner talks. Real listening is distinguished by your *intention*. If your intention is to understand, enjoy, learn from, or help your partner, then you are really listening.

For many couples, real listening is rare. They indulge in pseudo listening. In pseudo listening, your intention is not to understand, enjoy, learn, or help. Your intentions are contaminated by one of the many blocks to listening that follow. As you read the descriptions below, check off the blocks that you can recall using to avoid listening to your partner.

Blocks to Listening

☐ **Mind reading.** You are mind reading when you disregard or distrust what your partner is actually saying and instead try to figure out what he or she "really means." Mind readers give too much importance to subtle cues such as tone of voice, facial expressions, and posture. They ignore the actual content of what their partner is saying in favor of their own assumptions and hunches.

Mind reading is deadly to intimacy because it ignores the obvious in favor of the imaginary. Paul says to Peggy, "I think you look good in both dresses—wear either one." Peggy tells herself, "He really means I'm so skinny and flat-chested that I wouldn't look good in anything."

☐ **Rehearsing.** You're so busy rehearsing what you'll say next that you never really hear what your partner is telling you. Sometimes you may rehearse whole chains of dialogue: "I'll say, then my partner will say, then I'll say ... "

Susie is telling Sebastian why he should be the one who takes their son to his piano recital on Saturday, but Sebastian isn't listening. He's rehearsing his objection to the idea, because he wants to go to the ball game. He completely misses Susie's deeper concerns about him spending more time with his son.

☐ **Filtering.** Filtering means that you listen to some things but not others. You may listen for signs that your partner is angry or sad or anxious and then tune out when you sense that your partner is okay and that you aren't expected to respond to any emotional trouble.

Filtering can also work to *exclude* things you don't want to hear. For example, your ears might work fine until your partner starts talking about your drinking, your mother-in-law, or moving out-of-state.

☐ **Judging.** Judging means that you have stopped listening to your partner because of some negative judgment, or that you only listen for the purpose of assigning blame and putting negative labels on your partner. If you think that your partner is stupid or bigoted or crazy, you stop listening. Or you listen only to gather fresh evidence of your partner's stupidity, bigotry, or craziness.

Randy thought Kirk was an egomaniac, so he seldom listened when Kirk talked about himself. This negative judgment kept Randy from really getting to know Kirk for who he was.

☐ **Daydreaming.** Everyone's attention wanders. When you've been with someone for many years, it's especially easy to stop listening and drift away into your own fantasies. If you find it harder and harder to pay attention to your partner, it may be a danger sign that you are avoiding contact or certain topics.

Ralph spaced out nearly every time Gloria talked about her art class. He ultimately realized that he was resentful of the time she spent in class and was avoiding a confrontation by daydreaming.

☐ **Advising.** Your partner barely has time to speak a complete sentence before you jump in with your advice. Your search for the right solution and your urge to fix everything deafens you to your partner's simple need to be heard.

When George started telling Marie about his frustrations and despondency over his dead-end job, she was all over him: "You need to get into a whole new line of work. Why don't you go over to the junior college and get some career counseling? Or you could set up some informational interviews with executives in interesting fields." George felt even more overwhelmed. What he really wanted was sympathy and permission to just be a little depressed for a while.

☐ **Sparring.** You listen only to disagree, argue, and debate. You take a position and defend it, regardless of what your partner says. In many troubled relationships, sparring is the standard mode of communication.

Whatever topic Joyce brings up—the kids, money, relatives—Ted starts a tirade, repeating his party line regardless of any new ideas his wife tries to explain. Ted is so argumentative that he is incapable of listening.

☐ **Being right**. This block protects you from hearing anything that suggests you are less than perfect. To avoid any suggestion that you are wrong, you will lie, shout, change the subject, justify, quibble, make excuses, accuse, or otherwise fight off criticism.

Jennifer expressed concern about overdue notices and asked Rudy if he had paid the dentist bill or if she should pay it. He took this as an implied criticism and blustered that paying bills on time was stupid. "Let them wait—we'll keep the money and collect interest till after the second notice. Now give it a rest." Rudy never heard how anxious Jennifer felt getting the overdue notices.

☐ **Derailing**. You change the subject or joke it off whenever the conversation becomes too personal or threatening. By misdirection or humor you avoid listening to your partner's serious concerns.

Sylvia said that she thought Anne should cut down on her drinking and staying up late. Anne laughed it off by saying, "Hey, with my stress, I'd be crazy not to drink. And late nights are the only times I have to unwind."

☐ **Placating.** You are too quick to agree. As soon as your partner expresses doubt, irritation, or anxiety, you jump in with, "Yes . . . you're right . . . I know . . . I'm sorry . . . I'll fix it." You are so concerned with being nice, supportive, and agreeable that you don't give your partner enough time to fully express his or her thought.

Molly tried three times to tell Jeff why she was fed up with his old cars blocking their driveway. He would "apologize her to death," and shuffle one or two cars into the street for a couple of days. He never got the message that she wanted him to *get rid* of them if he wasn't going to restore them in the near future.

Time for Mastery

You can begin immediately to become a better listener. Just reading the preceding information and doing the assessment exercise that follows will raise your consciousness so that you are more aware of opportunities to improve your listening. The instructions for the rest of the exercises in this chapter are simple and easy to understand. Positive results will accrue as soon as you begin to follow the instructions. Mastery is a lifelong adventure.

Assessing Your Listening Blocks

In the space below, describe three situations where communication broke down between you and your partner. Indicate which blocks kept you from really listening to your partner. You may find that you used two or three different blocks in the course of the same conversation.

Here is a quick review list of the listening blocks:

Mind reading   Advising
Rehearsing   Sparring
Filtering   Being Right
Judging   Derailing
Daydreaming   Placating

Situation   *Blocks to Listening*

Situation   *Blocks to Listening*

Situation   *Blocks to Listening*

Over the next two days, notice how often you use your favorite listening blocks. Review every conversation with your partner.

Which blocks do you use most consistently?

Are the situations similar?

What topics do you have the most trouble listening to?

Do you block other people as well as your partner?

Did your greater awareness of listening blocks change your usual style of listening?

When you start noticing your listening patterns, you may feel anxious or irritated. You may decide to stop mind reading and find that you start rehearsing or derailing instead. You may also find that you start hearing or sharing information that you never expected to talk about.

Don't be alarmed or discouraged. The next exercise will give you some powerful listening skills with which to replace your usual blocking strategies.

Active Listening

It's not enough to shut your mouth and open your ears. Your brain must also be actively engaged in listening. There's really no such thing as a passive listener. Communication is a two-way, collaborative process, even when one person is ostensibly doing all the talking. To listen actively, you must paraphrase, clarify, and give feedback.

Paraphrasing

Whenever your partner says something important to you, you should state in your own words what you think your partner just said. This is the most important part of good listening. If you learn only one thing from this chapter, learn to paraphrase.

You can preface your paraphrase with lead-ins such as "What I hear you saying is that ... In other words ... Let me get this straight ... So you felt that ... If I understand you correctly ... Do you mean ... Would you say that ... "

If you consistently paraphrase, you will:

- Prevent most listening blocks.

- Correct false assumptions and misinterpretations on the spot.

- Give your partner the priceless gift of being heard and acknowledged.

- Keep angry feelings from escalating.

- Help yourself remember what was said.

Try paraphrasing the next time your partner tells you anything of note. You may be surprised at how long it takes to completely understand even the simplest statement. For example, Joel decided to paraphrase what Cindy was telling him about her mother:

Cindy: My mother wants to come up and stay with us over
          Easter break.

Joel:	Your mother asked if she could come up for Easter?
Cindy:	Yeah. Well, she didn't ask—I suggested it, and she thought it sounded like a good idea.
Joel:	*You* want your mother to come up.
Cindy:	Sure.
Joel:	And stay with *us*.
Cindy:	Well, she usually stays with Cathy, but I want her here, so we can have more time.
Joel:	You're hoping for more time with her than usual?
Cindy:	Uh huh. We could relax for a few days, play with the kids, and—you know—just talk.
Joel:	Just hang out.
Cindy:	And talk about how things are going with her. Being alone down there.
Joel:	You want to talk about her loneliness?
Cindy:	Yes, she's all by herself in that big house. If she moved up here, she could be close to us, close to her grandkids.
Joel:	You want her to move in with us for good, not just Easter?
Cindy:	Well, not with us forever. Just a trial week, to see if she likes it, how it works out. Then look for a place nearby.

As you can see, Joel's gentle paraphrasing has uncovered an agenda much vaster than a simple Easter visit. If he had not been a good listener, this issue could have lain dormant and unexplored.

Clarifying

Paraphrasing leads naturally to clarifying. You tell your partner what you thought you heard, find out you were wrong, and start asking questions to clarify. In phrasing your questions, remember that your intention is to understand, enjoy, learn, or help. Your intention must not be to interrogate, to pressure for your own point of view, to blame, to belittle, or to manipulate in any way.

Asking questions will give you a broader picture that includes more specific details, finer shades of feeling, and greater understanding of your partner's point of view. Ask for the facts—who, what, where, when, how. And also ask questions like "How did you feel about that?" and "What were you thinking then?"

Feedback

Feedback comes after you have paraphrased what your partner said and asked questions to clarify your understanding. Then you "feed back" your own reactions. You calmly relate, without judgment, your own thoughts, feelings, opinions, desires, and so on. You share your inner experience of your partner's account, without falling back into listening blocks such as sparring or advising.

Feedback accomplishes three things. First, it is another chance to check out your perceptions with your partner, so that he or she can correct any misconceptions. Second, your feedback provides your partner with information about the accuracy and effects of his or her communication. Third, your partner gets the benefit of your fresh point of view.

Good feedback is immediate, honest, and supportive.

Immediate means that you don't waste any time. As soon as you think you understand your partner's story through paraphrasing and asking for clarification, give your feedback right away. A delay of even an hour will lessen the impact.

Honest means that you have to give your real reaction, undistorted by fears of offending, desires to manipulate, or unwillingness to reveal your own feelings. For example, if you think your partner is wrong or you feel threatened, you need to say so in your feedback.

Supportive means that your honesty must not become brutality. You need to find ways to soften negative opinions without destroying their meaning. For example, you might say "I think maybe you made a mistake" instead of "You really blew it this time." Or you could say "I'm feeling insecure about you leaving" instead of "I'll die if you leave me."

Exercises

Listening With Your Body

Your body can encourage your partner by conveying that you're listening. The next time your partner starts to talk to you, follow these simple instructions:

1. Maintain eye contact.

2. Move closer or lean slightly forward.

3. Nod or interject a "yes" or an "uh huh."

4. Smile or frown in sympathy with what is being said.

5. Keep your posture open, facing your partner, arms unfolded and uncrossed.

6. Actively move away from distractions. Turn the radio down, put the magazine away, and so on.

Reciprocal Communication

This simple but powerful exercise may seem very structured and artificial, but try it anyway. Agree to discuss a topic that is a source of mild conflict between you. Take turns being the speaker and the listener.
When you are the speaker:

1. Explain your point of view briefly and succinctly.

2. Talk in terms of yourself and your experience. Use "I" statements to express your feelings and needs.

3. Avoid blame and name calling. No "you" statements about your partner's failings.

Stop after five minutes. Your partner will summarize what you just said. Let your partner know if anything is left out.
When you are the listener:

1. Pay close attention to really understand your partner's feelings, opinions, and needs.

2. No disagreeing, arguing, correcting, or talking back.

3. You may ask questions for clarification only.

After your partner speaks for five minutes, summarize your partner's experience as you heard it. Your partner will add anything you left out, or clarify anything you may have misunderstood. Keep going back and forth until the speaker feels that he or she has been completely heard and understood.

Now switch places, letting the one who was the listener become the speaker and vice versa. Follow the same instructions until the second speaker has been thoroughly listened to and understood.

This is how Art and Evie did this exercise.

Evie: When I found out that your mom left us ten
thousand dollars, I was overjoyed. It felt like we

could have some cushion at last. We could pay off the credit cards, get the car fixed, and have something in the bank instead of living from week to week.

Art: Do you feel like we've been living from week to week?

Evie: Yes. I know we both make good money, and we don't have any kids to put through college or anything, but it seems like we always spend just a little more than we make. It feels to me like we're always in the red, always a bit behind. That's why I don't want to go to Hawaii or Jamaica or any of those expensive places. I love trips, but I'd love some money in the bank even more. I also feel a little guilty about dragging my feet whenever you bring up the idea of a trip. I mean, she was your mom and in that sense, it's your money to do with what you want.

Art: Hey, it's a community property state.

Evie: That's a comment, not a question.

Art: Sorry.

Evie: That's okay. I was finished anyway.

Art: So let me summarize this: You feel nervous about living week-to-week. You want to save the money and not blow it all on trips and stuff. But you feel guilty about telling me what to do with my mom's money.

Evie: You got the feelings right, but not the plans. I want to pay down the credit cards and get my car fixed. To me that would be money well spent.

Art: And you'd like to save what's left.

Evie: Yes. Even if it's enough to go to some exotic beach place, I'd rather save it.

Art: I got it.

Then it was Art's turn. He explained that his desire to get away wasn't entirely frivolous. After the expense and worry of his mom's illness, he felt drained. He wanted to go somewhere warm and just sit around for a while, get in touch with his grief, and think about being an "orphan" in the world now that both his parents were dead. He also explained that he didn't feel much pressure about being somewhat in debt, since he had a secure job with good chances of advancement.

This exercise was the first time Art really listened to Evie's insecurities about money. And it was the first hint Evie had of how much Art was affected by his mother's death. They eventually compromised by catching up on bills, taking a more modest vacation, and investing some of the money in a CD.

Empathy

Empathy helps you understand your partner's position more clearly. To increase your empathy, consider that both of you are just trying to survive physically and emotionally. Everything you both do—including the violent, inconsiderate, outrageous, or stupid things—is done to minimize pain or threat and maximize pleasure or safety. From this point of view, everything people do is some kind of coping strategy. Some coping strategies are better or more appropriate than others. Some are clearly self-destructive. But all serve the same purpose—to ensure the survival of the self.

In the space below, describe and analyze a disagreement that you frequently have with your partner.

My Position	My Partner's Position

My Coping Strategies	My Partner's Coping Strategies

My Needs	My Partner's Needs

My Fears	My Partner's Fears

Here's how David did this exercise:

My Position	My Partner's Position
I want to stay home and work on my motorcycle this weekend.	Lisa wants us to go away and visit friends.

My Coping Strategies	My Partner's Coping Strategies
I delay talking about it, complain about the expense, get angry, sulk.	Lisa hints, whines, nags, cries, threatens to go without me (without ever intending to).

My Needs	My Partner's Needs
I need relaxation, and time alone, but don't want to look like I'm being selfish.	Lisa needs to be with friends, be with me, feel connected.

My Fears	My Partner's Fears
If I go, I'll be bored, restless, stressed out. If I stay, I'll be guilty.	If we stay home, she'll feel lonely, isolated, unloved, angry. If we go, she'll feel guilty about forcing me.

David shared his analysis with Lisa. His description cleared the air by showing that they both had real and legitimate needs that they were trying to meet and real fears that made them fight desperately for emotional survival. They were able to hear each other better and stay calm enough to compromise and take turns getting what they wanted.

Reversal

This is an exercise to build empathy and improve listening skills. Pick an old, minor disagreement that is not too explosive. Take turns stating your position. Listen carefully to each other's argument. Then reverse sides and each argue for the other's position.

See how it feels to fight for the opposite point of view. It should increase your understanding of your partner's position and perhaps show you how your own point of view sounds from the receiving end.

Afterwards, discuss your experience and how well you each represented the other's position.

When Melissa and Brad tried the reversal exercise, it went like this:

The Usual Money Argument

Melissa: I don't see why you're so tight. We've got the money in the bank. Let's just buy a new refrigerator instead of patching up the old one.

Brad: You're damn right I'm tight. If I didn't keep a tight rein on you and the kids, you'd spend us into Chapter Eleven. There's a lot of life left in the old refrigerator.

Melissa: It's always like this. No matter how much we have, you don't want to spend it. All our bills are current, and we've both got secure jobs. Let's enjoy our money—buy a new couch, a refrigerator, join the health club, go to Mexico.

Brad: We're in good shape *because* of my careful budgeting. If we start spending impulsively, we'll get into trouble. My family was poor when I was growing up, and I learned the value of a dollar the hard way.

The Reversal

Melissa: Okay, here goes: I hate to spend money on glitz and glamour. Keeping the money in the bank is better. It's there for an emergency. It makes me feel secure.

Brad: Yeah, but you go too far. You don't even want to buy basic necessities like shoes for the kids. You won't even replace a worn-out refrigerator.

Melissa: I'm afraid if we spend too much, we'll end up like my dad. He never bothered to save anything, so it was total disaster when he lost his job.

Brad: But the way we live is just too miserly. We don't have much fun. We could afford to go to Mexico or join the health club. But we don't.

The Critique

Melissa: When I pretended to be the tightwad, I realized how scary it is to feel poor, like there's not going to be enough to go around.

Brad: When I took your part, I felt *controlled*, held down by you.

Melissa: I could feel a little how you must feel—that if I relaxed control, if I gave an inch, you'd take a mile and we'd lose everything.

Brad: And I felt how dreary it is for you and the kids to do without and plead for every nickel, when there's money sitting in the bank.

Melissa: You know, I don't want to spend it all. Just a little, now and then.

Brad: Maybe I can loosen up a little.

Melissa: Mexico?

Brad: Well, let's start with the refrigerator.

2

Expressing Feelings and Scripting Needs

This chapter teaches two related but distinct skills. Expressing feelings is a matter of first identifying and then giving appropriate voice to your emotions. Scripting needs means planning in advance how you will ask for what you want, so that you can be assertive rather than passive or aggressive.

If you are weak in one of these skills, your relationship will be impaired. If you lack both, it may be doomed.

For example, Bill often felt vaguely irritated by the toys and junk mail all over the living room, but he never examined his feelings or tried to express them to his wife Sally. But about every other month he would express his need for more order in his life by going on a rampage. He would shout "This place is a pigsty!" and then scoop up toys and papers at random and toss them into the trash. Sally and the kids would invariably respond with tears and rage at his uncaring impulses. Remorse would set in and Bill would retire to the garage to cool down. Until the next time.

History

The techniques in this chapter grow out of Harry Stack Sullivan's concept of the self-system and forbidding gestures (1953), Sidney M. Jourard's observations on the inherent value of self-disclosure (1971), and assertiveness training methods developed by pioneers such as Robert E. Alberti and Michael Emmons (1974).

Theoretical Background

Psychological theorist Harry Stack Sullivan defined the self-system as the total of all your conscious experience: everything you sense, think, desire, and feel. As you were growing up, your self-system was shaped by what your parents said was okay to sense, think, desire, and feel. They shaped you by using "forbidding gestures." If your mother grabbed your wrist and scolded you every time you cried because you were feeling shy, you may have learned to stifle any expression of shyness. You may even have become boastful or belligerent in new social situations as a way to handle your forbidden shyness.

Forbidding gestures train you to identify certain forbidden feelings—shyness, anger, fear, pride—as "not me." For example, in our culture men are often taught that stubbornness, anger, or competitiveness are okay, but that sadness, fear, or uncertainty are "not me." Even though feelings like these are edited out of your conscious self-system, they still remain as unconscious influences.

Your self-system also determines how you ask for what you want. Alberti and Emmons described how some people fail to get important needs met by being too passive, while others fail by being too aggressive. They outlined steps whereby you can script your requests ahead of time and learn to ask for what you want assertively and appropriately.

Time for Mastery

It takes a week to keep a feelings diary, and about another week to take your first steps toward expressing unfamiliar feelings. Learning the steps to assertively scripting your needs may take another few days. Mastery depends on the frequency with which you practice your new skills.

Identifying Your Feelings

Good or bad? Sometimes a situation makes you feel *something*, but it's hard to say what that feeling is. In those cases, begin with the simple question, "Is it good or bad?"

Close your eyes, take several slow, deep breaths, and focus on the experience that causes the ambiguous feeling. Is the overall sensation positive or negative? Are you drawn toward the situation or repelled?

Location, size, shape, and color? Once you have decided whether the feeling is good or bad, try to give it a location in your body. Close your eyes again, focus on your breathing, and relax. Scan your body while feeling the feeling. Does it seem to reside in your chest, your stomach, your hands, your neck?

Now concentrate on that area most closely associated with the feeling. How much space does the feeling take up? Is it large or small?

As you begin to get an idea of the size, try to sense a shape. In your mind's eyes, trace the feeling's all-around shape. Is it a regular shape, like a ball or a cone? Or irregular?

What color comes to mind as you contemplate your feeling? Is it a warm red or orange? A cool blue or green?

Don't evaluate or judge your feeling or your performance in this exercise. Just observe whatever comes up for you when you try to identify location, size, shape, and color.

What does it say? Imagine that your feeling can talk by itself. What does it say? Let words come spontaneously, without forcing or judging them. You may hear meaningful clues to the nature of your feeling such as the words, *loss, gone, unfair, sad, bad*, and so on. Or you may hear only silence, or a phrase whose meaning eludes you.

What do you want to do? When you feel this feeling, what action are you drawn to? What do you see yourself doing—running, hugging, hitting, hiding, crying, shaking, screaming? Imagine that you are performing the action. This is just fantasy, so you don't have to restrain your actions the way you might in real life. Let your imagination go.

The action urged by your feeling is a good clue to the nature of the feeling. If you want to hug or comfort someone, you may be feeling sympathy, remorse, love, or desire. If you want to hit or shake someone, you're probably feeling anger or frustration. If you want to cry, hide, or turn away, you may be feeling sadness, depression, or anxiety.

What past experience does it remind you of? Have you had this same feeling before? Let your mind drift to the past and focus on a time when you felt something similar. Who were you with? What was happening? Were you able to identify the feeling? How did you express or fail to express this feeling in the past?

Sometimes it's easier to identify feelings by looking for a repeated pattern in your life. For example, Mary Jean felt ill at ease and distracted. Her husband Bob was out of town and she had a million things to do, but no energy or motivation to do them. She looked into her past and remembered feeling the same way when her college roommate moved away. She realized that she was feeling lonely and abandoned, even though her intellect knew that Bob's business trip was a necessary absence from home.

Name your feelings. By now you should be able to give your feeling a name. The list on the next page can help by reminding you of the many words available to describe feelings. Don't be surprised if you need several words to accurately describe your feeling. Most feelings are combinations of several component feelings.

Go through the list slowly and put a check next to the words that best describe your feeling.

Feelings diary. For the next week, make a note of each time you interact with your partner or think about your partner and you are aware of a particular feeling. This practice will train you in noticing and clarifying your feelings from moment to moment. Here's how Diane kept her diary.

Date	Situation	Feeling
8/3	Keith mowed over my poppies	Enraged, sad
8/4	Keith brought me flowers to apologize for mowing the poppies	Loved, tender, resigned
8/4	Wanting to visit my nieces upstate, knowing Keith won't want to go	Nervous, apprehensive, irritated
8/5	Talking about visiting nieces	Upset, put down, guilty
8/7	Driving upstate alone	Determined, guilty, lonely
8/8	Taking nieces to the zoo, thinking about how much more fun it would be if Keith were with us	Sad, depressed
8/9	Explaining why Uncle Keith didn't come	Embarrassed
8/10	Back home, telling Keith how much fun I had, how I missed him, trying not to beg him to come with me next time	Nervous, suppressed anger

Feelings List

Affectionate
Afraid
Amused
Angry
Annoyed
Anxious
Apprehensive
Bitter
Bored
Calm
Capable
Cheerful
Comfortable
Competent
Concerned
Confident
Confused
Contemptuous
Controlled
Curious
Defeated
Dejected
Delighted
Depressed
Desirable
Despairing
Desperate
Determined
Devastated
Disappointed
Discouraged
Disgusted
Distrustful
Embarrassed
Enraged
Exasperated
Excited
Fearful
Frantic
Frustrated
Fulfilled

Furious
Generous
Glad
Gloomy
Grateful
Great
Guilty
Happy
Hateful
Helpless
Hopeless
Horrified
Hostile
Impatient
Inhibited
Irritated
Isolated
Joyful
Lonely
Loved
Loving
Loyal
Melancholy
Miserable
Muddled
Needy
Nervous
Out of control
Outraged
Overwhelmed
Panicky
Passionate
Peaceful
Pessimistic
Playful
Pleased
Powerful
Prejudiced
Pressured
Proud
Provoked

Put down
Relaxed
Relieved
Resentful
Resigned
Sad
Safe
Satisfied
Secure
Sexy
Silly
Strong
Stubborn
Stuck
Supportive
Sympathetic
Tender
Terrified
Threatened
Thrilled
Touchy
Trapped
Troubled
Unappreciated
Uncertain
Understood
Uneasy
Unfulfilled
Unloved
Upset
Uptight
Used
Useless
Victimized
Violated
Vulnerable
Wonderful
Worn out
Worried
Worthwhile
Yearning

Find a notebook or pad you can carry around with you for a week. You can use the three-column technique that Diane used, or any other format that pleases you.

Expressing Your Feelings

The Key Affective Word

"Affective" means pertaining to the expression of emotion. The first step in expressing your feelings is to pick the key word that describes your emotional state: depressed, angry, anxious, guilty, worried, and so on. The feelings list presented earlier can help in this.

Modifiers

One word does not expression make. You need to expand on the key affective word to define what it means to you, to explain the intensity of your feelings, the duration, the context, and any historical information that will help your partner understand precisely how you feel.

1. Definition.   When Joan says "upset," she means that she is very worried and frightened. When her partner Gail says "upset," she means that she feels angry and irritated. You have to define your key affective word to clarify your meaning. Pick synonyms that will make your meaning clear: "I'm annoyed . . . irritated and stressed out." "I feel depressed . . . sad and lonely and not interested in anything." "I'm worried about my job . . . concerned that the company isn't doing well, afraid I'll get laid off."

2. Intensity. Use modifying words or synonyms to express the intensity of your feelings. If you are a little angry, say "a little" or "slightly." Choose synonyms that denote mild anger: "annoyed, irritated." If you are extremely angry, say so, or choose synonyms that make the intensity of your anger clear: "enraged, outraged, furious."

3. Duration. Explain how long you have been feeling this way: "all my life," "since last week," or "after I got up this morning." Seeing your feelings in a time frame can be another indicator that helps your partner gauge the seriousness or intensity of your feelings.

4. Cause and context. Avoid describing your partner as the *cause* of your feelings:

"You made me so mad."
"I'm worried about your reckless spending habits."
"You left me here all alone and I got depressed."

It's very tempting to blame your partner for any negative feelings you may be experiencing. This is especially true if your bad feelings really do stem directly from some unfair or inconsiderate action by your partner. But blame never solves problems. When you identify your partner as the cause of your unhappiness, your partner hears only the blame, not the unhappy feelings. Your partner is moved to self-defense, not sympathy and problem solving.

It's better to choose your words carefully so that you describe the *context* of your feelings without directly ascribing blame or causation:

"I felt mad after you broke the dishes."

"When I get an overdraft notice from the bank, I get very worried."

"When I was home alone today, I started to get depressed."

5. Historical precedents.   Often it is helpful to share what this feeling reminds you of—some time in your past when you felt the same way.

"It feels like the time my first wife left me."

"I haven't been this confused since I was applying to graduate school."

"I remember feeling like this when my mother was in the hospital."

6. Putting it all together.   Here's how Alicia put these steps together.

> I feel very angry *(key affective word)*. I'm upset and disappointed and I really feel let down *(definition)*. This trip was a big deal for me *(intensity)*. The moment I realized that you had forgotten to make the reservations *(duration)*, I had this sinking feeling, just like when my sister didn't show up for my birthday *(historical precedent)*. When I don't get something I've been counting on *(context)*, it really hits me hard.

Exercise

In the space below, express one of your common feelings fully, using the key affective word and each type of modifier. Write in short, complete sentences and in a conversational style. Don't hesitate to connect modifier sentences that go together in the same way that Alicia did with her expression. Imagine that your statement is a short speech you'll be making. Read the complete statement out loud to see how it sounds.

Key affective word:

Definition:

Intensity:

Duration:

Cause and context:

Historical precedents:

Guidelines for Expressing Your Feelings

These four guidelines are the best insurance that you will express your feelings clearly and that your partner will remain receptive.

1. Use "I" statements. Take responsibility for your feelings by using "I" statements rather than "you" statements. Notice how blaming these "you" statements sound:

"You make me furious."

"You're driving me crazy."

"You never let me get a word in."

Recast as "I" statements, these versions are less inflammatory, put responsibility for the feelings on the speaker, and are much more likely to be heard:

"I'm furious."

"I feel confused and crazy."

"I want to talk now."

Beware of the "you" statement in "I" statement clothing: "I feel *that* you are a jerk" does not qualify as a legitimate "I" statement. When you hear the word "that" in an "I" statement, it is usually a disguised "you" statement.

Take a moment right now to change the following "you" statements into "I" statements in the space provided.

"You never pay any attention to me."

"I feel that you are an hysterical nit-picker."

"Your careless spending habits make me furious."

2. Be honest. It is tempting to describe dinner with your in-laws as "fine, very pleasant," when actually you were bored and irritated the whole evening. It is tempting to say that you're tired and just want to go to bed when actually you are worried about the kids and afraid to broach the subject. It is tempting to invent important work you must do in the office when actually you just want to be alone.

Resist the temptation to describe your feelings in ways that manipulate or distort or hide the truth. When you cut your partner off from your true feelings, you also cut yourself off and make it that much harder to genuinely express emotions.

3. Be congruent. It's very confusing when your tone of voice and body language don't match your words. If you say "I'm sad" while you're smiling and dancing around, which is your partner supposed to believe, your words or your actions?

If you notice that your body language is incongruent with your statements, this may indicate that you actually do feel differently about the topic than you think you do. Spend some more time looking inside and see how you really feel. On the other hand, you may just have developed a habit of smiling when you deliver bad news or frowning when joking or some other incongruent style. If necessary, practice in front of a mirror until your posture, tone of voice, gestures and so on match the way you feel.

Scripting Your Needs

You have a right to ask for the things you need in your relationship. In fact, you have a responsibility to yourself and to your partner to be clear about your needs. You are the expert on yourself. No one else, not even your partner, can read your mind and know what you need in the way of support, intimate contact, time alone, domestic order, in-dependence, sex, love, financial security, and so on.

On the other hand, everyone else, especially your partner, is trying to get his or her own needs met. Your needs don't have automatic priority. You have a right to ask, but that doesn't necessarily mean that you are entitled to everything you ask for. You have to balance your right to seek your needs with your partner's right. Your needs may at times be in conflict: you want the sedan and your partner wants the pickup, you want another child and your partner thinks that two are enough, you want to move for better employment opportunities and your partner wants to stay in the same neighborhood. Compromise and cooperation are often the essential keys to resolving conflicting needs.

Exercise

It's best to write out your request ahead of time. This sounds very artificial, but it's important. When you have a serious need that you want your partner's help in satisfying, it's always worth the time it takes to write out your request first. You will get things clear in your mind, and, most importantly, you can make sure that your communication has all the elements of a good request. Use the needs script that follows to make sure that you have included the situation, your feelings, your request for behavior change, and your self-care alternative if appropriate.

Needs Script

Situation (specific, objective description of facts):

Feelings (non-blaming "I" statements):

Request (for behavior change):

Self-care alternative (how you could take care of yourself):

Guidelines for Scripting Your Needs

The situation. Be very objective. Describe just the facts, without analysis or interpretation. Avoid inflammatory language. Don't say, "This place is a dump." Instead, just say, "Sometimes there are dirty dishes in the sink and dirty clothes on the floor."

Feelings. Apply all you have learned in the first part of this chapter to clearly express your feelings.

Request. Ask for a change in behavior only. This is a very important rule. Don't expect your partner to change his or her values, attitudes, desires, motivations, or feelings. These characteristics are very hard to change. It's like asking someone to be taller or more intelligent. People feel personally threatened if you ask them to try to change intangibles that are seen as part of their very nature and largely beyond their conscious control. For example, what does it mean to ask someone to be "more loving" or "less critical" or "neater"? These kinds of requests are heard as attacks, and little real change is likely to result.

Stick to observable behavior. If you want your spouse to be more loving, describe the actions that loving means to you: "Hug me when I come in the door." "Sit next to me on the couch when we watch TV." "Take me out for dinner on my birthday." If you want your partner to be less critical, you're going to have to spell out the desired behavior: "Don't kid me about the phone bill or my driving when other people are around." "Don't comment on my driving in the car, and help me pay the bills this month so we can balance the checkbook together." If you want someone to be neater, put it in terms of desired behaviors: "Put all dirty clothes in the hamper, hang up the tools when you're done with them, and bundle all the newspapers by Wednesday night."

Don't ask for too much all at once. Sigmund told his longtime girlfriend Robin that he was willing to marry her if she would do 135 sit-ups a day to tighten her stomach muscles, allow him to buy her a more stylish wardrobe, read fewer novels so she could pay more attention to him, and send her son to therapy. This particular request broke up the relationship.

You have to stick to one situation and just one or two behavioral changes at a time. A laundry list of changes will be overwhelming to your partner. Concentrate on one request, get agreement, and try the new arrangement for a while before you go on to ask for something else.

Your self-care alternative. This is otherwise known as the "or else." Your self-care alternative is what you intend to do for yourself if your partner isn't willing to grant your needs request. For example, if you are tired of doing the dishes by yourself every night, but your partner doesn't agree to help you, your self-care alternative might be to stop going out to the movies on Fridays and use the savings to buy a dishwasher.

A self-care alternative isn't meant to be a punitive ultimatum. Your alternative is meant to be your plan for solving a problem if you can't get your partner's help in a preferred solution.

Don't spring your alternative right away. Save it until you see how negotiations are proceeding. But have an alternative ready, just in case.

Here is how Ben scripted his need for time alone.

> *Situation:* Since we started the tax-preparing business, we've been spending almost all our time together. I notice that I don't read or listen to music by myself like I used to.

> *Feelings:* I really enjoy working together, and I feel like we're closer than we've been in years. But I've also been feeling a little stressed out and nervous, like I'm on stage all the time or under pressure.

> *Request:* I need a little time each week by myself. What do you think about reserving one morning or one afternoon a week for things we can do separately? For instance, I'd like to get my camera out on Saturday and go off to take some pictures.

There are several things to notice about Ben's statements:

- He keeps the facts of the situation separate from the feelings.

- There is no blame. He uses "I" statements that take responsibility for his feelings.

- His request is specific and behavioral in nature. Rather than saying "I want you to stop breathing down my neck and talking about the business all the time," he requests an afternoon off.

- Although he didn't need to mention it, he had a self-care alternative in mind. If necessary, he planned to enroll in a meditation class so that he would have a set time each week to be off on his own without his partner.

When you have your request polished and ready, pick a time to talk to your partner. Make sure that he or she has the time and is in the frame of mind to listen attentively to your request. Commit yourself to a calm, cool request. Any tone of anger or irritation will severely limit your chances of getting what you want.

If you run into resistance with your first request and your self-care alternative doesn't work, see the chapter on negotiation for help in resolving conflicts.

3

Reciprocal Reinforcement

Relationships can gradually run down. Early pleasures become commonplace and boring. Minor flaws become major faults. Charming eccentricities become incredibly irritating. To counteract this trend, you need to give each other new pleasures from time to time. Reciprocal reinforcement can help.

Reciprocal reinforcement simply means that each person does more of the things that the other person likes—small, obvious things such as back rubs, washing dishes, giving flowers, fixing a lamp, making a favorite dessert, or returning a video tape.

This sounds too simple to be a serious therapeutic technique, but it works. If your relationship has become boring, irritating, and unsatisfying, reciprocal reinforcement may be the ideal starting place. It has five advantages:

1. It establishes collaboration—you will both be working together to make improvements.

2. It works fast, increasing pleasure, commitment, and caring immediately.

3. It builds confidence by giving each of you a sense of control over the relationship.

4. It's easy—you don't have to learn any new skills. You already know how to cook favorite dishes, give a hug, make a phone call, or attend a PTA meeting.

5. It can set the stage for future change on more significant, long-standing issues.

Reciprocal reinforcement works best to reverse dissatisfactions that have been building up for a long time. When you have a serious and immediate problem such as a rage reaction or an impending layoff that must be dealt with right away, you are better off using some other intervention such as Time Out (see chapter 11), separation, or formal problem-solving techniques (see chapter 7).

History

Reciprocal reinforcement in couples therapy was introduced by R. B. Stuart (1969) as a way of countering the low rates of reinforcement he observed in troubled marriages. He had each partner pick three pleasing behaviors that the other could perform more frequently.

In 1973, Azrin, Naster, and Jones developed the Marital Happiness Scale, from which they selected three behaviors to reinforce in each partner.

In 1979, Neil S. Jacobson and Gayla Margolin showed how the principle of reciprocity not only explains why reciprocal reinforcement works so well, but also provides an excellent starting point for couples entering therapy. They explained to new clients how couples shape each other's behavior over time by unconsciously rewarding some behaviors and punishing others. When couples see how they already exchange positive and negative behaviors all the time, in roughly equal measure, it provides a rationale for consciously altering behavior.

In 1980, Stuart elaborated on his original technique with the "Caring Days" intervention, in which each partner makes a list of small behaviors that the other could perform. Each agrees to do five items from the other's list daily, for one-to-two weeks.

Theoretical Background

Common sense says there are two kinds of changes that you can make to improve a relationship: increase pleasure or decrease pain. To put it in a behaviorist's terms, you can eliminate undesirable behavior or increase desirable behavior.

The latter approach is easier and more effective. Most people find it much easier to do more of something their partner likes than to stop doing something their partner hates. And research indicates that this approach works better. Studies show that while removing annoying behaviors won't increase pleasing ones, adding pleasing behaviors *will* reduce annoying ones.

Time for Mastery

Reciprocal reinforcement takes about five weeks:

- Week one—make pleasers list
- Week two—provide pleasers
- Week three—ask for pleasers
- Week four—exchange contracts
- Week five—mutual pleasers

Allow extra time for inevitable delays, interruptions, relapses, and setbacks. Realistically, you can expect to take a couple of months to work through all the exercises in this chapter, although beneficial results will begin immediately.

Instructions

Week One—Make Pleasers List

For one week, carry around a piece of paper and a pen. Keep a running list of what pleases you and what pleases your partner. Add to your list whenever you think of something. If you forget during the day, be sure to add something to your list before retiring each night.

Look for pleasers in these areas of your relationship:

Considerate acts	Sensuality, touching
Communications process	Leisure activities
Child care	Household management
Financial decision making	Employment
Education	Personal habits
Appearance	Independence

Guidelines for Reciprocal Reinforcement

1. Omit items that have been areas of serious conflict for you. If most of your arguments involve money, leave out financial matters.

2. Cross out items involving giant expenses or effort. The ideal pleaser costs nothing and is easy to do, like a kiss. New cars, losing weight, and major remodeling should not be on your pleasers list.

3. Don't include anything you are not really willing to do. For example, don't plan to visit your mother-in-law in a rest home daily or to itemize *all* your personal expenses unless you are really willing to do those things.

4. Add details to be more specific. For example "Refinish the green dresser" is more detailed than "Spruce up the house." "Shave Saturday and Sunday mornings" is more specific than "Improve grooming."

5. Use wording that focuses on behaviors, not attitudes. For instance "Hug her when I come in the door" is a specific behavior, while "Be more loving" is a vague attitude. "Consult him on New Year's party plans" is an obvious behavior that you can remember to perform, whereas "Be less bossy" describes a change in attitude that is much harder to act on.

Keep track of what pleases you and your partner until you have at least ten items for each of you. Rank each item according to this scale:

1 = Nice

2 = Better

3 = Great

Example.   Rod and Linda developed the following lists over the course of a week.

Rod's List

Pleases me

Offer a drink and a hug when I come home   3

Leave me alone in front of TV for 15 minutes before
dinner   3

Dump garbage daily   1

Keep cat out of our bedroom   3

Kiss good night   2
Leave notes—where she's gone, when she will return   3
Write full information in checkbook   2
Wear my favorite perfume   1
Dance together in the living room   2

Pleases her

Fix things   3
Hugs   2
Eat more veggies   2
Pay attention to her stories   1
Birthday and anniversary gifts   3
Refinish dresser   2
Wax her car   2
Notice her outfits, give compliments   2
Support her Weight Watchers efforts   2
Make my own breakfast   1
Do recycling   2
Be nice to her sister   3

Linda's List

Pleases me

Hugs   2
Compliments   3
Pay attention, check in daily   3
Keep up yard   1
Listen to my opinions and let me know he understands
       what I'm saying   2
Cook his own breakfast   1
Clean up closet   1
Keep books and magazines off couch   3
More affectionate touches that don't lead to sex   3
Take cooking course   2
Notice when I look good   3
More balanced meals when he cooks   3

Pleases him

Perfume   3
Initiate sex   2
Meat and potatoes   3
Balance my own checkbook   3
Hugs and kisses   1
Neck rub   1
Keep kitchen tidier   2

Help with yard work   3
Watch TV with him   1
Be quiet when he's reading   2
Return his library books   1

Don't share your lists with each other until the end of week two. Unexpected pleasures are doubly satisfying. And at this stage you shouldn't raise your partner's expectations about what you plan to do, just in case you forget to provide some of the pleasers you have planned.

Week Two—Provide Pleasers

Based on your revised list, pick four or five highly-rated items that you are willing to provide. Look for things that you have not been doing recently, pleasers that it will be easy for you to give. Every day of the next week, give your partner at least one item from your list that you think will be most pleasing.

Set a modest target number of pleasers that is a little higher than the number you were providing before. For example, if you usually do three things a week that your partner likes, plan to do one thing per day for this week. Start slow and don't try to become a perfect mate overnight.

Keep track. At the end of each day, write down the pleasers you performed and the ones you received. Don't try to second-guess yourself or your partner—include everything pleasing that you do or have done for you, even things that you and your partner "would have done anyway."

Keep track, but don't keep score. There may be discrepancies in the average number of pleasers already existing or being added in this week. There is really no way to tell if this is a reflection of one person putting out more effort, or a perception problem on the part of the other partner. Don't compare rates and make it a cause for argument. Assume that any apparent discrepancy is a *mutual* problem: one partner has trouble giving enough pleasers *and* the other has trouble perceiving and reinforcing pleasers. Concentrate on meeting your own target. You can depend on the fact that when you find the pleasers that really work, you will start getting pleasers coming back from your partner.

Don't tell each other what you have picked from your lists. Just give what you think will be pleasing to your partner and see what happens for a week.

In the second week of their experiment with reciprocal reinforcement, Rod hugged Linda several times, complimented her on how well she was doing with her Weight Watchers program, fixed a vegetarian meal, repaired her umbrella, and washed her Pontiac. Linda helped with some yard work, gave Rod a neck rub, made two meat and potato meals, joined Rod in front of the TV news, and kissed him goodnight when she went to bed first.

Feedback. At the end of week two, give honest feedback to each other about which pleasers you noticed and appreciated the most. It's important to let your partner know which pleasers worked and that you appreciate the effort in general. Giving positive feedback is essential to keep the flow of satisfaction coming your way. If you find giving feedback awkward or can't remember everything that happened, just read your daily lists of pleasers received to each other.

When Linda and Rod gave each other feedback, they learned some interesting things. They both appreciated the hugs. Linda especially valued Rod's vegetarian dinner, but she didn't even notice that Rod had fixed her umbrella. Rod appreciated help with the yard work and the neck rub, but found that watching the TV news together was irrelevant to him. He realized that his TV watching was a way of avoiding contact with Linda, not a relaxing activity in itself.

Week Three—Ask for Pleasers

At the beginning of this week, each of you gets to ask for three special things that you want the other to do during the next seven days. Be sure to follow these important guidelines:

1. The items should come from your lists. If you must ask for a new, untried pleaser, it should be very similar to the pleasers you already know are satisfying and easy to give.

2. Be specific. "Put all dirty clothes in the hamper and shoes away in the closet" is better than "Keep the bedroom neater."

3. Ask for behaviors, not attitudes. "Give me a nicely wrapped birthday present, with a card, on time" is better than "Be more caring."

4. No blaming. Be careful to make your requests in a way that doesn't imply blame. "Keep a running balance in the checkbook" is better than "Stop throwing away money we don't even have."

5. Pick behaviors that have no negative emotional history. Reciprocal reinforcement will improve your day-to-day relation-

ship and prepare you to tackle your heaviest problems, but it will not solve them by itself.

6. Pick behaviors that can be performed at minimal cost and effort.

7. No negotiating at this point. When your partner asks you to do something, just say whether you are willing and how likely you are to do it. If you are unlikely to do it, your partner should pick another item. If your partner is unwilling or unlikely to do what you would like, don't press, don't even ask why. Just pick something else.

When Rod and Linda made their requests, Linda opted for compliments about things she does around the house, more affectionate touches, and for Rod to make his own breakfast. Rod wanted a hug when he got home, the cat kept out of the bedroom, and notes left by Linda whenever she would be gone.

Evaluation. At the end of the week, evaluate by asking yourselves these questions:

• Was each requested pleaser carried out?

• Was it satisfying?

• How did each of you feel?

• If it wasn't done or wasn't satisfying, why not?

• Did one of you do something to undermine the interaction?

• Did you ask for something you didn't really care about?

• Did you agree to something you weren't really willing to do?

• Did you discount a pleaser because it was done by agreement and not spontaneously?

If a pleaser didn't pan out, don't blame anybody. Just don't ask for it again. Save it for later problem solving at a time when your relationship is stronger. There is probably some underlying conflict that prevents easy reciprocal reinforcement.

When Linda and Rod evaluated their week, they had managed to perform all their pleasers, and most were satisfying. Rod noticed that he actually enjoyed the touching without sex, although he had assumed it would be meaningless or frustrating. Linda found that leaving notes about where she was and when she'd be back was difficult. At first it felt like she was giving up some of her independence. Then Rod thanked her for making it easier for him to plan his activities and explained that he felt more secure knowing how to find her in an emergency. Linda realized that the notes were a communication tool, not a way of controlling or judging her. Rod realized that to keep getting the notes, he had to express his appreciation once in a while and refrain from criticizing how she spent her time.

Week Four—Exchange Contracts

You now have a repertoire of pleasers that you both enjoy receiving and are willing and able to give. You are ready to codify your best pleasers in the form of a contract. List what you will do and when and how often you will do it. Limit your contract to two or three really important behaviors at first. Put your contract where you will see it frequently and be reminded of your agreement. Keep the contract in force for a week, then open it up for renegotiation. Change or add pleasers.

Here is the contract that Rod and Linda developed.

I, Rod, will compliment Linda on her dress or appearance and things she does around the house. I'll cook my own breakfast. I will listen to Linda without interruption when she has an opinion and I'll let her know that I understand what she's saying.

I, Linda, will keep the cat out of the bedroom, give Rod a hug when he gets home, and give him time to relax quietly right after work.

They posted their contract on the inside of their medicine cabinet door, where they would see it a couple of times every day. Note that some of the items had changed from week three because they wanted to try some new things from their lists.

Week Five—Mutual Pleasers

If your exchange contract works out, you're ready to move up to mutual pleasers. Plan to do more activities together that both of you consider pleasurable. This can be the most powerful form of reciprocal reinforcement because you are working *with* each other rather than *for* each other. Mutual pleasers are especially good for busy people with divergent interests and those who have been avoiding each other to avoid conflict.

Start by each writing down possible activities on a list and then combine the lists into one list. The rules of brainstorming apply here:

anything goes on the list at first, no matter how crazy or unlikely. No criticism is allowed. Just generate as many ideas as you can, regardless of their apparent merit. Often two poor ideas can be combined into one good idea, or a wildly impractical notion might make you think of a really creative and more likely activity. Don't hold back in fear of sounding ridiculous and don't ridicule your partner's suggestions.

When looking for mutual pleasers, consider things you used to enjoy together but haven't done in a long time. For instance, if you met on the horse trail but haven't been riding in years, try a short ride together.

Another promising area is to look for new hobbies and avocations you can explore together—things neither of you has done before: antique collecting, skin diving, tennis, singing, political action, and so on. Learning and exploring something new can be less threatening than just planning to be alone together, with no particular focus. Also, a new activity will have no history of failure or contention for you as a couple.

Avoid things you have tried recently that didn't work. If you have been fighting every time you attend one of your daughter's soccer games, don't choose your children's sporting activities as a mutual interest to develop. Let such activities slide in favor of something genuinely interesting to both of you.

Once you have settled on a shared activity to try, nail down the details: when, where, how long, baby-sitting, rescheduling time conflicts, making reservations, how you will pay for it, and so on. It's all too easy to agree to go on a bird-watching hike some time, then never get around to it.

There are a few hurdles that you may need to watch out for:

1. If one of you typically makes all the social arrangements, make sure that the other one takes some active role in setting up your mutual pleaser.

2. If one or both of you tend to agree just to be agreeable, make sure you each genuinely want to do the activity you choose. It won't work if one of you "goes along" with the other's plan, or if one of you says yes to an activity just because it is too hard to say no.

3. Watch out for hidden agendas. Rachel got Henry to go for a long walk in the woods, ostensibly to get some exercise and enjoy nature together. Rachel's hidden agenda was to use the time alone to quiz Henry about his level of commitment to their relationship. Henry ended up feeling trapped and fooled and angry. Rachel ended up feeling sneaky and disappointed.

Special Considerations

If reciprocal reinforcement is not working for you, it may be because of one of these common pitfalls.

Victimization

Victimization means that you feel your partner is at fault, that your mate does things to you or fails to do things for you, that you're the victim and there's nothing you can do about it.

For example, Dorothy wanted Jim to reveal his feelings more. He seemed to hang back, unwilling to open up and share himself on any meaningful level. She tried to pry and coax information out of him, but the more she tried, the more he resisted. Dorothy just gave up. She was sick of being snubbed and shut out of his inner life. Even a marriage counselor couldn't get Jim to open up. It didn't seem like there was anything anybody could do to change the relationship. When the counselor suggested they try reciprocal reinforcement, Dorothy thought, "What's the use?"

The way around victimization is to approach reciprocal reinforcement as a scientific experiment. Follow the steps of reciprocal reinforcement even if you don't believe it will work. Then objectively evaluate the outcome. See if anything has changed.

When Dorothy and Jim started reciprocal reinforcement, she was surprised. In the first couple of weeks, she watched the news with him, rubbed his feet, and asked "How was your day?" when he got home from work. He brought her chocolates and stopped to pick up groceries on his way home from work. Gradually, Dorothy realized that she was getting information about Jim's feelings: what he felt about world events, how he loved her touch, his anxiety about work, and his growing appreciation of how much effort it took to keep the larder stocked.

The Spontaneity Paradox

You may believe that only spontaneous acts have value. You may feel that pleasure given out of obligation or by agreement is no good. You may say to yourself that your spouse "should really *want* to do it, not just do it."

For example, Greg told himself, "If Carl goes to the tennis courts with me by agreement, it doesn't count. He must really *want* to exercise and play together."

The truth is that it's quite common for people's thoughts and behaviors to change first, and the feelings to change later. When Carl finds out how much fun it can be to play tennis with Greg, he may end up wanting to play as much as Greg does.

But even if your partner never comes to want exactly what you want, even if your partner never feels exactly the way you feel about something, so what? You can still have much of the fun of shared activity. You can take comfort in the fact that acts performed by agreement or out of obligation at least indicate that your partner "wants" to please you.

To emphasize this "want to please," you can try the cookie jar technique. Each of you has a cookie jar into which you have placed slips of paper. On each slip is a pleaser that you would like to have done for you. The pleasers should be simple, specific behaviors that can be done quickly and easily, almost any time, any place: draw a bath, sort socks, help make a shopping list, address Christmas cards, put photos in an album, make a cup of tea.

At unscheduled times you or your partner pulls a slip out of the other's cookie jar and does it. If the pleaser isn't appropriate at the time, put it back and pull another out. Both of you should add new items to your cookie jars from time to time.

Mind Reading

Oneness of mind is a romantic myth. It leads to self-defeating interchanges like this:

Jane: He should know by now what I like. I shouldn't have to tell him. If he loved me, he'd know without being told.

Robert: I do love her, but I can't read her mind. I'm not good at picking up subtle clues. I need things spelled out.

Don't expect your partner to read your mind. Assume that you can only get what you ask for and that the quality of what you get will depend on how clear and detailed you can make your request.

Blaming and Labeling

Don't let your pet theories about your partner's personality keep you from wholeheartedly participating in reciprocal reinforcement. Bill thought that Jim had some serious character defects. He said that Jim was "cold, distant, and harsh with criticism." In fact, Jim didn't lack loving feelings. He just lacked skills of self-observation and expression. Giving Bill his pleasers and watching the results showed him how to express his love concretely and how to observe the effects of his behavior on others.

Can't Get Started or Remember To Follow Through

Perhaps a five-to-six week effort is just too much for you to begin or see through to the end. In that case, try a love day or care day. Or start even smaller with a love hour or a love evening. Take turns giving each other an hour, an evening, or a day in which you double your pleasing behavior. You'll still need to have a long list of pleasing options, and you'll also need to discuss exactly what it is about each option that makes it pleasing.

Habitual Low Spots

Is there a time of day or a particular day of the week that is stressful for you as a couple? For some it's the evenings right after work. For others it's the kid's bedtime or Sundays.

If you hit an habitual low spot, focus your efforts on that time. Find mutual pleasers for these stressful times and make an exchange contract that gives you each a precise script to follow. For example, Tara and Harry had this contract for weekday evenings at home:

> Whoever gets home first will collect the mail, take
> the messages off the machine, and start dinner. Whoever
> gets home second will give a big hug and kiss, set the
> table, and make sure the kids are set up with what they
> need for homework. No phone calls until after dinner.
> Whoever does the dishes, the other puts the kids to bed.
> No matter what we want to do separately, we will have a
> cup of tea together after the kids are in bed, and talk
> about what happened during the day.

When you have practiced reciprocal reinforcement for a couple of months, you should have a basis of mutual pleasure, cooperation, and control on which to build. Then you can tackle your more serious conflicts by learning some of the other skills in this book, such as problem solving or intervening in your system.

Advanced Skills

4

Clean Communication

Mary had been anxiously watching the clock since 6:30, aware that dinner was rapidly drying up in the oven. When Larry's key turned in the door an hour and a quarter later and Mary heard his nonchalant "I'm home," her wave of relief was instantly replaced with rage. "Where the hell have you been," she stormed. "Dinner's totally ruined." "Don't start with me," Larry began coldly. "Don't start with me," Mary mimicked sarcastically, then yelled, "Maybe I'll finish with you instead." "Fine," seethed Larry. "You do that. Life would be a helluva lot easier without your constant bitching." "Asshole," screamed Mary. "Get out of my face, bitch," yelled Larry. While he grimly opened his newspaper, Mary slammed into the bedroom.

Kevin and Natalie had spent the day at the beach. It had been a long week and both were tired. The warm sand and the lapping of the waves lulled them, and for a few hours they lay and read in amiable companionship. Natalie began thinking about how nice it would be to try to continue this state of harmony: "Hey, Kev, let's eat dinner at that little French restaurant around the corner." Kevin meanwhile was beginning to feel restless. His thoughts strayed to the unwritten report sitting on his desk: "Nah, I'm going to do some work tonight." "Work!" exclaimed Natalie. "You're always working. Make some time for me for a change." "Jesus!" shouted Kevin. "What have I been doing all day? Besides, some of us aren't dilettantes, we have jobs that require some dedication." "What's that supposed to mean?" demanded Natalie. "Since when is your precious job so much more important than mine?" "Since I bring home twice the money you do," Kevin retorted. "What a jerk, what sexist crap," Natalie exploded.

Exchanges like these leave scars, but it's not just the screaming fights that damage your relationship. It's the sarcasm, the put-downs and name calling. It's the body language of hostility, the folded arms and clenched jaw. After each interaction, you feel more alienated. Your anger, hurt, and disappointment grow.

Pejorative communication between a couple erodes each partner's self-esteem and makes mutual problem solving almost impossible. Clean communication, on the other hand, protects self-esteem and creates a safe place for working on problems. Clean communication means taking responsibility for the impact of what you say. It means being honest rather than lying or telling half-truths; it means being complete rather than leaving important pieces of the communication unspoken; and, most importantly, it means being supportive: fostering closeness and understanding rather than defensiveness and distance.

History

The importance of complete communication has been stressed by many authors. The term *whole messages* was introduced by McKay, Davis, and Fanning (1983). Whole messages have four components: observations, thoughts, feelings, and needs. Intimate communications are cleaner and more likely to fully convey what you mean when all four parts of a whole message are included. Partial messages (those that leave out one or more of the components) or contaminated messages (those that mix or mislabel parts of a whole message) create serious communication problems.

Time for Mastery

The assessment process takes one week. You can begin following the ten commandments for clean communication immediately, but the skill of delivering whole messages may require four to six weeks of rehearsal and practice.

Ten Commandments of Clean Communication

If you follow these basic guidelines, you'll virtually eliminate pejorative communication in your partnership. In the process, levels of hurt and anger will greatly reduce.

1. Avoid judgmental words and loaded terms. These are the zingers, the words that convey to your partner that he or she is flawed. *"Total lack* of effort ... *childish* behavior ... *uncooperative* ... that *self-involved* style of yours ... acting *helpless* ... *poor me* attitude ... *thoughtless* as usual ... a *total crock* ... playing *cute little Shirley Temple."* These words attack and undermine feelings of worth. They have no place in a relationship between caring partners.

2. Avoid global labels. Global labels are generalized condemnations of a partner's identity. He or she is "stupid, sexist, crazy, selfish, lazy, useless, evil, a bitch or an asshole." Notice the attack is not on your partner's behavior, but on your partner's person. It conveys the message that he or she is bad—not just at this moment, but always. When they're delivered, global labels feel correct and just. They feel like proper punishment. But the outcome is a loss of trust and a loss of closeness.

3. Avoid "you" messages of blame and accusation. "You're never home on time ... you never go anywhere with me ... you leave me all the work ... you never ask what I want ... you're a lot more interested in your work than me." The essence of a "you" message is simply this: "I'm in pain, and you did it to me." And there's usually this subtext: "You were bad and wrong for doing it to me." Consider how the "you" message contrasts with an "I" message.

"You" message: You're always spoiling our evening by showing up late.

"I" message: When you come home late I feel sad about missing the evening with you.

"You" message: You're never here when there's work to be done.

"I" message: I feel tired and irritated when I put the groceries away alone.

Notice in the "I" message that there's no direct statement of causation, there's no blaming of your partner.

4. Avoid old history. Clean communication sticks with the issue at hand, pejorative communication throws mud from the past. "You did this to me last week and a month ago at Barbara's house. And then there was New Year's, the same damned thing." The message is: "You're bad, you're bad, you're bad. You've always had this flaw, and it's not getting any better." Sometimes the past can provide a useful perspective, a longitudinal view of a problem. But references to old history are usually just building a case against your partner. You're collecting evidence to underscore the seriousness of his or her faults. A simple rule to follow: never bring up old history when you're angry. Anger turns references to the past into a club, rather than a source of enlightenment.

5. Avoid negative comparisons. Clean communication doesn't make your partner feel bad about him or herself. It's designed to help, not hurt. It's supposed to resolve, rather than reject. Negative comparisons *never* resolve anything. Their sole function is to punish and attack.

6. Avoid threats. The basic message contained in a threat is: you're bad and I'm going to punish you. "If you go to your sister's, don't expect me here when you get back ... If you can't do a simple fun thing like go to the movies with me, I know plenty of other men who will ... If you can't say something nice when I get home, maybe we should just forget going away this weekend." The "you are bad" message is painful enough, but the deliberate intention to hurt is tremendously destructive to your relationship.

7. *Describe* your feelings rather than *attack* with them. When you describe your feelings, you use clarifying words to make them understood. "I'm sad and tearful ... I feel a yearning to be closer ... I'm feeling rather hurt and withdrawn ... I'm stunned and embarrassed." Notice that the description directly identifies the emotion. Attacking with your feelings means using your affect as a weapon. Your voice gets loud, harsh, threatening, coldly hostile, sarcastic or needling. When you're communicating cleanly, you keep your voice as close as you can to normal volume and inflection. As a result, your partner can hear what you're feeling without being overwhelmed or bludgeoned by it.

8. Keep body language open and receptive. Your body says how open and willing you are to communicate. When you have pinched lips, a tight jaw, when you are frowning, squinting, or looking away in a dubious or disgusted manner, your body is saying loud and clear that you don't want to communicate. You are also blocking communication when your arms are folded or when you're leaning away or pointing an accusing finger.

If you want your body to say yes to open communication, keep good eye contact, nod while you're listening, keep your arms uncrossed, lean slightly forward if you are sitting, and keep your face loose and relaxed.

9. Use whole messages.   As described earlier, whole messages consist of observations, thoughts, feelings, and needs or wants.

Observations are statements of fact that are neutral, without judgment or inference. "Yesterday it rained nonstop from 10:00 till 3:30 . . . Chemistry classes start tomorrow . . . I'm going to find out what Beth is wearing before I go tonight."

Thoughts are your beliefs, opinions, theories, and interpretations of a situation. Thoughts are not conveyed as absolute truth, but as your personal hypothesis or understanding of a situation. "My idea was . . . I wondered if . . . I've suspected that . . . . I worried that . . . The way I saw it was . . . " "You're spending too much time at work" is not an appropriate way to express thoughts in a whole message. It turns your opinion into absolute truth. "My sense is that the balance is off; I think you need to spend more time at home." Here the speaker takes responsibility for her own opinion and doesn't try to make it the word of God.

The feelings part of the whole message can often be the most important component, especially between intimate partners. Feelings don't blame, they are simple descriptions of your emotional state. See chapter 2 for a detailed discussion of expressing feelings and needs.

The fourth part of a whole message is your needs. No one can know what you want unless you tell them, so expressing your needs clearly is very important. Not even the people closest to you can read your mind, no matter how much they love you. "I feel terrible. Would you please get up with the baby? . . . I need a break. Let's get some lunch. . . . Let me have an hour alone to recover from work" are all statements of needs or wants.

Important communications to your partner should always be in the form of whole messages that clearly separate your observations, opinions, feelings, and wants. Leaving out one of these components results in a *partial message*. When you take your coat to the dry cleaners or your car to the garage or when you're buying a new pair of shoes, you can communicate quite effectively without including information about your feelings and emotional needs. But when it's crucial that you and your partner understand each other, you can't leave anything out— you need to describe the observations that led to certain conclusions, the feelings about an event, and your desire for something to change. When there's a lot at stake emotionally and you need to be understood, a partial message becomes dangerous.

10. Use clear messages. Clear messages separate observations, opinions, feelings, and needs. Contaminated messages mix or mislabel these components to create hurt and confusion. A woman who sarcastically says to her partner at the dinner table, "You're talkative as usual," may pretend her statement is a simple observation. But the observation is contaminated with judging thoughts, feelings and needs. A more accurate statement would include all four components of a whole message: "I notice you're pretty quiet tonight (*observation*). It makes me think you're not interested in me (*thought*), and I feel hurt and a little angry (*feeling*). I'd really like you to talk with me more (*need*)."

Contaminated messages lead to alienation and distance. You know there's more to the message than is being clearly stated, but you're not really sure what it is. It's not so much that something is left out, as in a partial message, but what's said is covert or disguised.

An effective way to contaminate your message is to disguise it as a question, especially a "why" question. "Why are you looking at me like that?" might be labeled as a simple request for information. It could more accurately be described as a judging thought, ("You shouldn't be looking at me like that") or a feeling ("I don't like the way you're looking at me"). "Why don't you ever clean up after yourself?" is, even more clearly not a simple request for information. It could more accurately be stated using all four elements of a whole message: "You tend to leave your clothes on the floor when you get undressed (*observation*). It makes me think that you want me to pick them up (*thought*). And I end up feeling taken for granted and unappreciated (*feeling*). I'd like to talk about our expectations with respect to housework (*need*)."

Assessment

Now you need to take a look at your own patterns of communication. Divide several pieces of paper with a line down the right-hand side. During the next week, keep a log on the left half of the paper of each significant conflict or angry exchange that you have with your partner. If you don't have much data at the end of a week, go back in time to other significant conflicts or fights that you remember well and add those to the events listed on your log. As clearly as you can remember, write down the things that *you* said to your partner. Include anything you remember about your tone of voice and body language. Try to be as accurate and truthful as you can. The more complete your answer, the better you'll be served by this exercise.

At the end of the assessment period, look at each of the statements you wrote down on the left-hand column of the page. In the right-hand column, write down the number of the commandment or commandments that each statement broke. If you are engaging in blaming "you" messages, write a 3 in the right-hand column. If you are attacking with your feelings rather than describing them, write a 7. Don't bother noting anything about commandments 9 and 10, since you're still in the process of learning more about whole messages.

Notice which of the commandments for clean communication you tend to break repeatedly. Were these same commandments typically broken in the family where you grew up? When you use pejorative communication, what's the outcome? Do you get what you want? Are you aware of long-term negative consequences for using pejorative communications? How do you feel about yourself when you communicate pejoratively?

Laura's case.   During the week that Laura kept her journal, she logged three significant conflicts between herself and Ann. Here's what her journal looked like.

Conflict	Broken Commandments
Monday: Told Ann she was stupid to pay a gardener for something we could do ourselves. I was talking loud and pointing at her. Told her if she couldn't make better decisions, I was taking over the checkbook. She's a spendthrift like her mother. Three hundred dollars for planting a few flower beds. I told her there was a big hole in our collective wallet, and she was it.	1, 2, 3, 6, 7, 8
Tuesday: Ann calls me at work regarding what flight to book. Told Ann she was neurotic about decisions. What the hell difference does it make if we take the 6:00 or 7:30 plane? What's an hour and a half? It's stupid. Just order the tickets and leave me alone about it. I said, "Why don't you take responsibility and figure it out instead of expecting me to help you with every ridiculously minor decision?" Kind of shouting.	1, 3, 7

Friday: In the hotel room in Detroit she wants   1, 3, 4, 7
a room service dinner. It's about three times
as expensive as a coffee shop. Told her to
think about what we have to give up because
we're wasting money on this shit. She wants
another car, for example. How can we save
for it? I said, "Is this saving? Is it, Ann? Is
this planning for the future, Ann? Or is this a
big waste? You might as well throw our
money down the toilet, Ann, like you did last
month with those ridiculously expensive
drapes. I was supposed to be surprised. I was
surprised, all right, surprised at the idiotic
waste." Very loud, sarcastic.

When Laura looked back over her journal, she noticed that she was using a lot of judgmental language, blaming "you" messages, and was attacking with her feelings rather than describing them. Her family had communicated in exactly the same way. In addition, Laura's family was very prone to making threats. She noticed that she sounded like her father when she threatened Ann on Monday that she would take over the checkbook.

Laura thought seriously about her log. Was she getting what she wanted? What were the outcomes when she used pejorative language? The immediate consequence was that Ann often got very hurt and cried. But the long-term consequence was even more serious: Ann was becoming very tentative about making decisions and initiating anything for fear of Laura's anger. Laura suspected that her anger over Ann's decision with the gardener just made it harder for Ann to decide other things like which flight to take.

Laura already knew that her outbursts were not only hurting Ann, but were also undermining Laura's own self-esteem. She hated the angry, sarcastic tone she used. And she felt a sense of wrongness about wounding Ann. A single week of keeping her journal served to convince Laura that she needed much cleaner communication with her partner.

How To Communicate Using Whole Messages

Getting some practice. In the following exercise, try making whole messages out of each partial or contaminated message. Write your new message out using first-person sentences ("I notice that you've been out a lot . . . "). At the end of the exercise, you'll find suggested whole messages for each example.

1. "You've been working in the yard a long time." Imagine this said in an annoyed, tired voice, implying that the time was too long and may have been better spent helping to get dinner ready and attending to the kids.

    Observations:

    Thoughts:

    Feelings:

    Needs:

2. "Jimmy's been waiting for you. Another late one, huh?" This cold voice vibrates with anger and concern that Jimmy is very disappointed at going to sleep without seeing his parent. The class ended at 8:30, but recently there has been a pattern of staying late and socializing with other students.

    Observations:

    Thoughts:

    Feelings:

    Needs:

3. "I think you're ready to go home. Isn't it time for you to withdraw into your hole? The big silence? Drop your shit and run?" The voice is loud and bitter; the face looks angry and hurt. They've just finished an argument where her boyfriend characteristically shrugged, folded his arms, said "This is too

irrational," and fell quiet. Now he's gathering his things to leave.

Observations:

Thoughts:

Feelings:

Needs:

4. "What's the matter with you? We're supposed to be having fun here. At least we're spending enough money trying to." The scene is a fancy restaurant and the voice is a hiss. The speaker was resentful about being there to begin with and now is further upset that his partner is angry and withdrawn. She's reacting to his foot-dragging about coming and is speaking in one-word sentences.

Observations:

Thoughts:

Feelings:

Needs:

5. "What the fuck? There's nothing in the house but cereal. You wanna eat Raisin Bran for dinner?" The tone is disappointed and annoyed. They had agreed to take turns shopping, and the partner whose turn it was hadn't shopped all week.

Observations:

Thoughts:

Feelings:

Needs:

Suggested whole messages.

1. *Observations:* You've been gardening all afternoon.
   Thoughts: And I've had to cope with a lot in here by myself—dinner, the kids.
   Feelings: I feel tired and a little irritated.
   Needs: I'd like you to check in with me and find out what needs to be done.

2. *Observations:* You arrived after Jimmy was already asleep. He was disappointed and misses seeing you in the evenings.
   Thoughts: I think Jimmy needs to see you before he goes to sleep.
   Feelings: I feel angry and worried that he isn't seeing enough of you, that he's missing you.
   Needs: Please, can you get here before 9:30 so he can see you and get tucked in?

3. *Observations:* You've gotten quiet, and you're apparently ready to leave.
   Thoughts: When we have conflict like this, you often withdraw when I believe we need to hang in and keep talking.
   Feelings: I feel incredibly hurt and abandoned, and I'm angry about this.
   Needs: I need you to stay and talk this through with me.

4. *Observations:* You wanted to come here and now you're very quiet; you're not responding.
   Thoughts: I assume you're upset because I resisted the idea of an expensive place like this.
   Feelings: I'm irritated myself.
   Needs: I'd like us both to try putting this behind us. Let's start over and enjoy our evening.

5. *Observations:* It was your turn to shop this week, and you
   haven't yet gone. There's no food for dinner.
   Thoughts: I thought we had an agreement; that both of us were
   committed to keeping up our end.
   Feelings: I'm disappointed and irritated that there's no food.
   Needs: Could you shop so we can have something in the house
   tomorrow?

Laura's case again.   Laura went back to the three conflict situations she had written in her journal and developed whole messages for
each issue. Here's what she worked out.

1. *Observations:* The gardener was paid $300 to plant flower
   beds.
   Thoughts: That feels like too much money to me for something
   we could have done ourselves.
   Feelings: It's scary to me to see the money go out like that; I
   feel helpless, like I have no control over it.
   Needs: I'd like us to make decisions together, beforehand,
   when an outlay will be over $100.

2. *Observations:* You're asking me to decide between the 6:00 and
   7:30 flight, but it's hectic at work right now.
   Thoughts: I don't think it really matters too much between the
   two.
   Feelings: Truthfully, I feel irritated to have to stop and think
   about this at work.
   Needs: I'd like you to sort it out and make the best decision
   you can; just try to work it out on your own.

3. *Observations:* A room service dinner would cost $60 or more.
   Thoughts: It feels like too much money to me, particularly
   when we're trying to save for another car.
   Feelings: It scares me to spend money like that, and I guess
   I'm irritated that you want to.
   Needs: Look, how about dinner down in the coffee shop, but
   we'll treat ourselves to room service dessert later? (This last
   compromise occurred to Laura only after she'd thought
   through her entire whole message.)

Your turn.   Now you need to do some of the work that Laura
did. Go back to your journal and develop whole messages for each of
the conflict or anger situations that you noted. Divide and clearly
separate your experience into observations, thoughts, feelings, and
needs. After you've practiced with the items in your journal, it's time

to select an ongoing issue with your partner that you'd like to explore using whole messages. Write a description of the problem and then describe it again in the whole message format. While writing your whole messages, be sure to keep the other commandments for clean communication. Above everything, whole messages do not blame, do not attack. Their aim is to describe your experience and keep your communications open.

Now look for a time to practice your newly developed whole message with your partner. Rather than just waiting for the issue to come up again, you may want to select a time to express yourself when you're not angry and there isn't a big emotional charge.

5

Identifying and Changing Cognitive Distortions

In a high rise apartment building in New York, Elaine, Sean, Dick, and Nell happened to be riding up in the same elevator around 8:00 p.m. When Elaine arrived home, her husband was angry. Sean's wife had feelings of guilt when his key turned in the door. Dick's partner felt sad. Nell's boyfriend was hurt and a little anxious as she strode in.

These four people, arriving simultaneously, entered vastly different emotional climates. The reason was simple. Their partners had very different thoughts as they walked in. Let's listen in:

Elaine's husband:	She doesn't give a shit whether I'm waiting. How I feel means nothing to her. I'm just a piece of furniture around here.
Sean's wife:	They're making him work long hours again. He's keeping up a brutal pace, while I've already had a bath and had a chance to relax for a couple hours after work.

| Dick's wife: | We'll never have a life. They use him up there. That's the way it goes. |
| Nell's boyfriend: | She's not as interested in me as she is in her work. I wonder if she's bored and thinking of pulling out. |

Each partner's emotional reaction was largely determined by his or her thoughts. Blaming thoughts made Elaine's husband angry. Thoughts about her relatively lighter load made Sean's wife feel guilty. Thoughts of passive acceptance made Dick's wife sad. And Nell's boyfriend scared himself with thoughts of abandonment.

Many of your strongest emotional reactions are generated in the same way. They are created by your *internal monologue*—that constant stream of thoughts which helps you interpret and understand the world. Your internal monologue includes assumptions about your partner's feelings and motivations and your own interpretations of events.

In this chapter you can learn to listen in on your thoughts and begin to recognize their role in your emotional life. After you get skilled at hearing your internal monologue, you'll also have a chance to evaluate its accuracy. Not everything you say to yourself about your partner or your marriage is absolutely true. Sometimes you leave out important parts of the picture, sometimes you exaggerate, sometimes you make things too black and white. These common distortions can so alter your sense of an event that your emotional reactions may get skewed. Like a picture that's been retouched, the original experience is lost beneath your assumptions and interpretations. And you may end up responding to something you've largely made up.

Learning to recognize and change inaccurate and distorted thinking can make a huge impact on your relationship. It can help you be less emotionally reactive. And it can open new, more accepting ways of seeing yourself and each other.

History

Cognitive behavioral therapy, a relatively new and growing branch of psychology, has studied the relationship between thoughts and feelings. The internal monologue that helps you interpret your experience has been called *self-talk* by rational-emotive therapist Albert Ellis (1975). Cognitive theorist Aaron Beck used the term *automatic thoughts* "because it more accurately describes the way thoughts are experienced. The person perceives these thoughts as though they are by reflex—without any prior reflection or reasoning; and they impress him as plausible and valid" (Beck 1979).

Beck and A. Ellis, along with theorists Michael Mahoney (1974) and Donald Meichenbaum (1977), have made a strong case for how your thoughts shape the way you feel and ultimately how you act. They have also developed tools for changing your thoughts and feelings. Beck has employed such strategies as the Daily Dysfunctional Thoughts Record (1988) to help couples identify distorted automatic thoughts and the Three Column Technique to challenge and change distorted thinking.

Theoretical Background

A woman sees her husband walk to the window and gaze out. She starts to feel hurt and then angry. She says sarcastically, "What's so wonderful out there. Are you gawking at the school girls again?" On the surface, the sequence doesn't make sense. But cognitive theorists would argue that there's something in between the event and the feeling that explains everything. Events don't cause feelings and behavioral reactions. Thoughts do. The woman is thinking, "He doesn't want to be here. He's sick of this house and of me." That makes her feel hurt. Then she thinks, "He's put nothing in this marriage. You put nothing in, you get nothing out." Then she feels angry and begins to craft a hostile remark.

The relationship between events, thoughts, and emotions has been called A B C theory (Ellis and Harper 1961). A is the event. The event is a catalyst for B—thoughts that attempt to assign meaning to what's happened. Once you've made some assumptions and interpretations about the event, they may trigger C—feelings. The woman who watched her husband at the window (A) could not possibly have felt hurt and anger (C) without B—her assumptions about his feelings and desires and her judgment about his efforts in the marriage.

Thoughts are always the mediating factor—they explain your sense impressions and provide the "real" picture of every event. And the picture they provide is so compelling that it is almost always believed and relied on. You decide to act based less on what you see and hear than on the meanings that you overlay on your experience.

Beck (1988), along with Dattilio and Padesky (1990), have identified the particular *cognitive distortions* that most affect intimate relationships. These distortions are specific thinking errors that act as a lens, filtering and changing the real event.

Time for Mastery

Assessment is a two-week process. The process of actively challenging distortions will take another four weeks, at a minimum, to get significant results.

Listening to Your Thoughts

The first step is to listen—not to what your partner says, but to the monologue inside. It's nearly continuous, a constant stream of thought seeking to make sense of things. For the next week, keep a *Thoughts Diary* that records your automatic thoughts during times when you are reacting emotionally. Whenever you are feeling angry, sad, anxious, guilty, or hurt in relation to your partner, make an entry in the diary.

Your Thoughts Diary can be set up on a piece of typing or binder paper that you divide into three columns. Above the left hand column, write *Event*. Above the middle, write *Thoughts*. Above the right hand column, write *Feelings*.

Arlene kept the following diary during a "typical" week with her husband.

Arlene's Thought Diary

Event	Thoughts	Feelings
Dresser drawer still sticks.	He doesn't care because only my clothes are affected. Lazy.	Anger
Late notice for car insurance.	That's real responsible!	Anger
Talking about his ex-girlfriend when he finds a book with her name in it.	Sounds like he misses her.	Sad/anxious
Back banister is wobbly.	He doesn't do a damned thing to keep up this house.	Anger
Doesn't ask how my first jewelry class went.	I'm invisible.	Hurt
Invites his sister over.	Boring, boring, boring. Shit, I'm so ungenerous.	Guilty

Dog's barking and going crazy in the backyard when I get home.	The neighbors are going to be in a rage. It's so incredibly stupid for him to leave the dog out there.	Angry
He's reading, then he says, "I love you, Sweetie," and turns out the light. He's asleep in a minute.	I'm lonely. We never talk.	Sad
He does the laundry but leaves the wet clothes out to get moldy.	Stupid, stupid. Never thinks, does it half-assed. (This isn't going to change.)	Depressed/ resigned
He falls on the floor laughing.	Unbelievable. He acts like a four-year-old.	Contempt

Arlene's Thought Diary surprised her. She had always assumed that her feelings came in direct response to her husband's behavior. But now, after recording her automatic thoughts, she was beginning to see things differently. The wet clothes that he left out weren't making her depressed. It was saying to herself, "This isn't going to change." Those words had incredible power and sent her mood to the cellar. When he said, "I love you," Arlene's response was to feel depressed. It was the thought, "We never talk," that really colored the moment for her, suggesting a life of emotional isolation.

Identifying Cognitive Distortions

An axiom in the computer world is: "Garbage in, garbage out." If you program in something that's wrong or inaccurate, the computer will serve up an answer that doesn't make sense either. The same is true of your emotional life. If you think inaccurate, distorted thoughts, your emotional reactions will be painfully exaggerated.

There are eight *cognitive distortions* that can greatly impact your relationship:

1. Tunnel vision. Here you filter out all the positive aspects of your partner's behavior or the relationship itself and focus exclusively on the parts that feel hurtful or deficient. It's a kind of selective attention where some parts of the picture receive intense, almost obsessive attention while other parts drop totally out of awareness. Notice how these examples work:

"There's a coldness in our marriage." She's forgetting all the head rubs, kind favors, and hours of patient listening to problems.

"I look back, and I mostly see her typing her damned papers." He's forgetting the weekend trips to the wine country and the elaborate dinners they've always enjoyed cooking together.

"I've tended to rely on other people, not him." She's forgetting the times he was rock solid during childbirth and at her mother's death.

2. Assumed intent. This is mind reading. It's the tendency to make assumptions about the feelings and motives of a partner. Without any direct knowledge, you form negative assumptions that explain why your partner acts the way he or she does. Assumed intent is a deadly mental error. Unconfirmed beliefs about your partner's motives can make you extremely angry, hurt, or discouraged. And if they're not true, you end up making strong responses to a phantom reality that may be tragically removed from your partner's real feelings and motives.

"He's just washing the dishes because he got home late last night." In fact, he's washing them because he noticed she looked tired.

"She doesn't want to go with me to the reunion." In fact, she's hoping to come, but is afraid to ask.

"She's been unusually pleasant, she's softening me up for something." In fact, she's trying to improve the climate of the relationship with deliberately positive remarks.

3. Magnification. Here you make things worse than they are. You exaggerate the effect of your partner's behavior or you focus on future catastrophic possibilities. Magnification relies on words like *terrible, awful, disgusting, horrendous, ridiculous*, and *unbelievable*. Another way to magnify is to use words that overgeneralize. Key words that indicate overgeneralizing are *always, all, every, never, everyone*, and *no one*. Magnification takes a grain of truth and builds a mountain on it.

"We had a *hideous* vacation." In fact, four days were lovely, and one day was spent in conflict.

"You're *constantly* unhappy with the amount of time we spend together." In fact, the issue has only been brought up twice in the last month.

"You *never* say anything nice to me." Only yesterday there were compliments about the garden and the good job supervising the kids' homework.

"You're *always* in a hurry." In fact, the rush is only once a week for church.

4. Global labeling. Here you paste a negative name tag on your partner, a label that acts as a global indictment of his or her personality or performance. Global labels don't just criticize behavior, they tar the core identity of a spouse. "He's a dictator ... she's a liar ... totally irresponsible ... selfish ... a depriver ... crazy ... a complainer ... he's neurotic ... a jerk ... narcissistic ... stupid ... I'm stuck with an asshole." Global labeling is really a particularly damaging form of over-generalization. A generalization such as "He has no concern about money" gets reduced to the label "spendthrift." Or "She talks every subject to death" is summarized by the term "motor-mouth."

5. Good-bad dichotomizing. You sense reality in simple black and white. Your partner's behavior is good or bad, wrong or right, and nothing in between. Good means that it meets your needs, bad means that it doesn't. Right is when your partner is generous, wrong is when he or she is self-focused. Once these labels are attached, it's hard to see all the complex motivations and needs that influence every interpersonal event.

"It was wrong of you not to tell me Margaret wasn't doing her homework."

"What's the matter with you, sitting like a stone in that chair all night? Why can't you do something productive?"

"When we were away, you were pleasant; now it's the big sour puss."

6. Fractured logic. This is where you take one small event and build a large, unsubstantiated conclusion on it. The old saying, "Take a button and sew a vest on it" is a perfect description of fractured logic.

"Because he went home early, it means he isn't interested."

"Because she's been late coming home from work, it means she's having an affair."

"Because they sent him on a business trip, it means he'll probably get a promotion."

"Because we had a fight, it means we're heading for divorce."

7. Control fallacies. Here your automatic thoughts pull you in one of two extremes. Either you see yourself as totally responsible for your partner's needs, feelings, and happiness (and therefore a failure if there are problems in any of these areas), or you feel out of control and helpless to make positive changes for yourself or your partner. Either end of the control continuum gets you in trouble. If you assume responsibility for everything that happens in the relationship, you are to blame for every difficulty. On the other hand, if it feels like your partner is in control of everything and you are powerless, then your partner gets the blame for everything that goes wrong. Control fallacies dictate which way the finger of blame points—to you or to your spouse.

"There's nothing I can do about our distance. Emotionally, he's on Pluto."

"She just blows up without cause, without reason; she's just a bomb waiting to go off."

"He's been under stress, and I could be making things much smoother for him here at home. I could get him to relax."

"I should never have let her get so sad."

8. Letting it out fallacy. At the core of this fallacy is the belief that your pain is always someone else's fault. They have done it to you, made you hurt, and they *deserve* to be punished; justice demands that they be paid back for the pain you've suffered. Another aspect of this fallacy is the belief that you need anger and emotional violence to get a partner's attention or cooperation.

"I'm hurting and he's done it; and he's going to damned well know about it."

"She's so inconsiderate, it makes me want to scream at her until she finally listens to me."

Exercise

Write in the distortion or distortions for each of the situations listed below. (Note: Most of the situations exemplify more than one distortion.)

Event	Thoughts	Feelings
1. Bill's off to the store to buy a new lens.	He's always spending money on his cameras; but he thinks it's a waste to spend anything fixing up the house.	Anger
Distortions:		
2. Brother-in-law gets belligerent during family dinner.	He's ruined what should have been a lovely day with his stupid insistence on having his drunken brother for Thanksgiving. When this is over, he's going to wish he was born deaf.	Sadness/ anger

Distortions:

3. Cheryl leaves note.	She's crewing again on Bill's boat. It means that whole group is getting very close and leaving me out.	Sad/anxious/jealous

Distortions:

4. Rebecca's staring vacantly at the floor.	I'm making her sad. She used to sparkle; now the light's gone out.	Sad

Distortions:

5. Floor strewn with extra coat hangers and junk from closet.	It's wrong of her to leave this god-awful mess.	Angry

Distortions:

6. Talking to Sid during dinner.	Sid's clueless. Last week at the Brady's, and then with Carol, and yesterday with Rene. Totally clueless.	Angry/helpless

Distortions:

7. Jean gets angry over the meat left out.	There's nothing I can do. Everything pisses her off. It's constant.	Sad

Distortions:

8. Arlene's reading a novel after dinner.	Why is she always reading a book? She's angry, she's trying to avoid me. But she has no right to withdraw from the whole family like that. It's no way to be a mother.	Angry

Distortions:

9. Jim's tools are on the floor of the laundry room.	He's finally fixing the dryer. He must be getting laid off again.	Anxious

Distortions:
_____

| 10. Having sex. | She touches me in this kind of flitting way, like it's distasteful. She doesn't speak. She gets up quickly for a shower. It seems like she's trying to get it overwith. | Sad/angry |

Distortions:
_____

Distortions answer key

1. Magnification, assumed intent.
2. Magnification, global labeling, letting it out fallacy.
3. Fractured logic.
4. Control fallacies.
5. Good-bad dichotomizing, magnification.
6. Global labeling, tunnel vision.
7. Control fallacies, magnification.
8. Assumed intent, good-bad dichotomizing, magnification.
9. Fractured logic.
10. Tunnel vision, fractured logic, assumed intent.

(Some of the distortions are similar to others and may be open to interpretation. Sometimes personal associations may give a phrase a special meaning to you. For instance, what we identify as magnification may seem more like tunnel vision to you.)

Keeping Track of Cognitive Distortions

Because cognitive distortions can be so damaging to your relationship, it's important to learn to recognize them when they occur. On the next page is a quick summary of the distortions for you to refer to. During the coming week, add a fourth column to your Thoughts Diary and label it *Distortions*. Try to identify which distortion or distortions are present in some of your thoughts. Since you only make entries in the diary when you are feeling some emotion in relation to your partner, you may be surprised to find distortions more often than you thought. Don't be discouraged about this. Right now your job is to learn more about your patterns of thinking. Change will come later.

Cognitive Distortions—Quick Reference

1. **Tunnel vision:** filtering out important parts of the picture, usually the good part.

2. **Assumed intent:** mind reading, making assumptions about the motives, desires, and feelings of your partner.

3. **Magnifying:** exaggerating, making things worse than they are. Overgeneralizing with words such as *all, every, always, none, nobody, everyone.*

4. **Global labeling:** pinning a negative *identity* tag on your partner—stupid, lazy, crazy, selfish.

5. **Good-bad dichotomizing:** labeling behavior good or bad, right or wrong, instead of seeing the complex needs, feelings, and motives that lie behind most behavior.

6. **Fractured logic:** making a big conclusion from very little evidence. "Because he did _____ , it means _____."

7. *Control fallacies:* assuming you're responsible for all the problems, or that you're helpless and your partner's responsible for fixing things.

8. *Letting it out fallacy:* assuming that your pain is your partner's fault and thinking that he or she deserves to be punished for it.

Here's the diary that Clark kept during the week when he was trying to notice his distortions.

Clark's Diary

Event	Thought	Feeling	Distortion
Julie complains that we never eat out.	She's a total yuppie spendthrift. We'd be in Chapter 11 if she'd have her way.	Anger	Global labels, magnifying
Julie looks sad.	I'm bringing her down. This (the relationship) isn't working for her.	Sad/ anxious	Assumed intent, control fallacies, fractured logic
Julie very passive during sex.	She's totally withdrawing, doesn't care.	Hurt/ anxious	Assumed intent, magnifying
Julie late getting ready for the movies.	She's never on time.	Irri- tated	Magnifying

Julie quiet at night.	She doesn't trust me with her feelings, doesn't want to be close anymore.	Sad/ anxious	Assumed intent
Julie takes a walk.	She never walks, she must be doing some heavy thinking about us. Things are bad.	Sad/ anxious	Assumed intent, magnifying, fractured logic
	Doesn't seem like we have fun anymore. No spark. No life.	Deep sadness	Tunnel vision
Julie out walking again, late.	Stupid, dangerous.	Angry	Global labels, magnifying
Julie out walking again.	Maybe she's got friends I don't know about.	Jealous	Fractured logic
Big discussion. Julie says she's down because her mother was recently diagnosed with MS.	It's not right to with-hold that from me. She was driving me crazy.	Some-what angry	Good-bad dichotomizing, control fallacies
	It's one problem after another. We can never relax and enjoy our lives.	Depres-sion	Tunnel vision

After you've completed your Thoughts Diary, keeping track of distortions for one week, notice any emerging patterns. Are there certain distortions you tend to use over and over? Do certain situations produce one or more characteristic distortions? Which distortions seem to trigger which emotions? By focusing in on the particular distortions you use most, you can sharpen your awareness and listen for those specific thought patterns in the future.

Clark realized that he frequently made assumptions about Julie's feelings and motives, and those assumptions often triggered sad or anxious feelings. Tunnel vision also produced a deep sadness. Anger, on the other hand, seemed associated with global labels or magnifying. The diary helped Clark zero in on specific distortions he needed to work on.

Exercise

In the space provided, identify the distortions that seem most typical of you. Give examples of three situations for each one.

Distortion	Examples
	1.
	2.
	3.

Distortion	Examples
	1.
	2.
	3.

Distortion	Examples
	1.
	2.
	3.

Distortion	Examples
	1.
	2.
	3.

Here are a few of Clark's entries.

Distortion	Examples
Assumed intent	1. Julie looks sad and I assume that I'm bringing her down.
	2. Julie is passive during sex and I assume that she's withdrawing from me.
	3. Julie is quiet at night and I assume that she doesn't trust me with her feelings.

Distortion	Examples
Magnifying	1. Eating out would bankrupt us.
	2. Julie's "never" on time because she's late for the movies.
	3. Things are "bad" with us because she takes a walk.

Seeing the Relationship between Thoughts and Behavior

Go back over your Thoughts Diary for the past two weeks and on a separate piece of paper write down your behavioral reaction to each event. What did you say? How did you act? What mood did you display? Everything on this piece of paper is a direct consequence of your thoughts. If you want to know what your cognitive distortions are costing you and your relationship—this is it.

Here are a few of Clark's entries.

Event	Behavior
Julie complains that we never eat out.	I yell at her and tell her that she needs to examine her values.
Julie's late getting ready for the movies.	I shout up from the bottom of the stairs that I'm leaving without her. She's very withdrawn that night.
She's out walking late.	I tell her that she's stupid to risk her life. Zero conversation the rest of the night.
She's out walking late again.	I grill her about what she's doing. I get very angry. She threatens to go to her sister's house.

Challenging Cognitive Distortions

Now comes the hard part—change. Altering those old thinking patterns that so often create upset. Every time you notice a distortion, you need to go through the "Clear Thinking Drill." This is a group of questions that help you evaluate, clarify, and restructure your thoughts. Here's the drill.

Clear Thinking Drill

1. What evidence supports my interpretation?

2. What evidence might be contrary to my interpretation?

3. Is there an alternative explanation for my partner's behavior? Are there any other motives or feelings that might lie behind his or her actions?

4. Have I checked my assumptions about my partner?

5. Is this *always* true? Are there exceptions?

6. What is the *balancing reality*—the positive part of the picture (our relationship or my partner's behavior) that I have left out?

7. If I am generalizing or labeling, how can I describe the situation *specifically* and *accurately*?

8. Rewrite one of the distortions from your diary using the information you've gathered above.

Here are examples of people who have used the Clear Thinking Drill to explore and challenge their cognitive distortions. Bill, an attorney, had just been yelled at by one of the senior partners for filing his motions late. He was shocked and down on himself for being "too lazy" to get things done on time. He told his wife, Carrie, about the incident when he got home, announcing that he was in a rotten mood. While he talked, Carrie kept humming and smiling as she adjusted the living room curtains. Bill's automatic thoughts: "She likes to see me unhappy. She thinks I'm lazy too."

Later in the evening, Bill used the Clear Thinking Drill to examine his automatic thoughts.

1. *What evidence supports my interpretation?*
   Her cheerfulness, and the fact that she's always after me to do the dishes and clean the yard.

2. *What evidence might be contrary to my interpretation?*
   She's been very supportive in the past when I had problems at work, and she certainly seemed concerned when I had all that stomach trouble a few months ago. Regarding laziness, she tells the kids I'm a "hard working Daddy" and appreciates my doing all the bills.

3. *Is there any alternative explanation for my partner's behavior? Are there any other motives or feelings that might lie behind his or her actions?*
   She might just be in a good mood, or she might be trying to cheer me up.

4. *Have I checked out my assumptions about my partner?*
   No. I can't assume anything till I ask her directly.

5. *Is it always true; are there exceptions?*
   Doesn't apply.

6. *What is the balancing reality—the positive part of the picture (our relationship or my partner's behavior) that I may have left out?*
   Carrie loves me, even if she complains about things. She doesn't want me in pain.

7. *If I am generalizing or labeling, how can I describe the situation specifically and accurately?*
   Doesn't apply.

8. *Rewrite the distortion.*
   Carrie complains about things I don't do, but she loves me and

supports me when I'm down. I can't assume anything; she may just be in a good mood.

Sophie was annoyed that Troy kept "boasting about all this great shit he can cook. He's the cock of the walk, so proud of himself, like what I do is nothing, of no importance. He can barbeque some smoky old lamb, but it's totally without meaning that I cook three zillion meals for the kids." Sophie did the following work on her Clear Thinking Drill later that night.

1. *What evidence supports my interpretation?*
   Just that he's so full of himself about certain things he does. And he rarely expresses much appreciation for what I do.

2. *What evidence might be contrary to my interpretation?*
   He liked the dinner I cooked when his brother came over. He can be affectionate; he appreciates *me* even if he doesn't say much about specifics. He's never put me down for the work I do, so he probably isn't trying to show me up, or say he's great and I'm not.

3. *Is there an alternative explanation for my partner's behavior? Are there any other motives or feelings that might lie behind his or her actions?*
   I think he just wants to feel good about himself. And he gets this manic enthusiasm when he's around friends. Everything's a big exaggeration.

4. *Have I checked out my assumptions about my partner?*
   I kidded him about his boasting. He got hurt and said it's just social nervousness.

5. *Is it always true? Are there exceptions?*
   Boasting doesn't happen much. But I frequently feel my work is unnoticed.

6. *What is the balancing reality—the positive part of the picture (our relationship or my partner's behavior) that I may have left out?*
   He may not notice, but he will thank me if I point out something I've done.

7. *If I am generalizing or labeling, how can I describe the situation specifically and accurately?*
   Forget "cock of the walk." Let's say he's *very* excited about his cooking skills.

8. *Rewrite the distortion.*
I don't think he's trying to show me up by boasting. With friends he's very excited about things he does well, he's sort of nervous and manic around people. He rarely acknowledges work I do, unless I point it out. He appreciates *me*, but he's oblivious to all the things I do.

Sophie's Clear Thinking Drill softened her angry feelings. It still wasn't an ideal situation—she wanted more acknowledgement. But she no longer felt in a rage either. After the drill she decided to be more direct with Troy about the things she did to keep their lives running.

Solomon walked into the bathroom. The hair dryer, along with various tubes, lotions, and brushes were lying next to the sink. His automatic thoughts: "Denny's a slob. He never cleans up after himself." Here's Solomon's Clear Thinking Drill.

1. *What evidence supports my interpretation?*
The mess in the bathroom; dropping his clothes by the side of the bed.

2. *What evidence might be contrary to my interpretation?*
He usually cleans the kitchen when he cooks; his desk is neat; he doesn't dress like a slob; he organized the big whirlwind cleanup of the garage.

3. *Is there an alternative explanation for my partner's behavior? Are there any other motives or feelings that might lie behind his or her actions?*
Maybe Denny just doesn't realize what a mess it is and how annoying it is to me. He uses all this junk in the morning—when he's always out of it and half awake—maybe it's beyond him to clean up then.

4. *Have I checked out my assumptions about my partner?*
Doesn't apply.

5. *Is it always true? Are there exceptions?*
See # 2.

6. *What is the balancing reality—the positive part of the picture (our relationship or my partner's behavior) that I may have left out?*
He's easygoing about my stuff—the art supplies I leave lying around, snacks left by the TV, and when I forget the dishes.

7. *If I am generalizing or labeling, how can I describe the situation specifically and accurately?*

Delete "slob." Let's say he doesn't clean around the bathroom sink or the bed unless we do it together.

8. *Rewrite the distortion.*
   He doesn't usually clean around the bathroom sink or pick up unless we do it together, but he does keep other areas clean, and he's easygoing about my messes.

Tanya saw Randy getting out of his car in the driveway and thought: "If he cared about the kids, he'd get home earlier so we'd be on time for the parent-teacher's conference. It's wrong. He's totally uninvolved with his children. He spends all his time fooling with his stupid computer." Here's Tanya's Clear Thinking Drill:

1. *What evidence supports my interpretation?*
   None—I don't really believe he doesn't care.

2. *What evidence might be contrary to my interpretation?*
   He reads to the kids at bedtime; gets upset if they're hurt or get mistreated at school. Sometimes he takes them to the doctor, takes them to visit friends. He built a playhouse for Sarah.

3. *Is there an alternative explanation for my partner's behavior? Are there any other motives or feelings that might lie behind his or her actions?*
   Yes. He's stressed at work and doing a lot of overtime because he's trying to prove himself to his new boss. Then he comes home fried and falls into the computer to relax.

4. *Have I checked out my assumptions about my partner?*
   Doesn't apply.

5. *Is it always true? Are there exceptions?*
   See # 2.

6. *What is the balancing reality—the positive part of the picture (our relationship or my partner's behavior) that I may have left out?*
   He's hard working; he knows how to relax. He's civil rather than mean when he's overworked.

7. *If I am generalizing or labeling, how can I describe the situation specifically and accurately?*
   He's not totally uninvolved. He's late about three nights per week, and he spends up to an hour on the computer.

8. *Rewrite the distortion.*
   I know he cares, he does quite a bit with the kids. He works

hard, often comes home late, and unwinds with the computer. I wish he did more, but he is *involved*.

The Clear Thinking Drill is a tool for training yourself to respond to distortions you may uncover in your Thoughts Diary. At this point, your diary needs to have some new sections so you can "talk back" to the distortions effectively.

Take a piece of typing paper and turn it sideways. Make six columns down the page, and label the columns *Event, Thought, Feeling, Distortions, Alternative Response,* and *Outcome.* Under the word *Thought,* write: "Rate belief in thought, 0-100%." Under the word *Feeling* write: "Degree of emotion, 1-100." Under *Alternative Response,* write: "Rate belief in alternative response, 0-100%." Under *Outcome,* write: "Re-rate belief in original thought, 0-100%. Rerate degree of emotion, 1-100."

This seems complex, but it really isn't. When you write your thought down in the thoughts column, just rate how much you believe the thought. If you're convinced 90 percent that it's true, that's what you put down. If you're only 50 percent convinced in its veracity, write that. Rating degree of emotion is also simple. 100 is the most intensely you've ever felt the feeling; 1 is the barest noticeable amount of the feeling. Just assign a number between 1 and 100 that reflects how strongly you experience the emotion. Under *Alternative Response* you'll rate the belief in your new response using percentages, in the same way you did your thought.

The *Outcome* column in your new Thoughts Diary is extremely important. After thinking about and developing a new alternative response, you re-rate your belief in the original thought. If the strength of your belief in the original thought goes down, it's a clear indication that you're having some success. It helps motivate you to continue the work. If the intensity of your emotion also goes down, it provides clear evidence that changing your thinking can have a real impact on how you feel.

Try to use your Thoughts Diary any time you have a strong emotion regarding your partner. Sometimes you'll be able to develop an alternative response without using the Clear Thinking Drill. But often, particularly in the beginning, you'll need to do the entire drill to develop an alternative response that feels believable and helps to change how you see things. Use this new, more elaborate version of the Thoughts Diary for at least four weeks to get maximum results. Remember Bill, who got chewed out at work and came home in a rotten mood? Here's how he filled out his Thoughts Diary after that incident.

Bill's Diary

Event	Thought Rate belief in thought, 0-100%	Feeling Degree of emotion, 1-100%	Distortions	Alternative Response Rate belief in alternative response, 0-100%	Outcome Rating Re-rate belief in original thought, 0-100%. Re-rate degree of emotion, 1-100%.
Carrie humming and smiling while I tell her about my lousy day.	She likes to see me unhappy. She thinks I'm lazy too. 90%	Angry. Rating: 60.	Fractured logic; assumed intent	Carrie complains about things I don't do, but she loves me and supports me when I'm down. I can't assume anything; she may just be in a good mood. 70%	Original thought: 40%. Degree of emotion: 20.

Notice how Bill's work to develop an alternative response pays dividends. Both his belief in the original disturbing thought and his degree of emotional upset go down considerably. You can achieve this too. Be consistent and keep at it. Use your Thoughts Diary whenever you have strong negative feelings towards your partner. If you can't easily generate an alternative response, use your Clear Thinking Drill to modify your automatic thoughts.

6

Negotiation

Whenever you and your partner discuss how to discipline your children, where to go on vacation, how to divide household chores, or how to spend your money, you are negotiating. People negotiate with their partners more often than unions negotiate with management. Negotiation is not a cold, calculated process limited to diplomats, corporate lawyers, and terrorists. Everyone negotiates, especially in couples.

Simply stated, negotiation is a special kind of communication. It's a skill. If you follow the guidelines in this chapter, you can become a fair and effective negotiator in your relationship. You will be able to get what you want more often, without manipulating or alienating your partner.

History

People have been negotiating for centuries: boundary disputes, peace treaties, trade agreements, collective bargaining contracts, and so on. Historically, negotiation has all too often involved a heated exchange of insults and ultimatums, mutual manipulation, and the defense-at-all costs of entrenched positions.

In the 1970s the Harvard Negotiation Project began to ask the question, "What is the best way for people to deal with their differences?" They developed the "one text" mediation procedure, which was used in the 1978 Camp David Middle East peace negotiations.

The Harvard Negotiation Project also devised the method of principled negotiation, explained in Roger Fisher and William Ury's 1981 book *Getting to Yes*. They suggested that the old way of bargaining over positions was unproductive and unnecessarily hostile. A better approach is to separate the people involved from the problem needing to be resolved. By focusing on mutual interests instead of positions, you can brainstorm options for mutual gain and work out compromises in which both parties benefit.

Pair a lawyer trained in principled negotiation with a family therapist and you have a divorce mediation team. Mediated divorce is becoming more popular as separated couples become more aware of the high cost—both emotional and financial—of the divorce battles waged by opposing legal counsel.

But the best time to learn to negotiate is before your relationship is on the rocks. Negotiation is a distinct and valuable communication skill that deserves to be taught alongside the more commonly available training in assertiveness, active listening, or empathic expression.

Theoretical Background

The theory behind successful negotiation is fairly straightforward. There are eight principles of good negotiation.

1. Conflict is inevitable. All couples fight from time to time. Conflict doesn't automatically mean that your relationship is in trouble.

2. No name calling, threats, anger, and so on. See also chapter 4 on clean communication and chapter 8 on avoiding aversive strategies.

3. Negotiation involves two parties with important, legitimate, but opposing interests. Not all conflicts and arguments will require negotiation. For example, your partner's interest in getting stinking drunk may seem important to him or her, but it's hardly legitimate. Your interest in occasionally playing country western music on the radio may be perfectly legitimate, but not important enough to require negotiation. Save negotiation for the really important conflicts in which you have opposing, legitimate interests.

4. Separate your feelings from the issue. Chapter 2 on expressing feelings and scripting needs is helpful preparation.

5. Focus on interests, not positions. This chapter will give you ample practice in seeing your conflicts as interests to explore rather than positions to defend. This is the key to successful negotiation.

6. Seek mutually agreeable options. The idea is to reach a fair compromise that benefits you both, not to win your partner over to your position.

7. Be flexible. There are almost always several solutions that will benefit you. Don't be blinded by preconceived notions of only one acceptable outcome.

8. Be persistent. Often the final solution involves several trial periods and refinements. Don't give up.

Time for Mastery

You can work through this chapter in a couple of days and get a good understanding of the steps involved. The time it takes to complete your first negotiation will depend on the conflict involved. If you pick a minor conflict to start, you should be able to work out a compromise in a week.

It's important to note that the skills taught in this chapter will improve your relationship even if just one of you learns them. If both of you learn to negotiate better, the results will come more quickly and be even more dramatic.

No matter how complicated a negotiation may seem, it can be broken down into five stages: preparation, discussion, proposal/ counterproposal, disagreement, and agreement.

Preparation

Before you talk with your partner, determine what you want ideally, what you could live with, and what's unacceptable. During breaks from the discussion, you can prepare further by brainstorming more options, looking up information, and making up counterproposals. Use this form to prepare for a negotiation.

Preparing To Negotiate

Ground rules (read and check off before continuing)

☐   *I accept conflict calmly.* I know that conflict is natural and inevitable in all relationships. Everyone has disagreements. Disagreement is not a disaster. Conflict is an opportunity to change and grow. This conflict gives us a chance to exercise our creative powers of problem solving.

☐ *I want a fair, mutually agreeable outcome.* I want something that's good for both of us. This is the proper goal of negotiation. I have let go of the idea of getting my way at all costs, of winning, getting revenge, punishing my partner, venting my anger, and so on.

☐ *I'm flexible.* I will let go of my entrenched positions. I am clearing my mind of my preconceived solutions. I am open to creative, unexpected resolutions.

The situation. Briefly describe the situation dispassionately, objectively, without feeling or interpretation or argument.

My feelings. This is the place to label your feelings. Jot down a few words that best describe your emotional state in this situation: depressed, angry, scared, sad, resentful, excited, guilty, ashamed, nervous, or whatever. By clearly acknowledging your feelings, you can keep them separate from the facts of the situation and the rest of the negotiation.

Our interests and needs. In the first column, list what you ideally want in this situation—the interests, actions, and outcomes that you assume your partner will not readily agree with. Include the intangible needs that so often complicate negotiations between intimates: respect, trust, security, freedom, power, and so on.

In the middle column, list what you think your partner wants that opposes your interests. Include the intangible needs that you think your partner may have in this situation.

In the third column, list your shared interests. This may be the most important column. Look for sources of agreement in this situation—things you and your partner both want and can agree on.

My interests	My partner's interests	Our shared interests

Tentative solutions.   Now consider the situation again. What is your ideal solution? What could you live with? What outcomes are unacceptable?

My ideal solution:

What I could live with:

Unacceptable:

Here's an example of how Marion completed the preparation exercise.

Preparing To Negotiate

Ground rules (read and check off before continuing).

☒   *I accept conflict calmly.*

☒   *I want a fair, mutually agreeable outcome.*

☒   *I'm flexible.*

The situation.
Thanksgiving is coming up. My mom has invited us to her house. I'd like to drive out and stay for the weekend as well. Ken would rather stay home this year.

My feelings.
Love for mother.
Fear she could die before I see her again.
Guilt that we seldom go to Ken's family on Thanksgiving.
Yearning to see my sister and cousins.
Resentment for Ken's stay-at-home, loner attitude.
Nervous that even if we go, Ken will be grumpy.

Our interests and needs.

My interests	My partner's interests	Our shared interests
See mom	Stay home	Keep peace between us
See sister	Read, watch TV	Relax
See cousins	Work on tool shed	To feel close, like we really belong together
Preserve family ties	To be himself, not have to put on the face of the good son-in-law	
Look good to my family		
Celebrate		
Know that Ken wants me to be happy		

Tentative solutions.

My ideal solution: Drive out Wednesday, stay at mom's, come back late Sunday.

What I could live with: Shorter visit.

Unacceptable: Not going at all.

Discussion

In this stage, you and your partner start talking. It helps to begin by sharing the information you have prepared, in the same sequence you followed for the last exercise:

- The facts as you each see them.

- Your feelings and your partner's feelings in the matter.

- How you see the problem in terms of your interests, your partner's interests, and your mutual interests.

- How the problem is complicated by intangible needs for support, trust, closeness, contact, freedom, or whatever.

- Hold off on possible solutions until all your interests and needs are clear. Present your ideal solutions as tentative proposals, subject to revision.

If you get stuck in a discussion, you can return to this basic formula to summarize the negotiation and get back on track:

I think (facts) _____

I feel (emotions) _____

I want (interests) _____

I need (intangibles) _____   _____

Perhaps we could (tentative solution) _____

_____

It's important in negotiation to use healthy communication skills. If you review the chapters 1, 2 and 4, on listening, expressing feelings and scripting needs, and clean communication, you'll find important guidelines for communicating cleanly in your relationship. To summarize here:

- No blaming, labeling, threatening, belittling, guilt tripping, discounting, raking up past disputes.

- Empathy—put yourself in your partner's shoes to better understand your partner's interests.

- Active listening—paraphrase, summarize, and ask questions to best understand your partner's point of view.

- Keep restating the goal—"I want a fair, mutually agreeable solution."

Here is an example of how Marion and Ken began their discussion.

Marion:	Let's figure out what we want to do for Thanksgiving. It's coming up and Mom has invited us again. I really should call her by the end of the week and let her know.
Ken:	(*groaning*) Oh, I wish we could just stay home this year. We go to your mom's every year.
Marion:	I realize we visit her nearly every year. But Thanksgiving at my mom's is special for me, and I'd really like to go again this year. In

	fact, what I'd really like is to drive out Wednesday and stay through the weekend. Come home Sunday.
Ken:	When am I supposed to work on the tool shed? We've got to get the lawn mower and stuff under cover before it snows.
Marion:	Well, let's discuss it. The way I feel, my mother's been sick and she isn't getting any younger. I want to see her again while she's still relatively healthy and up to handling a family crowd. I want to have enough time there to also see my sister and cousins, too. But at the same time, I feel guilty that we almost never visit your family at Thanksgiving. Plus I know that you get fidgety at my mom's.
Ken:	Well, I'm not saying I want to go to *my* folks. It's not that important in my family. But you're right, it's dead boring at your mom's. I just don't feel up to five days of hanging out in that scene. It's not relaxing for me, and I have things I want to do.
Marion:	Let's compromise, then. It's not worth going to mom's if you and I end up arguing and resenting each other. I want a Thanksgiving that we both can enjoy.

Notice how Marion was careful to avoid blaming or complaining. She felt like accusing her husband of being antisocial and a hermit at heart, but she knew that such labels would only create more problems, not solve anything. She kept her focus on a clear statement of her interests and her desire for a mutually agreeable decision arrived at jointly.

Proposal/Counterproposal

In this stage, you move from discussion of interests into actual suggestions for action and change. You make a suggestion or an offer. Your partner comes back with a different idea. You counter with a variation on your first offer. Your partner responds with a proposal that is closer to what you want. Along the way you will probably revert to more general discussion or take time out to do more preparation. Eventually, you reach a compromise that you both find acceptable.

To facilitate this process, you should jointly and separately consider these classic methods of compromise to see if they fit your situation.

I'll cut the pie, you choose your piece first. This works for many situations, from kids pouring juice to divorcing adults splitting up a household. For example, when Marla and Stan broke up, they had to divide their Christmas tree ornaments. Compared to the whole divorce it was a minor issue, but it recapitulated many of their past arguments about fairness and power. They resolved the conflict by having Marla divide the ornaments into two groups that she considered of equal value, then Stan chose one of the groups and Marla took the remainder.

Take turns. I'll stay home with the kids Saturday so you can take your class, and you will watch the kids Sunday so I can play golf with my Dad.

Do both, have it all. Let's take out a loan so we can get a new car *and* go to Hawaii. Let's get up an hour earlier so you can exercise *and* I can cook a real breakfast.

Trial period. Let's limit Janie to an hour's television a day and see if her homework improves after a month.

My way when I'm doing it, your way when you're doing it. When you're driving, we'll go the fastest way on the freeway and I won't complain. When I'm driving, we'll go the scenic route and you will relax and try to enjoy it.

Tit for tat. If you clean the bathroom once a week, I'll do the laundry once a week.

Part of what I want with part of what you want. I get to have the worst two sides of the house reshingled, you get to put the money we save away in the college fund.

Split the difference. You want to buy a five-piece bedroom set for $3,000. I'm happy with what we've got. Let's split the difference and get a new bed and dresser for $1,500.

In the case of Marion and Ken, they used the "Part of what I want with part of what you want" method. They went to Marion's mom's house on Wednesday, Thursday, and most of Friday, so Marion had some time to visit with her family. But they drove home late Friday night so that Ken would have the weekend to rest, watch sports, and make a start on the new toolshed.

Exercise

Choose an area of conflict to practice on. Use the form below to apply as many of the compromise strategies as possible to your area of conflict.

Describe conflict:

Possible compromises

I'll cut the pie, you choose your piece first:

Take turns:

Do both, have it all:

Trial period:

My way when I'm doing it, your way when you're doing it:

Tit for tat:

Part of what I want with part of what you want:

Split the difference:

If you have trouble figuring out good compromises, photocopy this form and use it with two or three of your common conflicts until you gain more skill at spinning out compromise ideas.

Disagreement

This is the hardest stage. The way to survive and get past disagreement is to remind yourself that it is not the end. It's just another natural and expected stage of negotiation.

When you come to disagreement, take it as a sign that it's time to return to an earlier stage:

- Try a new counterproposal, using a different compromise strategy.

- Return to discussion of interests and needs.

- Brainstorm together to invent more creative solutions—the more bizarre and unusual, the better. See chapter 7 on problem solving.

- When you're really stuck, take a time out (see chapter 11).

- Return to solitary preparation. Spend more time looking for common interests and creative resolutions. Reexamine your feelings. Gather needed information.

Agreement

Finally you both agree on an option that gives you each a maximum of what you want with a minimum of what you don't want. Before you send up skyrockets and declare the negotiating over, make sure the solution is clear to both of you. Each of you should say the full agreement out loud, to verify that you both mean and intend the same thing.

Special Considerations

There are some times when the course of negotiation doesn't run smoothly. When intimacy breaks down, you must negotiate with your partner as though you were strangers or adversaries. Here are a few of those times.

When your partner has control over the situation, money, kids, possessions, and so on. In this case, there is not going to be a discussion as equals. Your best approach is to figure out your most promising alternative. For example, Jill wanted to go back to school to become a marriage, family, and child counselor. But she had no money and her husband, Howard, refused to pay for her tuition. He thought her idea was misguided and that she would never persist long enough to get a degree, much less a license to practice. Jill's best alternative was to get a job, save up some money, then start taking some classes at night.

If your best alternative is fairly strong, you might be able to use it as a bargaining chip. In Jill's case, she put it this way to her husband: "If you won't cover the tuition, I'll have to get a job and go to school at night. That means you're on your own here at home. You'll have to cook your own meals, do the cleaning and laundry, the yardwork, and whatever comes up. I'll be too busy to do much around here."

Howard suddenly heard Jill loud and clear. He decided that if he didn't let go of some of his hoarded savings, his quality of life was going to decline drastically.

When your partner takes a hard line. When your partner is entrenched in a position and refuses to budge, your best strategy is to use leading questions coupled with silence. For example, Bob really wanted Annie to go to a marriage enrichment workshop with him. She refused outright and wouldn't budge. Bob got through to her by asking this series of leading questions:

"If you won't do the workshop with me, then please explain your plan for how we can add some passion and fun to our relationship . . . "

"Tell me more about why you don't want to go. I don't under-stand . . . "

"It seems to me that we fight over and over about the same stuff—money and Susie's temper tantrums and Jack's grades. I'm ready for some outside input. Have you got some new solutions to these problems that I don't know about?"

Annie eventually began talking about her fears of being ridiculed or overwhelmed by more articulate workshop participants, of feeling dumb or inadequate, of being thought of as a failure at marriage. She got to explore and reduce these fears when they attended the workshop.

When your partner is hostile. Handle attacks by time out (see chapter 11), postponement, and redefinition. For instance, you can say, "Let's take a time out and talk about this tomorrow morning. All this yelling isn't getting us anywhere." In the morning, if it's appropriate, you can redefine your partner's anger as evidence of concern: "You know, I appreciate the fact that you take this problem seriously. When you get angry I can tell that it really concerns you, that you're really fired up about working this out."

When your partner uses dirty tricks. Handle dirty tricks by "call-ing process." Shift the subject from *what* you are talking about to *how* you are talking about it. This lifts the conversation up one level of abstraction, moving from the subject matter at hand to the style of com-munication. This allows you to interrupt the flow of argument and in-sist on a return to the rules of fair play, like a lawyer raising an objection in a courtroom.

For example, if your partner calls you names, say, "Wait a minute. You're calling me names and pasting labels on me that I don't deserve.

Let's at least try to be accurate here." If your mate rakes up past transgressions and throws them in your face, say, "That's not fair. I'm not on trial for everything I ever did. The subject is here and now, and the past has nothing to do with it. Please don't cloud the issue."

If hostility is too high or your partner persists in dirty tricks, consider calling in a neutral mediator such as a family therapist.

7

Problem Solving

Couple problems are often more difficult to solve than individual problems. When conflicting desires, standards, and expectations must be reconciled, two heads are not necessarily better than one. For example, just consider the relative difficulty of budgeting for a single person compared to budgeting for a family of five. Sometimes even simple problems can't be solved effectively because old conflicts and resentments interfere with a clear, calm appraisal of the situation.

Many chapters of this book are dedicated to healing old conflicts and resentments. This chapter focuses on dealing with current situations. Where other chapters deal with more emotional issues, this chapter presents proven intellectual techniques for solving joint problems. The steps are simple and straightforward:

1. State the problem
2. Set goals
3. Brainstorm solutions
4. Trial period
5. Evaluate results

History

From the early fifties through 1963, A. F. Osborn produced three editions of *Applied Imagination*, laying out the principles of creative problem solving in business, government, the arts, and everyday life. Osborn's brainstorming techniques were adapted by behavior modification researchers Thomas J. D'Zurilla and Marvin R. Goldfried (1971), who devised a five-step strategy for generating novel solutions to any kind of problem.

Problem solving as a therapeutic strategy was explored further in Jay Haley's *Problem Solving Therapy* (1976), his other writings on the intuitive interventions of Milton Erickson, and *Change* by Watzlawick, Weakland, and Fisch (1974). These authors showed that the best solutions emerge when problems are viewed in terms of your previously unsuccessful solutions.

Theoretical Background

The most important thing to understand about problem solving is that "the *problem* isn't the problem, the *old solution* is the problem." This means that a problem is defined as a persistent failure to find an effective response. In problem solving the first and most important step is to describe the problem, in detail, in terms of what you have done so far that has not worked.

If you and your partner live in a very small apartment, that isn't necessarily a problem. It only becomes a problem if your response is ineffective: if you leave dirty dishes and craft projects and junk mail and laundry strewn all over; if you keep collecting more and more antiques or books or motorcycles; if you agree to store your friend's trampoline; if you decide to start breeding Great Danes. The way to start solving the space problem is to turn your focus away from "this tiny apartment" and describe what you have been trying to store and do in the apartment.

Often a situation becomes problematic because you use a response that seems okay at the time, but doesn't work in the long run. For example, if you are a little short of money one month, that in itself may not be a big problem. But it can become a problem if you apply short-term solutions like paying the phone bill with a rubber check, hiding bills from your partner, or applying for new credit cards because the old ones are beyond their limits. In the long run, your response will not be effective in keeping the phone connected, keeping your partner happy, or reducing your debt. So the situation becomes "problematic" for you. This is why an important step in problem solving is to assess the long-range consequences of possible solutions.

Time for Mastery

You and your partner can learn the steps of problem solving in a single session together. However, problem solving as a couple requires what psychologists call a "collaborative set." If either of you is harboring old resentments, private agendas, or looking more for someone to blame than for solutions, the process is doomed. Each partner must be open, cooperative, and reasonably objective for mutual problem solving to work.

Lifelong mastery of problem solving is a matter of adopting a viewpoint that sees life as a series of situations requiring you to respond as a couple. With practice you can acquire the skill of setting emotion aside for a moment to analyze situations in terms of effective and ineffective responses.

State the Problem

In the space below or on a separate sheet, write your problem situation and your usual responses. The "who, what, where" format is a helpful guide. It's the way newspaper reporters are trained to organize the details of a story. Go into as much detail as you can. Don't worry about getting each aspect of the situation into the right space or sequence. Just get as much about your situation and responses down as you can.

Be objective like a newspaper story: just the facts, with no blame or interpretations that are critical of either partner.

Problem situation and usual responses

Who

What

Where

When

How

Why

Feelings

Other

Here's how the Needleman family stated their problem:

Who: Dad Peter, mom Polly, son Rob, daughter Shelley

What: We make plans for all of us to bike or walk or jog regularly together and don't do it. Then we bemoan being out of shape, how flabby the kids are, etc.

Where: We plan to exercise at home, the park, the municipal pool. Where doesn't seem to matter. When we plan or complain, we are usually in the car or at the dinner table.

When: After seeing the Johnsons, we all feel out of shape. Or after looking at ourselves in the mirror. When we make a new plan, we do okay the first time or two, then something comes up to distract us and we never get back to the exercise regimen.

How: We grimly agree to exercise. Lukewarm enthusiasm fades into indifference. We can always find an excuse not to exercise. Kids complain walking and jogging are boring. Adults complain kids are too wild on bikes.

Why: We want to be fit, healthy, attractive. Want to have fun together as a family. Why we fail is because we're over-scheduled? Weak willed? Wimps? Can't all agree on the ideal exercise? Some key element is missing—motivation, lifestyle, genetics?

Feelings: Feel proud & healthy when we exercise. Feel depressed, like failures as parents, and old when we don't.

Set Goals

In order to set goals, you need to analyze what you have done so far in terms of the basic problem solving principle: "the *problem* isn't the problem, the *old solution* is the problem."

A good way to do this is to look at every part of your description according to this formula:

The real problem isn't	The real problem is

Pair up every aspect of your problem with every other aspect. Try everything together, not just the parts that look like they go together. Tell yourself the real problem isn't who is involved, the real problem is how they react. Or the real problem isn't what happens, the real problem is where it happens. It's like sorting a big basket of black and navy blue socks. You have to match every sock up with every other one to find correct pairs. Keep going until you've laid every phrase in your problem/response description against every other phrase to see if you have a meaningful match. Doing this forces you to keep looking at every aspect of your problem as a potential starting point for new ideas.

Much of what you generate will be gibberish. But a few combinations will spark genuine new insights about the situation. Here are some of the enlightening combinations the Needlemans came up with:

The real problem isn't	The real problem is
Making plans	Following through
Not enough time	Not enough time together
Being flabby	Feeling wimpy

Get the idea? Keep putting the who's, what's and why's together until you have three or four good ideas for goals. By goals, we mean new directions in which you can go to find effective responses to your situation. Here are the Needleman's goals:

1. Make only plans we can realistically follow through on.

2. Get more exercise separately if we can't do it together.

3. Work on more accepting attitudes about our appearance and about each other.

The first goal, to make more realistic plans, was an obvious one. But the next two goals came as a bit of a surprise. By considering each little bit of their situation as the "real" problem, the Needlemans realized that their whole concept of the family exercising together was problematic. The fact was that they didn't really like to exercise together.

They realized that they could get their togetherness needs met by shopping or eating or camping together and do the exercising separately. Another insight was the degree to which they had all been buying into the commercial American ideal of the body beautiful and running each other down for not having perfect bodies.

Brainstorm

Brainstorming is making a long list of ideas, as fast as you can, until you can't think of any more ideas. The rules are simple:

No value judgments. Write down each new idea or possible solution just as it is proposed, without judging it as good or bad. Evaluation is done later.

Freewheeling is best. The crazier and wilder your ideas, the better. Freewheeling gets you out of mental ruts and allows you to break free of your old, stale way of viewing the problem.

More is better. Keep going until you have a very long list. Don't stop to think or evaluate. The more ideas you write down, the better chance of good ideas.

Collaborative set. Make sure you both come up with ideas for how both of you could behave to solve a problem. Don't just make suggestions for how your partner could improve, assuming that you are perfect as you are. And of course, pejorative, blaming language is out.

Combine and improve at the end. When you can think of no more ideas, go back over your list. Cross out the obviously unworkable ideas. Make the good ones better. Combine several good ideas into an excellent plan. When weighing one idea against another, consider the long-range consequences of each.

Brainstorm ideas to accomplish each of the goals you have set. Here are the results of the Needleman's brainstorming. (Ideas marked with an X were crossed out.)

Goal 1: Make plans we can realistically follow through on.

Write down all scheduled events on calendar, even tentative ones.

X Give exercise first priority, nothing can preempt it.

X Do only imaginary, pretend exercise.

No more "every Saturday at 10" plans—unrealistic.

Have contingency plans—e.g. roller rink if it rains.

Kids must have veto power—jogging is boring, boring, boring.

X Charge fines for missing exercise.

Cut out some parties, meetings, trips to free more time for exercise.

X Make written contracts agreeing to exercise.

X Sign up for a regular class.

Each sign up for a class that interests us as individuals.

For their second goal, they listed exercises each wanted to try. (Ideas marked with a * seemed suitable for classes they could take; a ✓ indicates exercises they could do in pairs.)

Goal 2: Get more exercise separately if we can't do it together.

Peter   Jogging
           * Yoga ✓

Polly   Walking with friends
           * Jazzercise
           Swimming ✓
           * Yoga ✓

Rob   Buy roller blades
           * Karate

Shelley Swimming ✓
           * Dance lessons

For their third goal, they marked ideas that they knew they wanted to do with a *.

Goal 3: Work on more accepting attitude about our appearance and about each other.

No more fat jokes.

* Polly buy some clothes that really fit.

Peter cancel *Penthouse* subscription.

Polly stop buying fashion magazines.

X Write a letter to the editor condemning "fatism" & body worship.

* Shelley do nutrition and body image for science fair.

Rob and Shelley lay off name-calling (lard-butt, pimple face).

X Daddy stop "sucking it in."

Put bathroom scale and old Weight Watchers stuff in the closet.

Cover up full-length mirror.

Give away all diet books.

* Get a self-help book on sane diet and exercise.

Trial Period

Next you have to put your chosen solutions into effect for a trial period. While you have the paper and pencils out, make a list of who will do what, when each item will be done, and how long you will try the new solution.

The Needlemans agreed to try their solutions for three months and then evaluate. In the first two weeks, they agreed to get started by doing the following tasks:

Peter: Cancel *Penthouse.*
         Sign up for yoga class.
         Sign Rob up for karate.
         Take down the mirror.
         Buy new running shoes.

Polly: Mark calendar.
         Set swimming dates with Shelley.
         Sign up Shelley for dance.
         Put away scale and diet books.
         Buy one outfit that fits.

Shelley: Get nutrition books from library.
         Check out self-help book on body image.

Rob: Find out about best roller blades to buy.
         Call roller rink for schedule.

Evaluate Results

At the end of the trial period, look back and evaluate how well your solution has worked. The Needlemans found that it was still hard to make enough time to exercise. It didn't work to have more than one activity at a time. Peter settled on jogging and did not sign up for the next series of yoga classes. Polly and Shelley concentrated on swimming, and Rob stuck with karate. The most important change was in their attitude toward each other. The guilt and recriminations of the past were gone. There was more support for the efforts they did make to exercise and less obsessing about body image.

When you evaluate your results, look especially for evidence that you were right about the long-term consequences. Make sure you are putting your efforts where they count the most.

Example

Roger and Sarah had different sexual rhythms and interests. Roger was a night person. He liked to stay up late and make love in the evening. Sarah got tired about eight p.m. She liked to go to bed early and have sex early in the morning.

Roger liked mild bondage rituals, but Sarah found them embarrassing and sometimes even threatening. She liked to talk during sex and Roger didn't.

Their ineffective solutions were to make vaguely accusatory complaints about how different they were sexually. Sarah would ask Roger to talk during sex, and he would try it but feel resentful and sometimes lose his erection. Each wanted the other to initiate sex, and neither felt like getting things started very frequently. Over time they had fewer sexual encounters, until they were making love about once a month. Roger would rent X-rated videos and watch them privately.

This is how they stated the problem:

Who: Us.

What: Sex.

Where: In bed.

When: The time is never right: Roger likes night time, Sarah likes mornings.

How: Roger likes silence, being tied up occasionally, and X-rated videos. Sarah likes talking and being swept off her feet, finds bondage embarrassing.

Why: We're mismatched. Declining desire.

Feelings: Frustrated, resentful, uncared for, deprived.

Other: We still love each other, but our sex life is dead.

They set goals by generating these novel ways of looking at the problem:

The real problem isn't	The real problem is
Sex	The time
Mismatched desire	Embarrassment

Their goals were to find creative scheduling ideas that would put them together when they were both alert and capable of feeling sexual, and to try to overcome their mutual embarrassment about the other's sexual turn-ons.

Here is their brainstorming list:

Creative scheduling

Make dates for weekend "nooners."

Trade off evening and morning times.

Go to bed early, before Sarah gets tired.

Stay in bed for a while weekend mornings, read or watch TV until Roger gets fully awake and able to feel sexual.

Reduce embarrassment

Sarah to experiment with some of Roger's sexual fantasies.

Roger to write out a description of his fantasies and Sarah will think about it.

Sarah talks and Roger listens during sex.

Watch X-rated videos together.

Roger can learn several "sweet nothings" he can say during sex without having to think.

Sarah can read *My Secret Garden* to explore women's sexual fantasies.

They decided on a trial period of a month. In that time they made love nearly as often as they had in the early weeks of their relationship, and both felt impassioned and revitalized. Over the long term, Roger became able to say his "sweet nothings" during sex and became more of a morning person. Sarah was able to stay up a little later to make love, and she came to a greater acceptance of the variety and validity of sexual fantasies. Roger never became the honey-tongued swashbuckler that Sarah dreamed about, and Sarah never became the bondage queen of Roger's fantasies. But they were each able to play these roles once in a while, with modest success.

Anger and Conflict

8

Assessing and Changing Aversive Strategies

The honeymoon phase of a relationship is formed largely of illusion: it is the beautiful hologram of two becoming one, of a man and woman merging in a love that can provide satisfaction for each important human need.

In time the image fades. The vision of an encompassing union without conflict or pain is replaced by the realization that each person has very different, even opposite, needs. This shattering of the dream of perfect merging, and the disenchantment that follows, are unavoidable steps in the building of true love.

People, no matter how close, frequently want very different things and pull in different directions. Even partners who are well matched often experience conflicting needs. The discovery of this fact triggers the most important challenge that a couple will face: developing a constructive method for resolving conflict.

The strategies you use in response to conflict largely determine the level of satisfaction in your relationship. Healthy strategies promote compromise and acknowledge the importance of each partner's need. *Aversive strategies* use shame and fear to force a partner into giving in or giving up what he or she wants.

Aversive strategies often yield very good short-term results: a partner is hurt or intimidated into giving you what you want. But over time, aversive strategies cease to work. People become numb and inured, or rebellious, or deeply alienated. Intimacy and trust are replaced with anger, detachment, or resistance. It's a high price.

In this chapter you will learn to identify the eight aversive strategies most frequently used to control others in relationships. You can assess which strategies you tend to use and become more aware of their impact on you and your partner. Finally, you'll have the opportunity to explore and practice the two foundation skills in healthy conflict resolution.

Theoretical Background

Much has been written on the role of the dysfunctional family in creating problems in communication (Bradshaw 1988a, 1988b). Dysfunctional families use shame and fear to coerce and control members. Parents who are themselves overwhelmed and out of control force their children to take care of the family's emotional and sometimes physical needs. The fear of attack or abandonment makes children disregard their own needs and feelings while focusing their energy on meeting a parent's demands.

"Put that stupid guitar down and pick your sister up at school. Do something useful for a change." "What are you doing going over to Joan's house? She dresses like a tart and spends all her time chasing boys at the mall. If you think you have time for that, we haven't given you enough to do here at home." "Tell me, how's my darling? Cat got your tongue? So you don't want to talk to your dad? Well, maybe now your dad doesn't want to talk to you either. Just get on out of here. We don't have to bother talking at all, now."

Notice how these children get shamed or frightened into doing what the parent wants. These mechanisms of control are extremely powerful. They literally beat children into submission; they force a child to surrender his or her needs in order to feel at all safe in a family.

As a child, you may have watched your parents threaten or humiliate each other or your siblings. You may have been a victim of aversive strategies yourself. The lessons are never forgotten. You may have learned that inflicting fear and shame will sometimes resolve conflict. You may have learned that pain can control people. This is called modeling, learning by observation. When Mom is tired and needs help with the groceries, she attacks you for being lazy and selfish. Grudg-ingly, you help her shop, but you also learn that people get their way by denigrating and guilt-tripping. When your dad explodes and threatens to make the house off-limits to your friends because you're giggling and talking too loud, you get the message. But you also learn that threats are quick, effective ways to get your needs met.

Now, as an adult, when you find yourself in conflict situations, when you want something very much, you may use methods that you watched as a child. You may resort to the same hurtful strategies that once were aimed at you.

Time for Mastery

Assessing the aversive strategies you use can take as little as one week. Practicing *the key attitude* in conflict resolution may take an additional one-to-four-weeks.

Learn To Recognize the Eight Aversive Strategies

The methods that follow are the most frequently used aversive strategies.

1. Discounting. The message to your partner is that his or her needs are invalid. They don't have the importance, the magnitude, or the legitimacy of your needs. The idea is to shame him or her into ac-quiescence.

"For God's sake, Honey, you've been home looking at Oprah all day. Why do you want *me* to do the bills?" (Basic message: My need to relax is more legitimate than your desire to avoid this task.)

"When we go to see your brother, all the two of you do is sit around playing backgammon. You never even go out for air. At least when we visit my mother's, people are talking to each other. It's a real family feeling, not just games." (Basic message: My need to visit my mother is more important because we do something real and valid.)

2. Withdrawal/abandonment. The message here is "Do what I want or I'm leaving." The threat of abandonment is so frightening that a partner may be willing to give up a great deal to avoid it.

"I don't think this is working, Ted. If you can't pick me up when my car craps out, I don't think I have any business being in this relation-ship." (Basic message: Pick me up or you will be alone.)

After being told that his partner was going to Boston for a three-day college reunion: "Do what you got to do." Grimace. "It's the heavy television for me tonight. I'll see you later." Grimace, slow nodding. "Don't wait up." (Basic message: If you go, I'm checking out for a while emotionally. Expect no intimacy from me.)

Sometimes withdrawal takes the form of the emotional deep freeze. Sometimes it's just a chilly gap in the conversation. But it has the effect of taking away something precious: the feeling of connectedness that is the lifeblood of any relationship.

3. Threats. Here the strategy is explicitly to promise harm to your partner.

"I've had enough of your high and mighty shit. No job is good enough for you. You can take this one, Bill, or I'm going to stop covering up for your sorry ass career with your family." (Basic message: Do what I want or I'll bad-mouth you.)

"Hey, OK, I won't ask you to do it again [a particular sexual behavior]. Maybe I'll ask somebody else." (Basic message: Give me what I want sexually or I'll no longer be monogamous.)

With this strategy, a partner commits to *actively* hurting the other as a means of control. It's a high-risk and high-gain strategy because, while it may get what you want, the price can be extremely high in the coin of resentment.

4. Blaming.   The method here is to make your need the other person's fault. "If you could say something real about yourself, I wouldn't have to live in this emotional void. Look, I'm asking, what's going on with you? Knock, knock. What's happening in there?" (Basic message: I feel empty because you're inadequate.)

Another use of blaming is to make your partner's need his or her own fault. "If you'd taken the kids to the zoo on the streetcar like I suggested, this never would have happened. The car wouldn't have been broken into, and you wouldn't have to do all this shlepping to get it fixed." (Basic message: You created the problem, you fix it.)

Notice that as long as a need can be blamed on your partner, he or she is expected to atone by meeting it.

5. Belittling/denigrating.   Here the strategy is to make your partner feel foolish and inappropriate for having a need different from your own.

"Why do you want to go to the lake all the time? All you ever do is get sinus headaches up there." (Basic message: Going to the lake is a stupid thing to want.)

"Your friends haven't got a brain between them. Why can't we be involved with people who can talk about something other than designer sunglasses and who's getting laid at the tennis club?" (Basic message: Your friends have no value; give them up.)

Once again, fear or shame is the lever used in this method of control. If a partner wants not to be devalued, he or she must relinquish an important need.

6. Guilt tripping. This strategy conveys the message that a partner is a moral failure for not supporting what you want. He or she is unfair, inconsiderate, or just plain wrong for having a conflicting desire.

"I've spent the whole day keeping this house going, and you can't even spend twenty minutes fixing the door on the oven. You're in love with that couch. Your main task in life is to keep your feet up." (Basic message: Your desire to rest is unfair; you're bad.)

"I always try to do whatever you say feels good sexually. I mean, I know why I'm here—so you can come. But I ask you to wear something that turns me on and all you do is tell me that it's too embarrassing or weird." (Basic message: Saying no to me is wrong and unfair.)

7. Derailing. You respond to your partner's need by switching the conversational focus. The covert message is that his or her desires aren't worth talking about.

"I know, I know, you want more time off from the kids. We're both going crazy. Listen, I've got only two nights to prepare that lecture for the Hornblowers' Society. Got some heavy work ahead in the library. Did you get my suit from the dry cleaners? Tell Susie I want to see a perfect spelling test this week." (Basic message: Everybody's got problems, but mine are more important.)

"You're not getting enough time to work on your song writing? Join the club. We've got a total meltdown at Salvadore's school. The language teacher quit. I always thought her accent was a joke anyway. But now the algebra teacher's got Lyme's Disease, and one of the aides hit a kid yesterday, and his parents ..." (Basic message: Your music doesn't count.)

8. Taking away. Here the strategy is to withdraw some form of support, pleasure, or reinforcement from the other person. You *take away* something your partner finds nurturing.

"I'm not really in the mood, hiking's getting boring for me." Said coldly after the partner was reluctant to spend money on a new PC. (Basic message: No PC, no fun with me.)

"It's time for everyone in this family to do his own laundry. Why don't you start taking care of yourself a little, Peter?" This is after Peter didn't want to diagnose the clacking noise made by his wife's car. (Basic message: I'll punish you if you refuse me.)

Assess Your Use of Aversive Strategies

Now's the time to find out how and when you use aversive strategies. The following *conflict log* can help you keep track of your behavior over the next week. Xerox more copies if you need them.

Whenever you find yourself in some form of conflict with your partner, record the appropriate information in your log. A conflict could be a shouting match, a few cold remarks, or just the awareness that you want different things. Start by noting the date of the event. Now look inside: What did you need in that situation? What were you trying to get for yourself? Was it rest, attention, help with something, some form of pleasure? Be honest. Write your answers down in the column headed *My Need*.

How did you try to persuade your partner to give you what you wanted? Literally, what did you do to influence him or her to have things go your way? Write that down in the column labeled *My Behavior*.

If you are aware of using an aversive strategy, note which one(s) in the column provided. If nothing comes to mind, go through the list and see if your behavior fits any of the eight strategies described.

The last column, *Consequences*, is very important. This is an opportunity to explore the outcomes of your behavior. What happens, in particular, when you use aversive strategies? *Do you get what you want?* Consider this carefully. Are your methods working? Do they create cooperation or angry resistance? Is there an emotional aftermath? Do one or both of you act hurt, vengeful, shut down? How long does it take to recover from the methods you have used to resolve the conflict?

Remember that this is a chance to look at your own behavior, not the behavior of your partner. It's quite possible, even likely, that your partner employs aversive strategies as well, but that isn't the point. Your partner's behavior is his or her responsibility. Your task here is to look honestly at what you do and begin to assess objectively how it affects your relationship. The only person you can change is yourself. And change starts with awareness.

Keep the conflict log for one-to-two weeks. Before you start, look at Joe's example to get an idea how a complete record might look.

Drawing Conclusions from Your Conflict Log

Notice in Joe's record that he tends to use the same aversive strategies repeatedly—belittling, withdrawing, and blaming. In terms of consequences, while he sometimes gets what he wants, the emotional after-

Conflict Log

Date of Conflict	My Need	My Behavior	Aversive Strategy	Conse-quences

Joe's Example

Date of Conflict	My Need	My Behavior	Aversive Strategy	Consequences
10/18	Stay home from PTA meeting; rest	Said the whole organization was a waste of time. Got angry and went down to my workshop.	Belittling With-drawal	Susan got very hurt and didn't go to the meeting either. Things were very cold between us (lasted two days).
10/21	Sex	Told her her tiredness is a turnoff. Rolled away from her.	Blaming With-drawal	Didn't have sex. Nothing changed.
10/22	Rest	Told Susan all the forms for a refinance application are a waste of time. Won't save enough to be worth the effort (she's hot to do it).	Dis-counting	She did most of it herself but made me fill in the stuff about my income. Very cold, clipped manner with me.
10/27	Go to the Jazz Festival	Told her she was a killjoy for not wanting to go. Told her she keeps us from expanding and growing and doing anything different.	Belittling Blaming	She got angry, then cold. I went alone.
10/29	Lighter toast	Asked her why she has to scorch the toast all the time.	Belittling	Agreed we'd both just reset the toaster.
10/30	Control	Told Susan her idea for a deck under the trees was stupid. Too dark and shady. Just kept working and didn't say anything. Cold.	Belittling With-drawal	No deck. Susan got angry and went to Sara's house.

math always includes coldness and withdrawal. The aversive strategies Joe uses are highly destructive—they are literally killing his relationship. The blaming and belittling are designed to shame Susan into giving up her needs. Sometimes she does, but the cost is a tremendous erosion of intimacy and emotional trust.

Taking a clear, hard look at your conflict log may make you more than a bit uncomfortable, but it could help you to start facing the ways you deal with conflict. Try to extract the following information from your record. (Note: If there aren't enough examples in your record to answer these questions, it might be a good idea to keep it one or two weeks longer.)

1. What kinds of needs tend to trigger your use of aversive strategies? Is there a pattern? Or does any need, large or small, lead to aversive methods of conflict resolution?

2. Which strategies do you most frequently rely on?

3. Are you generally getting what you want using your current strategies? Examine the *My Need* column and try to assign a percentage to your rate of success.

4. What are the typical emotional consequences for using each of your aversive strategies? How long does the aftermath last?

5. Are the aversive strategies affecting your relationship to the point that you are now ready to change them? Think a while about this one.

Consider that a yes answer is a commitment to some serious work on your part.

The Key Attitude

It's hard to develop healthy conflict resolution skills without establishing a *key attitude* that supports each partner in having different needs and desires. The key attitude has three components.

1. Conflict is inevitable between intimates; it's okay to want different things. This is just an acknowledgement that each person has unique needs and that even the closest companions will have their own tastes, preferences, fears, and goals.

2. Each partner's needs are equally valid. Your need to rest is as important as your partner's need to get something done. Your partner's need for newness and excitement is as important as your need for safety and familiarity. Your love of birds is as important as your partner's love of trains. Your partner's fear of ridicule is as important as your need for attention.

Trying to figure out which need is more legitimate, more deserved, or more significant undermines your relationship. After all, there's no judge or jury to tell you. You each see the situation through the lens of your own experience, your own feelings.

When you try to invalidate a partner's need through aversive strategies, you often create an impasse. Your partner resists the discounting or pressure to abandon his or her needs, and you resist any counterattack against your own. Rigidly adhering to the principle of equally valid needs is the best way out of this fix. By definition, both your needs become legitimate and important.

3. Conflict must be solved together as partners. When you use aversive strategies, there are winners and losers. You are adversaries rather than partners. The issue is resolved when the will of one prevails over the will of the other. In contrast, the key attitude requires you to regard conflict as a problem *both* partners must solve. Since your needs are equally valid, both require attention. Both needs figure into any solution. And no solution is acceptable that ignores either partner's wants and feelings.

When expressing the key attitude, it's often helpful to briefly state each partner's need. This allows you to acknowledge the main elements of the conflict in a direct, nonjudgmental way.

Here's how Helen expressed the key attitude toward Louise. "I can see that in the area of my studies we need different things. You need time to be together and enjoy the moment. I need to read an incredible amount to keep up with the demands of my graduate program. What we both want is equally important. Louise, we can figure this out; there's a way we can set things up so both of our needs are considered."

Notice how the three elements of the key attitude all get covered: (1) we have different wants, and it's okay, (2) they're both equally important, and (3) we can solve this together in a way that gives each of us some of what we need.

Exercise.   Go back to Joe's example. The following are some examples of *key attitude* statements Joe could have used.

Conflict 1: Joe wants to stay home from the PTA meeting.
1. Okay to want different things; identify separate needs.
   "Susan, it's okay. We want different things here. I want to rest, you want me to be with you at the meeting."
2. Equally valid needs.

"We both have reasonable needs."

3. Conflict solved as partners; needs of both considered. "Let's figure this out together, being aware of what we both want."

Conflict 2: Joe's interested in sex.

1. Okay to want different things; identify separate needs. "I sense we're kind of pulling in different directions here. You're tired and need to rest, and I'm turned on."
2. Equally valid needs. "There's nothing wrong with either of those things."
3. Conflict solved as partners; needs of both considered. "Can't we figure this out together? A time to be sexually close when we are both into it?"

Conflict 3: Joe wants to rest.

1. Okay to want different things; identify separate needs. "We each want something very different right now. You're hot to get this refinance application in, and I'm desperate to rest and not put any energy into it."
2. Equally valid needs. "This refinance is important to you, and relaxing and avoiding pressure right now is important to me."
3. Conflict solved as partners; needs of both considered. "I have misgivings about it, but let's set a time to sit down and sort it out together."

Conflict 4: Joe wants to go to the Jazz Festival.

1. Okay to want different things; identify separate needs. "I understand, Susan. I love jazz and you don't. I want to go, and you feel a lot more comfortable at home."
2. Equally valid needs. "My need to do new things isn't more important than your comfort."
3. Conflict solved as partners; needs of both considered. "But I'd like to work something out together. Some way we can compromise on things like this."

Now it's your turn. Try to develop a key attitude statement for Joe's last two needs—"lighter toast" and "control."

Conflict 5: Toast.

1. Okay to want different things; identify separate needs.

2. Equally valid needs.

3. Conflict solved as partners; needs of both considered.

Conflict 6: Control.
1. Okay to want different things; identify separate needs.

2. Equally valid needs.

3. Conflict solved as partners; needs of both considered.

If you've finished the exercise, go ahead now and read the next section which contains sample key attitude statements for the toast and control issues.

Toast:
1. "You like it dark, I like it light. That's okay."
2. "We're both entitled to our tastes."
3. "But what can we do so we both get toast the way we like it?"

Control:
1. "We've got different ideas about the deck. That's fine. You see it under the trees. I'm concerned about it being too dark and want it more in the sun."
2. "They're both valid ideas."
3. "Any way we can get to some sort of compromise?"

At this point, you are encouraged to go back to your conflict log and develop a key attitude statement for each entry. Be sure to include all three elements of the key attitude.

Making a key attitude statement is the beginning of conflict resolution, not the end. You've asked your partner to work together, but chances are you haven't solved anything yet. Chapters 6 and 7 on negotiation and problem solving will show you where to go from here.

9

Coping With Anger

Anger damages intimate relationships. Susan Hazaleus and Jerry Deffenbacher (1986) found in a study of angry men that 45 percent of their subjects had suffered a "terminated or damaged" relationship during the previous year. Deborah Weaver and Darlene Shaw, at the Medical School of South Carolina, found that hostile Type A women had significantly worse marriages than Type B's (Wood 1986). Divorce statistics provide further evidence of the role of anger in marriage breakups. Some 52 percent of U.S. divorces are granted on the grounds of either physical or emotional cruelty.

Repeated anger episodes have the same effect on a relationship that cuts have on the skin. The anger creates emotional scar tissue that grows thicker with each new wound. Like its physical counterpart, emotional scar tissue is inelastic and lacks feeling. Chronic anger makes people rigid and highly defensive, and the long-term effect is a loss of empathy and intimacy.

Angry partners feel helpless. If the other person would only change or improve, things would feel better. It always feels like the other person's fault. And when no amount of complaining and angry blaming induces a partner to change, feelings of helplessness, even paralysis, deepen. And the anger only gets worse.

While anger focuses on the other person, on how he or she does wrong and needs to change, healthy coping brings the focus back on you. This chapter will help you understand how you *make yourself angry*, and how you can change your thoughts and attitudes so the anger you feel is replaced by effective new coping responses.

History

Therapists used to think that ventilating angry feelings was healthy and appropriate. This idea was based on Freud's "hydraulic model" of energy. He believed that energy could get blocked or dammed up and would eventually build to the point that it began to spill over and flood the system. Suppressing anger was like keeping the lid on a pressure cooker: eventually the steam would build up to the point of explosion. The release was *catharsis*, an emptying of the emotional reservoirs through some form of intense outpouring. Catharsis in the form of angry ventilation is encouraged by those who believe in the hydraulic model. "Suppressed anger festers in the mind and body of the individual, creating both emotional and physical ailments; it insinuates itself between husband and wife" (Bry 1976). Theodore Rubin says in *The Angry Book* (1969) that expressing anger serves to create healthier and happier communication.

Modern research, unfortunately, does not support these theories. After summarizing the major studies on anger, Carol Tavris (1982) concluded that people who vent their anger tend to get more angry, rather than less. Whether the subjects were children, college students, or adults, the research consistently demonstrated that free expression of anger and hostility resulted in measurably increased angry and negative feelings. There's a reason for this. When you get angry, you tend to remember all the negative traits and behaviors of the target person. You review the failings and violations and the history of wrongdoing. And when you express your anger, when you say out loud all of these negative perceptions, you strengthen them and make them easier to recall next time. To put it simply, anger hardens negative perceptions. Anger begets anger.

As some therapists began to recognize that anger was frequently more destructive than it was helpful, methods of treatment began to emerge that focused on the way angry thoughts lead to angry feelings and behavior. Cognitive theorists began to follow Albert Ellis (1962) in looking at how anger is influenced by unrealistic expectations and "shoulds." When others break your rules for appropriate behavior, it feels like they've done wrong and ought to be punished. Aaron Beck (1979) showed how certain *styles* of thinking literally created the emotion of anger.

Once it was clear that thoughts play a big role in your anger response, several therapists developed pioneering methods for changing the thoughts that trigger anger. Raymond Novaco (1975), building on the work of Donald Meichenbaum, developed an anger treatment called stress inoculation. This technique helps you rehearse relaxation strategies and coping statements while imagining anger-evoking scenes. You'll have a chance to practice stress inoculation later in this chapter.

Theoretical Background

The two-step model of anger. Anger has two components. To become angry you have to (1) feel some form of stress or pain and (2) use trigger thoughts that act as a spark to ignite a hostile response. Both stress *and* trigger thoughts are necessary for you to really *feel* angry (McKay, Rogers, and McKay 1989). Trigger thoughts are the catalyst that transforms stress and pain into an angry, blaming reaction. If you have angry thoughts without stress, you'll never feel aroused enough to have an emotional reaction. Stress without trigger thoughts remains just an unpleasant feeling.

Why does stress get so easily converted into anger? When you're in emotional or physical pain, you're strongly motivated to do something about it. Pain creates physiological arousal that has the effect of mobilizing you to action. Anger helps you cope with pain in two ways. First, it can help you discharge the arousal so that your tension level decreases. If you feel hurt because your wife criticized your efforts in the garden, getting angry can give you temporary relief from emotional arousal caused by the hurt. The second way anger helps with stress is literally to block awareness of your feelings. A woman who was anxious about the possibility that her husband might leave her used an outburst about the clothes he'd left on the floor to push the fear out of awareness. The anger helped her defend against a much more painful feeling.

Anger as a choice. Because anger cannot exist without the presence of trigger thoughts, anger is something you can control. You can change the feeling of anger by changing the thoughts that ignite it. You can learn to recognize the thinking that begets anger and replace it with thoughts that lead toward a sense of empowerment and calm.

Time for Mastery

The Anger Assessment Record will take one-to-two weeks to complete. The stress inoculation program will take an additional one-to-two weeks of focused work. You should begin to see some reduction in your overall level of anger by the end of four weeks.

Complete an Anger Assessment Record

Before you can make any changes in your feelings or behavior, you'll need to get a clear understanding of how your anger arises. Over the next seven to fourteen days keep an anger assessment record (a blank form that you can xerox is provided on the next page). Each time you feel angry with your partner, under the column marked *Event* write what was happening, objectively and behaviorally. Put down what was said or what was done that you associate with your anger.

In the column marked *Stressors* write down the source of your pain. There are four categories of stressors that you should be aware of. *Painful affect* has to do with feelings that are negative or unpleasant: sadness, guilt, shame, anxiety, and so on. *Painful sensation* refers to things that you experience physically: toothache, joint pain, heartburn, headache, and so on. *Frustrated drive* is the stress that comes from having something you want blocked. You're striving for or needing something, but there's an obstacle in the way. *Threats* are stressors that derive from a situation where someone promises to cause you pain. Be sure to write down the specific stressor that impacted you, not just the category.

In the column marked *Trigger Thoughts*, write down everything you said to yourself that started and then intensified your anger. There are two kinds of trigger thoughts: blamers and shoulds.

Blamers label the target person as wrong and bad. The generic blamer is: "You deliberately did _____ to me." The key idea behind a blamer is that you've been intentionally harmed by the wrong behavior of someone else. Blamers always have at the core a belief that *they* did it to you. Your stress was caused by the offending person.

Shoulds are the second kind of trigger thought. The generic should is: "You should not have _____, but instead you should have _____." The idea is that the other person ought to know how to act correctly, but instead has deliberately broken the rules of appropriate behavior. Now the person becomes bad and wrong and deserving of punishment.

Anger Assessment Record

Event	Stressor	Trigger Thoughts	Anger Rating

The next section of this chapter will provide more information about these two categories of trigger thoughts.

It's very important that you make as complete a record as possible of your trigger thoughts. Try to remember exactly what was in your mind at the moment you got angry. How were you seeing the situation? How were you describing the offending person to yourself? If the situation escalated, what did you say to yourself to make your anger grow?

The last column in your Anger Assessment Record is the *Anger Rating*. On a 1-10 point scale, note how angry you felt in the situation. This scale is designed to help you recognize which stressors and trigger thoughts generate the greatest anger.

Keep the Anger Assessment Record until you have at least ten anger events. If seven days isn't enough, keep the record going until you reach the cutoff of ten episodes. Remember that an anger event isn't necessarily a blowout. You might not even express the anger openly. An anger event is merely a situation where you experience an anger response of at least 1 on the rating scale.

On the following page is the Anger Assessment Record that Lynn kept during an eleven-day period.

Analyze Trigger Thoughts

In this section you'll learn more specifics about the two main categories of trigger thoughts, and get some ammunition for resisting them.

Blamers

Blaming can take different forms. *Global labels* are perhaps the most damaging blamers. You accuse the other person of being foolish, incompetent, careless, and so on. Lynn, for example, labeled Bill as being irresponsible, lazy, stupid, selfish, and an asshole. These labels have the effect of damning Bill as a person; he's a failed human being.

Blame can also take the form of *assumed intent*. This is a common form of mind reading. You make assumptions about the motives, intentions, and meanings behind another person's behavior. Assumed intent creates anger when you come to the conclusion that your partner has deliberately tried to hurt you. The belief that your pain is the result of a conscious choice by someone else makes you feel victimized and gives you permission to punish and attack. When Lynn wonders whether Bill is making noise at night to annoy her or imagines that he "plays the good guy to make her look like a witch by comparison," she's assuming intent.

Lynn's Anger Assessment Record

Event	Stressor	Trigger Thoughts	Anger Rating
Bill misplaces the checkbook.	Anxious, back pain.	He never pays attention to anything. He spends more time worrying about his novel than me and Sharon.	3
He's late getting back from the writers' group.	Tired, back pain.	It isn't fair. He leaves me the whole job of getting the kids down. He takes time for himself but not for all the rest of the stuff that needs doing around here.	6
Bill wants to borrow my sunglasses.	Drained, depressed.	Why can't he keep track of his own damned glasses? Just put them away somewhere. Irresponsible.	2
Late notice from house insurance.	Anxious, frustrated that he doesn't listen.	It's the same shit always. He's too lazy & preoccupied with his own stuff to take the time to pay attention to the bills. It's stupid and irresponsible.	6
Report cards come in.	Anxious, embarrassed.	If he'd helped with Sharon's homework, things would get a lot better at school. He leaves me with the whole load. Sharon needs some real discipline, and he's too wrapped up in himself to bother.	8
Sharon mouths off. And when I get angry, he defends her.	Hurt, frustrated.	He's always playing the good guy so I'll look like a witch by comparison. He's sweet, irresponsible Dad; I'm the only one who ever says no to her.	9
Hear his computer beeping away.	Tired, lonely, back pain.	All he cares about is his fucking novel.	3
He comes to bed late, clumping around.	Tired, hurt.	He can't even keep quiet when I'm sleeping. Doesn't he know it'll wake me, or is he doing it to annoy me?	3

Lynn's Anger Assessment Record

Event	Stressor	Trigger Thoughts	Anger Rating
He talks about some character in his novel.	Anxiety about Sharon's school work.	Get a clue. Your kid's heading down the scholastic toilet, and you're lost in make believe.	8
Late from writers' group.	Tired, depressed.	I do the kids, he does the fun. I could do this by myself—I don't need him.	7
He gets home: tells me I'm riding him, squeezing the life out of him.	Hurt.	He's a selfish, irresponsible asshole.	10

A third kind of blamer involves magnifying. Here your internal monologue may include words such as *terrible, awful, horrendous,* and *disgusting.* Magnifying can also include words that overgeneralize: *all, always, every, never, nobody,* and *everyone.* Magnifiers expand your sense of being harmed. They make a subjective sense of injury worse and, as a consequence, you get angrier. Lynn is magnifying when she says "it's the same shit *always* . . . he leaves me the *whole* job . . . he *never* pays attention."

Combatting blamers with accuracy. Accuracy and nonexaggeration are keys to changing your anger response. It's crucial that you avoid global labels that brand your partner with a negative trait. A person may be irresponsible in some areas and very responsible in others. Rarely is a global label accurate for every aspect of a person's behavior. Accuracy also means avoiding magnifiers. It wasn't true that Bill "never paid attention to anything." He spent less time focusing on Lynn and their daughter than Lynn would have wanted. But words like *never* and *always* create instant exaggeration and greatly inflate the damage done.

Accuracy is particularly crucial when trying to understand the motives of your partner. Don't assume intent to harm without clear and direct evidence. Unless your partner has said why he or she is doing something, remind yourself that you have no certain knowledge of what he or she is thinking or the forces that influence hurtful behaviors. The motto for every marriage should be: "Assume nothing. Check it out." If you're puzzled or disturbed by your partner's behavior, open a dialogue to explore the possible motivations. Chapter 12 on identifying your partner's schemas will provide more specific help in the process of checking your assumptions.

Shoulds

Shoulds grow out of your sense of the correct and proper way to act. One variation is the *entitlement fallacy*. Here the underlying assumption is that because you want something very much, you ought to have it. But entitlement confuses desire with obligation. It implies that when you want something a lot, the other person loses his or her right to say no. Your partner no longer has the freedom to choose; his or her limits and needs are less important than yours. Entitlement says: "I want this a lot, and you're bad if you don't give it to me."

Lynn feels entitled to Bill's help with Sharon's homework, discipline, and the bedtime process. And when she doesn't get the amount of help she feels entitled to, it seems like Bill is breaking the rules. He's a bad person.

A second kind of should is the *fallacy of fairness*. Here the expectation is that relationships are governed by the same kinds of laws and principles that you find in court. It feels like there is some standard, hard and absolute, that determines what is correct. The fallacy of fairness is built upon an imaginary fulcrum where the tasks and obligations and rewards of a relationship are balanced. Unfortunately, between partners the concept of fairness is completely arbitrary. Each partner's balancing fulcrum is tilted at a different angle. Since there is no judge or jury to decide, partners define fairness to fit their needs and expectations of the other person. It isn't fair, Lynn thinks, that Bill leaves her with the whole job of getting the kids down. She's tired, her back hurts, and she wants his help. Bill would define fairness very differently, most probably in line with his desire to socialize with the writers' group. The partner who appeals to fairness will always define it to serve the needs of the moment.

The last type of should is the *fallacy of change*. Here the assumption is that when your partner does wrong, he or she can be punished and coerced into being different. The idea is that if you just apply enough pressure, you can mould your partner into a better person. Lynn really believes that if she complains enough, Bill may become a different kind of parent and husband. He'll shift his priorities away from his novel and attend more to his family responsibilities. While an angry insistence on change may feel righteous, the result is often disappointing. People change only when they are capable of change, and reinforced to change. Bludgeoning your partner with anger is more likely to result in alienation than in any healthy metamorphosis.

Shoulds and the principle of personal responsibility. The shoulds are a major source of anger and disenchantment in relationships. But there is an important weapon you can use to resist their influence. This weapon is the principle of personal responsibility, which states that (1) *you are responsible for your own pain*, and (2) *you are the one who must change your coping strategies to better meet your needs.*

If something feels very wrong to you, if you are struggling in your marriage with a situation that feels unpleasant or painful, you and not your partner has the responsibility to change it. There are four important reasons for this.

(1) You are the expert on your own needs. You know what hurts and what feels good; you are the authority on your own tastes, preferences, secret desires, aversions and pleasures.

(2) Your partner is the expert on his or her own needs. It is your partner's job to focus on those needs, and he or she has complete responsibility for meeting them. *It's not your partner's job to take care of you.* If a partner places your needs first, that choice hinders the primary responsibility of protecting and providing for him or herself.

(3) People's needs invariably conflict. This is a basic, unavoidable reality. You like suburban malls, your partner likes to shop downtown; you need help with the kids, your partner wants to work on his novel; you're tired and need rest, your partner wants you to go hiking. Many people resent this conflict and feel it shouldn't exist. But it's an unavoidable reality.

(4) How satisfied and happy you feel depends on the effectiveness of *your* strategies for meeting basic needs. *The amount of support, appreciation, and help you are getting now is all you can get, given the current strategies you are using.* What you're now doing to get more cooperation, more pleasure, or more intimacy in your relationship won't give you any more than you're presently getting. To get more of anything, you'll have to change strategies. Lynn wants more help, particularly with Sharon. The strategies she's using rely on blame and attack. The amount of support Bill now gives her with Sharon is all she can get as long as she sticks with the current strategies. If Lynn wants more support, she'll have to try something else. Maybe she needs to reward Bill in some positive way for helping Sharon. Whatever ultimately works, it's clear that the strategy of anger has gotten Lynn as much as it can get.

Six Steps to Personal Responsibility

Here are the ways you can take responsibility when you feel helpless and angry about your partner's behavior.

1. Develop more effective strategies for reinforcing your partner. How can you reward your partner for doing the things you want? Paul was often angry at Irene because she overspent the budget. Anger wasn't getting him anywhere, so he decided on a different strategy. Paul told his wife that he wanted to spend more time together doing fun things. If she could stay within the weekly budget, he'd like to go out for dinner and a movie Friday night. However, if they were over budget for the week, they'd have to skip going out.

2. Take care of the need yourself. Cynthia was angry because Arnie never trimmed the hedges in their front yard. She thought it made their place look run-down. Using the principle of personal responsibility, Cynthia decided to trim the hedge herself. It seemed to bother her a whole lot more than it did Arnie, so she figured it was up to her to solve the problem.

3. Develop new sources of support, nourishment, and appreciation. There are some things your partner may never be able to give you. Instead of feeling helpless, you can go elsewhere for what you need. Randall was a bird-watcher, and it irritated him that Barry was increasingly reluctant to join him on his hikes. He found that he went bird-watching less often and blamed Barry for losing interest in his hobby. When Randall decided to take responsibility for the situation, he joined a local bird-watching group and met several friends who enjoyed hiking in the same places he did.

4. Set limits. Many people feel pressured by a partner to do things they don't want to do. They're too tired, too stressed, too uninterested, or perhaps even too afraid. When you don't say no to these pressures, you may end up feeling angry. Setting limits by saying no is a crucial way of taking responsibility for situations you don't like. Leanne's husband continuously dragged her to baseball games. She didn't like the hot dogs, the crowds, or baking in the sun for three-and-a-half hours. And she had no particular love for the game itself. She often felt irritable after "blowing a Sunday" at the ballpark and found herself picking fights. When Leanne decided to take responsibility for the situation, she told her husband that she was willing to attend two ball games a year, period. He would have to find someone else to go with him if he wanted to attend more.

5. Negotiate assertively. This is the process of directly and calmly asking for what you want. It doesn't involve blame or anger. When you and your partner have conflicting needs, you can generate compromises that incorporate both your needs in the solution. See chapter 6 on negotiation for the specific steps toward building compromise.

6. Let go. There are two kinds of letting go. The first is built on an acceptance that the situation cannot change, and you will have to live with it. Taking responsibility in this way means letting go of the expectation that things will be different, that you'll have what you want. Leonard often made sexual overtures to his girlfriend late at night. She was very much a day person, however, and turned into a zombie after about 10:30 at night. For months, Leonard harbored a simmering anger about these nightly rejections. Taking responsibility meant accepting his girlfriend's biorhythms. He was clear he wanted the relationship, so for Leonard sex was going to have to be a daytime activity.

The second kind of letting go follows a recognition that a relationship may be too unrewarding or too painful for you to continue. The thought of letting go in this way can be frightening. There are frequently good reasons for holding onto a difficult relationship: your family depends on you, they will be hurt, there might be a serious financial loss, and so on. But if things aren't going to change, if you've tried to reinforce new behaviors and nothing works, the healthy response is not chronic anger. So it's important for you to weigh the cost of letting go against the feelings of helplessness and chronic anger that so thoroughly destroy your sense of well-being.

Exercise. Return now to your Anger Assessment Record and review your trigger thoughts. Next to each trigger thought write in the type of trigger you have used: entitlement fallacy, fallacy of fairness, fallacy of change, global labels, assumed intent, or magnifying. This exercise is important. It will help prepare you for the step ahead when you'll begin rewriting your trigger thoughts to make them emotionally neutral.

Rewrite Your Trigger Thoughts

Go back to your Anger Assessment Record and on a clean sheet of paper rewrite your trigger thoughts so they are accurate and reflect the principle of personal responsibility. To help you get a feel for this process, notice how Lynn reworked some of her trigger thoughts:

Lynn's Revised Triggers

Trigger Thoughts	Rewrite
He never pays attention to anything. He spends more time worrying about his novel than about me and Sharon.	I'm generalizing. Bill spends time with me and Sharon. But I wish the balance was different, that he'd spend less time on the novel.
It isn't fair. He leaves me the whole job of getting the kids down. He takes time for himself, but not for all the rest of the stuff that needs doing around here.	There's no such thing as fair. Bill is doing what he needs to do. I want more support from him, so I'm going to have to reinforce him to get more involved with the kids. Or maybe I'll take a night for myself.
Why can't he keep track of his own damned glasses? Just put them away somewhere. Irresponsible.	He's doing his best. I'm sure he doesn't want to lose things. If this bothers me, I don't have to lend him my sunglasses.
It's the same shit always. He's too lazy and preoccupied with his own stuff to take the time to pay attention to the bills. It's stupid and irresponsible.	He doesn't *always* screw up the bills. Most of the time it goes okay. He doesn't do it as carefully as I'd like, but a late notice is a relatively minor issue. Nothing awful is going to happen.
If he'd help with Sharon's homework, things would get a lot better at school. He leaves me with the whole load. Sharon needs some real discipline, and he's too wrapped up in himself to bother.	Sharon does need discipline, and Bill is frequently too busy to focus on her. If I don't like this (and I don't), I need to reinforce him to get more involved. Maybe we can agree to trade off supervising her homework, and on nights he's supervising her, he gets to his novel only *after* her homework is done.
He's always playing the good guy so I'll look like a witch by comparison. He's sweet, irresponsible Dad. I'm the only one who	I'm assuming things. I don't know why he plays the good guy; maybe he *is* trying to be a good dad. I do most of the dis-

Trigger Thoughts	Rewrite
ever says no to Sharon.	ciplining, but he does try oc-casionally.
All he cares about is his fucking novel.	He obviously cares about Sharon. I'm exaggerating to say he only cares about his novel.
Can't even keep quiet when I'm sleeping. Doesn't he know it'll wake me, or is he doing it to annoy me.	I think it doesn't occur to him that I'll wake up. He doesn't realize how loud it is.
Get a clue. Your kid's heading down the scholastic toilet, and you're lost in make believe.	I'm exaggerating. Sharon strug-gles with math and science but she's doing all right in other things.
I do the kids, he does the fun. I could do this by myself—I don't need him.	I'm exaggerating again. He spends time with the kids, but I do a lot more supervising of chores and bedtimes. I wish he'd help more, but he does help some.
He's a selfish, irresponsible asshole.	I won't use labels. I don't want him to accuse me of squeezing the life out of him. It hurts.

The work you've done rewriting trigger thoughts from your Anger Assessment Record lays an important foundation for the next step. It's time to start dealing with trigger thoughts closer to the time they come up. Xerox the following form. Each evening, review the day for any situations where you felt angry. Use the form to analyze and rewrite your trigger thoughts.

Trigger Thoughts Worksheet

1. Trigger thought:

Shoulds:

_____

(Person's name)

should not have _____

(what they did)

but instead he or she should have _____

_____

(the right thing to do)

Blamers:

_____

(Person's name or global label—jerk, bitch, etc.)

deliberately did _____

(the offense)

_____to me.

Did your trigger statement include global labels? Which ones?

_____

_____

Did your trigger statement include assumed intent? What did you imagine about the other person's intentions?

_____

_____

Did your trigger statement include magnifications? Which magnifying words did you use?

_____

_____

2. Rewrite your trigger statement without global labels, assumed intentions, or magnifiers. Try to make the statement absolutely accurate, without any form of exaggeration.

_____

_____

_____

3. Applying the principle of personal responsibility to the anger-provoking situation, which of the following do you need to do in order to take control of the situation?

☐   Develop more effective strategies for reinforcing others.

☐ Take care of the need yourself.

☐ Develop new resources of support, nourishment, and appreciation.

☐ Set limits.

☐ Negotiate assertively.

☐ Let go.

4. Write a specific plan for how you will implement one or more of the six steps to responsibility listed above.

_____

_____

_____

_____

Lynn's husband, Bill, was doing his own work on anger. He used the Trigger Thoughts Worksheet to deal with a situation where Lynn asked him to cut down on the time he devoted to his novel.

Bill's Trigger Thoughts Worksheet

1. Trigger thought:

Shoulds:

_____*Lynn*_____
(Person's name)

should not have _____*tried to totally stunt my creativity*_____
                        (what they did)

but instead he/she should have _____*supported me and the things*

*that are important to me*_____
                    (the right thing to do)

Blamers:

____*My killjoy wife*_____
(Person's name or global label—jerk, bitch, etc.)

deliberately did _*tried to make me as miserable as she is*___
                        (the offense)

to me.

Did your trigger statement include global labels? Which ones?

killjoy

Did your trigger statement include assumed intent? What did you imagine about the other person's intentions?

1. Trying to make me as miserable as she is

2. Trying to totally stunt my creativity

Did your trigger statement include magnifications? Which magnifying words did you use?

Totally

2. Rewrite your trigger statement without global labels, assumed intentions, or magnifiers. Try to make the statement absolutely accurate, without any form of exaggeration.

Lynn wants me to cut down the hours I devote to writing. It will mean the novel goes a lot slower, with less focus and consistency. I want her to support my creative process. I'm not going to mind-read why she's saying this. What she tells me is that she needs more help with the kids.

3. Applying the principle of personal responsibility to the anger-provoking situation, which of the following do you need to do in order to take control of the situation?

   ☐ Develop more effective strategies for reinforcing others.

   ☐ Take care of the need yourself.

   ☐ Develop new resources of support, nourishment, and appreciation.

   ☐ Set limits.

   ☒ Negotiate assertively.

   ☐ Let go.

4. Write a specific plan for how you will implement one or more of the six steps to responsibility listed above.

She's got her needs; I've got mine. I'm going to stay calm and negotiate for at least an hour-and-a-half of writing time per night.

Bill's worksheet helped calm him down. It stopped the global labels, the mind reading, and the magnification. His decision to negotiate helped him feel less victimized and gave him a plan for taking care of his own needs. You can achieve many of the things that Bill did when you use the Trigger Thoughts Worksheet. Make a commitment to yourself right now to use it every time you feel any significant anger towards your partner.

Self-Instruction

How well you handle anger has a lot to do with how well you can talk yourself down from high levels of arousal. Talking yourself down involves reminding yourself to stay calm and cope rather than blowing up.

Instruct yourself to relax.   Reminding yourself to relax is a key component to anger control. You need to know how to do two things: (1) take deep, diaphragmatic breaths and (2) relax the tense "hot spots" in your body. The deep breath is easy. Put one hand on your upper chest and the other on your abdomen just above your belt line. Now take a breath way down into your abdomen so that only the hand above your belt moves, while the hand on your upper chest remains relatively still. Practice this for a while. If you have trouble making the hand on your abdomen move or if both hands are moving simultaneously, there are a couple of things you can do to get the knack of it. First, imagine that a heavy weight is pressing down on your abdomen (as heavy as an iron frying pan, for example). And try to push the weight up with a deep, abdominal breath. If this doesn't work, literally push down on your abdomen with your hand and try to push that hand up with your breath. Once you can reliably push up the hand on your abdomen, you don't have to hold it there anymore. But practice is still important. Do three minutes of deep breathing three times a day until it becomes an automatic, well-learned skill.

The second thing you need to learn is to relax those tight "hot spots" in your body. It's a lot easier to get angry when you're tense, and, as anger builds, you may have noticed certain areas of your body that characteristically tighten. Right now scan your body for tension; look particularly for hot spots in your forehead, jaw, neck and shoulders, forearms, abdomen, and thighs. When you find a tense area, take a deep, abdominal breath and say, "Breathe it away" or "Breathe and let go." Focus the relaxing feeling from the breath into that tight area and watch it relax.

Here are some examples of self-instructional coping statements that can cue you to relax instead of hit the boiling point. Pick two or three that might work for you.

- Take a deep breath and relax.

- When my muscles get tight, it's time to relax and slow things down.

- Stay calm and relaxed.

- It's time to check my body for tension and relax what's tight.

- Relax the hot spots.

- It's time to stretch my jaw.

- It's time to shrug and relax the shoulders.

- It's time to stretch my arms.

- Loosen the legs.

- Breathe it away.

- Breathe and let go.

Coping with arousal. When you're starting to feel emotionally aroused, it's crucial to be able to say calming things to yourself. The following is a list of coping thoughts that will help you stay calm and cool. Many of them won't be useful; most of them probably won't feel like your style. But try to select at least two or three that you might be able to use when you start to get angry. If you want, change the phrase around so it really feels right to you.

- No one is right, no one is wrong, we just have different needs.

- No matter what is said, I know I'm a good person.

- Just as long as I keep my cool, I'm in control.

- Just roll with the punches. Don't get bent out of shape.

- Stay away from blaming and judgments.

- Neutral words only.

- Keep your voice calm and flat.

- No sarcasm, no attacks.

- Getting mad will cost me _____
  _____. (Insert the negative consequences of anger in this situation.)

- If I start to get mad, I'll just be banging my head against the wall, so I might as well relax.

- Getting upset won't help.

- It's not worth it to get so angry.

- I'm annoyed, but I can keep a lid on it.

- I'll stay rational. Anger won't solve anything.

- Anger is a signal of what I need to do. It's time to cope.

- Don't escalate. Cool it.

- There's nothing gained in getting mad.

- Easy does it. Remember to keep a sense of humor.

- If I'm stuck in a bad situation, I'll think about how to handle this in the future.

Coping with an angry person.   When somebody provokes you, it's natural to start pumping up your anger with trigger thoughts. But you can use self-instructional coping statements to keep you from acting out your anger. As before, pick out two or three that feel like they might work for you. Modify them so they feel exactly right.

- I'll let him make a fool of himself.

- He'd probably like me to get real angry. Well, I'm going to disappoint him.

- I don't need to prove myself to him.

- I'm not going to let her get to me.

- It's really a shame that she has to act like this.

- For her to be that irritable, she must be awfully unhappy.

- There's no need to doubt myself. What he says doesn't matter.

- I can't change it with anger. I'll just upset myself.

- I've acted this way in the past myself. I can give him some slack.

- Stay cool. Make no judgments about her.

- I don't have to take shit. I'll simply withdraw from the conversation.

- I won't be manipulated into blowing up or losing my cool.

- Blowing up only gives her what she wants.

Coping statements from *When Anger Hurts* (McKay, Rogers, and McKay 1989).

Now, take the two or three coping statements you selected from each category (coping with tension, coping with arousal, and coping with an angry person), and write them down on a 3 x 5 file card. Try to memorize them. But also carry the file card with you so you can review your coping thoughts whenever an angry situation starts to flare up. You also get a chance to practice these self-instructional coping statements in the Stress Inoculation section coming up.

Stress Inoculation

It's easier to practice anger-control skills by starting out with imagined scenes of provoking situations rather than struggling in the actual situations themselves. Stress inoculation is an opportunity to relax away anger and talk yourself through a visualized provocation. What you'll do is construct a hierarchy of anger-evoking scenes, stretching the continuum between mild irritation and total rage.

The first step to constructing your anger hierarchy is to review the range of situations where you tend to feel angry with your partner. Go ahead right now and list any situation that tends to set you off: conflicts about the kids, money, work around the house, personal habits, recreational activities, sex, dividing responsibilities, relationships to friends, and so on. Don't concentrate on just the major upsets; it's important to list the minor irritations as well. Keep going till you have at least twenty items on your list.

You can convert your list into a hierarchy by ranking the items in order, from the least to the most anger-provoking. Use a scale that runs from zero (no anger) to 100 (the angriest you've ever been). For your hierarchy to work, the items can't be too far apart on your anger scale. If you have a 20-item hierarchy, the items should increase by approximately 5 points on the anger scale—5, 10, 15, 20, and so on. At this point you'll often find your items bunched at either the high or low end of the scale. You've got a lot of 70, 80 and 90 point items, some 20s and 30s, but not many items in the middle. Some people end up with nothing but high-end items. Wherever you find gaps in your hierarchy, you'll need to develop additional items to fill in. If you have nothing between the item *Ted leaving his clothes on the floor* (35 points) and *Ted inviting people to dinner without consulting me* (65 points), you'll need five or so items to span the gap so you'll have a smooth progression up the hierarchy.

The following is a hierarchy that Roger developed after listing every situation he could think of where he felt anger with his wife Ruth.

Roger's Anger Hierarchy

Rank	Item	Anger Score
17	Ruth tries to hurry me when I'm in the shower.	5
16	Ruth cooks the kind of fish I hate and says she forgot.	10
15	Ruth wants us to go crazy rushing to church rather than be a few minutes late.	15
14	She keeps pressuring me to put in the new greenhouse window in the kitchen.	20
13	She's irritable and just disappears; goes to bed without saying good night.	25
12	Ruth leaves the gate open and the dog gets out of the yard. Running around the neighborhood looking for the dog.	30
11	Ruth criticizes me for not exercising and getting out of shape. She wants me to get on the scale so she can see how much I weigh.	35
10	She complains about my watching detective shows on TV and just switches the channel without asking.	40
9	We arrive at her parents' house and she wants me to go home and get something we forgot.	45
8	She says I'm just like my mother, always trying to control everything.	50
7	Ruth gets irritable about me reading in bed, says it keeps her awake. I put a newspaper over the light. She says, "Why bother?"	55
6	She takes the car down to that rip-off garage where I told her never to go. She says it's convenient.	60
5	Ruth says she's too busy to cook for my mother's birthday.	65
4	She wants to go on this dinner-dancing bay cruise. I think $120 is too much for one night's entertainment.	70
3	We're golfing, and she laughs when I hit it in the woods—and then won't help me find it.	75

| 2 | It's 8:00 and dinner isn't together. I ask her and she hands me a frying pan and says, "Here, you cook the shit for a change. I'm sick of it." | 80 |
| 1 | She gets in a snit and drives off, leaving me at the store. I have to walk 17 blocks home. | 85 |

You'll notice that Roger had only 17 items on a hierarchy that didn't go above 85 on the anger scale. Roger felt that the highest anger situations he experienced were not with Ruth. He simply couldn't think of anything with his wife that compared with some of the extreme anger situations that he had encountered at work.

Now that your hierarchy is set up, you can use it to practice coping with anger. Start with the first item, the one with the lowest anger score. Try right now to fix that scene firmly in your imagination. See your partner, and hear the sound of his or her voice. Really visualize and feel the scene—the colors, temperature, surroundings, and so on. As soon as you have a clear image of the anger-evoking scene, start using your new coping skills. Remind yourself to breathe away the stress. Then really take a deep breath. Scan your body and notice any hot spots of tension; then breathe again to relax the tense places. Use one or two of the coping statements that you memorized for dealing with arousal or an angry person. If the coping thoughts you've memorized don't seem appropriate for the scene, you may need to go back to the list and choose others that fit better.

Always follow through with any instructions you give yourself during a scene. If you tell yourself to loosen your jaw, really work on letting go of tension in that part of your body. If one of your coping thoughts is "Easy does it, remember to keep a sense of humor," imagine yourself smiling in the scene. See yourself looking relaxed.

After you've held a clear image of the scene for thirty-to-forty seconds, shut it off. Take a short rest before going on. You should continue repeating a scene, relaxing and using your coping thoughts each time, until you've imagined the scene twice without feeling any angry arousal. When you're finished with a scene, continue on to the next item on the hierarchy. Even though each step up the hierarchy will bring you in contact with angrier and angrier scenes, your growing ability to relax away anger and stress should make the next item no more difficult than the last.

Practice your hierarchy no more than thirty minutes at any one time. Over the course of three to seven days you should be able to move through the entire list of items.

It's not unusual to find that some items are more difficult than others, requiring far more repetition before you experience them without anger. This is a signal that you may need to modify your coping statements to make them more applicable to the scene. Or you may need to be more focused on the relaxation process, paying particular attention to specific hot spots. On occasion, you may struggle with a scene because your old anger-triggering self-talk is leaking through. Avoid trigger thoughts during a scene. Be accurate, don't exaggerate, don't use global labels.

If you do find yourself repeating a scene over and over without significantly reducing your anger, it may be in the wrong place in your hierarchy. Skip it for now, and insert it three or four scenes later, when you may be better prepared to deal with the angry feelings it evokes.

When you've successfully moved through your hierarchy, practicing the skill of relaxing away anger in each scene, you're ready to take these new skills into real life. Remember to use your coping thoughts; keep your file card handy to remind you when you forget. Make deep breathing an automatic response as soon as any anger situation starts to present itself.

Sometimes relaxing away and talking yourself through anger isn't enough. Other, interactive skills may be necessary when angry feelings start to escalate. Chapters 6, 10, 5, and 1 on negotiation, coping with an angry partner, identifying and changing cognitive distortions, and listening will help you respond more effectively while instructing yourself to relax and cope.

If new anger situations present themselves that put you off stride and make it hard to cope, you can use the same imagery technique you've practiced in stress inoculation to calm yourself. Select appropriate coping thoughts. Then visualize the scenes while breathing away stress and using the coping thoughts you've selected. Keep repeating the scene over and over until you feel no anger.

10

Coping With an Angry Partner

When your partner is angry, you probably hear a lot of criticism. And criticism hurts. It feels like a rejection. Even the most minor criticism can be painful when it comes from someone you care about, someone whose opinion matters. Whether the criticism is fair and accurate or completely wrong, you may still feel judged and attacked, your self-esteem may plummet, and you may end up feeling extremely defensive.

It's important to remember that angry people are often people who can't communicate effectively. They don't know how to negotiate for what they want nor how to set limits to protect themselves. They don't know how to encourage cooperation nor how to resolve conflict. They're frustrated and they're angry; they attack and belittle and criticize.

Your own anger can seem like a justifiable reaction, as well as a useful way of protecting yourself from the painful consequences of being criticized. Unfortunately, an angry response to criticism is likely to trigger even more anger and criticism from the other person rather than problem-solving communication.

Anger can be openly aggressive or disguised, and passive-aggressive. Both styles sabotage intimacy and trust.

Cassie and Michael were already a little late for his office party. Cassie was somewhat apprehensive about her first interaction with Michael's colleagues and had done her best with her appearance. As she emerged from the bedroom, Michael said bluntly, "You've got too much makeup on and that dress is really too brazen." Hurt, Cassie responded sarcastically, "Great! Since when did you become the resident fashion expert?" Michael snarled, "I may not be an expert, but at least I have the sense not to parade around wearing something so damn provocative!" "Oh yeah? Well at least I don't look like a potbellied mortician!" Cassie stormed back into the bedroom to change; Michael paced the living room knowing the evening was ruined.

On the other hand, Ed and George rarely yelled at each other. Although frequently hurt by George's criticisms, Ed considered it bad taste to respond in kind. He would try to hide his painful feelings by looking down, murmuring something inaudible, and waiting patiently till George's lecture was over. This strategy seemed to work—except that Ed's headaches, which had eased during the early months of their relationship, had reappeared in full swing recently. These, Ed argued innocently, were the cause of his apparently worsening memory—his missed appointments with George, his late arrivals picking George up, his forgetfulness about their agreements.

Whether you respond to criticism aggressively like Cassie or passively like Ed, your relationship will not be enhanced. In fact, it may be seriously compromised. Fortunately, there are alternatives to these strategies.

History

The concept of assertiveness was developed as long ago as 1949 by Andrew Salter. Joseph Wolpe (1958) and Arnold Lazarus (1966) further clarified the concept, differentiating between assertive and aggressive behavior, and suggesting that people tend to be assertive in some situations and ineffective in others. Major contributions to the field of assertion training include Robert Alberti and Michael Emmons (1974) who argued that "each person has the right to be and to express himself, and to feel good (not guilty) about doing so, as long as he does not hurt others in the process," and Manuel Smith (1975) who described ten "Assertive rights." Arthur Lange and Patricia Jakubowski (1976) defined assertion as "a direct, honest, and appropriate expression of opinions, beliefs, needs, or feelings." No matter which definition is used, assertive behavior allows you to stand up for your rights, express personal likes and dislikes, accept compliments comfortably, disagree with someone openly, and say no.

Theoretical Background

Aggressive, passive, or assertive? The three responses look very different and are based on very different attitudes.

Aggressive. The underlying stance of the aggressive response is that your needs are always right and always more important than everyone else's. You believe that you have the right to get what you want and to do what you want and you don't care whose toes you step on in the process. Your voice may be loud and strident or low and ice-cold. You may use humiliation, intimidation, guilt manipulation, and put-downs to achieve what you want. You're always on guard against someone trying to usurp your position of superiority, and you usually win the ensuing battles. But as the old saying goes, it's lonely at the top, and always being right doesn't inspire the closeness and vulnerability required for intimacy.

Passive. The underlying stance of the passive response is that your needs and wants are less important than those of everyone else. You believe that you don't deserve to ask for what you want; instead you must set aside your needs and focus on helping others meet theirs. Your voice may be soft and supplicating, your words hesitant and self-deprecating. You may tend to smile a lot, avoid eye contact, hint vaguely and indirectly at your thoughts and feelings, and qualify or apologize for many of the things you say. You may listen more often than you speak, and you may even rely on others to guess what you want to say. You may feel angry that no one knows or cares what you want, and you may find yourself resorting to manipulative strategies to get your needs met.

Assertive. The underlying stance of the assertive response is that you have the right to pursue your needs and that others also have the right to pursue theirs. Your pursuit of your needs takes into account the rights and feelings of others. When speaking assertively, your voice is firm and understanding; you often maintain eye contact. You make direct statements about your thoughts, feelings, and desires, and at the same time can listen attentively to the statements of others. You are willing to negotiate and compromise, but not at the expense of your own rights. Nor do you push others to give up theirs.

Time for Mastery

Understanding the steps involved in responding assertively to anger and criticism will take a few days. Learning to develop your own assertive responses may take another week. Mastery will depend on the frequency with which you practice your new skills.

Practicing Assertive Responses

Each of the following situations contains one aggressive response and one passive response. For each situation, develop your own assertive response. An example of a possible assertive statement follows each one.

1. *Partner:* I have a late meeting tonight so I won't be home for dinner. You'll have to deal with the kids on your own. I don't want any shit about this, OK?

   Aggressive response: Again! Your damn meetings are always more important than your family! This is outrageous.

   Passive response: Okay, dear. Have a good day.

   Alternative assertive response:

   Assertive example: Well, I'm sure I'll cope, but I want you to give me some notice in future. Then I can arrange to have some help.

2. *Partner:* I'm sick and tired of your mother dropping by unexpectedly and staying for hours. I don't want her here when I get home from work.

   Aggressive response: At least she's interested in talking to me for more than five seconds at a time! Which is more than I can say for you!

   Passive response: Well, I'll try telling her, but you know how she is.

   Alternative assertive response:

Assertive example: I know you don't like it when she's here late, but I really enjoy her company and sometimes we lose track of time. Perhaps you could call me when you're leaving the office and give us time to say our goodbyes before you get home.

3. *Partner:* This place is a pigsty! Can't you pull your load around here? Can't you contribute something besides the constant sound of the television?

   Aggressive response: If it's so bad, why don't you just shove off? And don't bother coming back!

   Passive response: I'm sorry, I'll get to it. It'll be okay.

   Alternative assertive response:

   Assertive example: It is a mess. I had a hard day today. Let's have a drink and talk, and we can straighten up later.

Responding to Criticism

In dealing assertively with criticism, you hold the attitude that although other people may have opinions about your behaviors, thoughts, feelings, and desires, you are ultimately the final judge of what's best for you. This attitude suggests that you don't need to respond to criticism by all-out aggressive warfare or by passive collapse. So what do you do with the criticism itself? This section presents a variety of different strategies that you can use.

Probing

When criticism is accurate and constructive, it can be useful to acknowledge it. When it's clearly manipulative and hurtful, it's important to both limit and deflect the damage. You may not be able to fully assess the criticism without first understanding exactly what the critic means. The way to assess this is to probe. Address the part of the criticism that the person seems to feel most strongly about. Try and elicit why he or she is bothered by that particular element. Ask for specific examples if it would help you understand what your critic is feeling or thinking or wanting. Continue to probe until you feel clear about your critic's intent.

Rosslyn and Eric had moved to San Francisco three months ago when Eric's company had offered him a promotion and transfer. Eric enjoyed his new responsibilities and loved the excitement of being in a big city. Although Rosslyn hadn't decided whether to look for a new job or make her long-dreamed-of career change and go to graduate school, Eric assumed she was also happy about their move. He was surprised when he arrived home one evening to an angry attack.

Rosslyn: If you come home one more time with that idiotic oh-so-cheerful look on your face I'm going to scream.

Before responding angrily himself, Eric decided to try and find out what exactly Rosslyn was so upset about.

Eric: What is it that bothers you about my being so cheerful?

Rosslyn: You're away all day doing a job you love and having a wonderful time.

Eric: What is it that bothers you about me enjoying my work?

Rosslyn: I'd like to be enjoying myself as well. You have all the new friends, you have the new job, and I just sit around all day and agonize over what I should do with my life.

Eric   So you're lonely and worried about the decisions you're facing?

Rosslyn: Yes. I've wanted to talk about it with you but you always seem so cheerful I've been afraid to ruin your happiness.

In probing, Eric learned that Rosslyn was less angry than lonely and in need of support. He realized he hadn't been as supportive of her as he could be and was able to make decisions about how to behave differently.

Acknowledging

Criticism hurts. Yet there may be times when you agree with what you hear. When the criticism you receive is accurate, it's best to simply acknowledge it. Your partner may be ready to launch an attack to prove his or her assertion, and your agreement can defuse the situation. "Yes, you're right, I did forget to tell you I'd be late again," "Yes, I did change my mind at the last minute," "You're right, I didn't prepare any dinner tonight."

Don't be tempted to use sarcasm in your acknowledgement. "Yeah, right!" may sound like agreement, but covertly it sends another message. Don't be tempted to apologize or to make excuses for your behavior either. You aren't a child; you don't have to justify yourself the way you did when you were one. If you think that it might help create more assertive communication and your partner seems open, you may choose to give an explanation of your actions. But you don't have to.

> *Partner:* Your new sweater—it's filthy! You've ruined it! That sweater cost a lot of money.
>
> *You:* You're right, it is filthy. (*pause*) One of the assembly line machines broke down, and I was trying to see what was wrong underneath it.

Deflecting

Deflecting is a useful strategy when the criticism you're hearing is manipulative and primarily a put-down. There are four techniques you can use to disarm your critic while preventing escalation.

1. Content-to-process shift. You shift the focus of communication from what's being said (content) to what's happening between you (process). This is a particularly useful strategy when voices are being raised, when strong emotions seem to be preventing effective communication, or when it seems that the real issue isn't being addressed. "I'm getting frustrated. It seems like every time we try to discuss finances, we end up raising our voices." "I'm not feeling like continuing this—we're getting upset and it's making me nervous." "I know you said you wanted to talk about our relationship, but I feel like I'm doing all the talking." "This is the third time today that you've criticized me for something trivial—what's going on?" "Your words are friendly enough, but your tone is so sarcastic—I'm really feeling attacked and I don't know why." This strategy often involves some self-disclosure about what you're feeling or thinking at that moment. Be careful not to phrase your statments as a criticism or an attack of the other person.

2. Assertive preference. This strategy is useful for politely telling your critic to stop bugging you. It involves acknowledging the critic without attacking and disagreeing without getting angry.

> *Partner:* Look at all the traffic! I told you we should have gotten on 280 at Alemany.

> *You:*   I know that you think your route is faster; I'd still prefer to go this way.
>
> *Partner:* I heard you making fun of me—how can you sit here and say you didn't?
>
> *You:*   I understand your perception of the situation, I guess my perception is just different.
>
> *Partner:* You're crazy to pass up the offer of help. He's had much more experience and could do a much better job than you'll do.
>
> *You:*   I appreciate your concern, but I'd rather do it alone.

You don't need to get involved in lengthy explanations; simply state your preference to do things your way.

3. Assertive delay. Rather than being compelled to respond instantly to criticism, assertive delay allows you to take a break. Whether for a few seconds or several hours, a time out lets you calm down, think carefully about what's being said, activate some coping strategies, and prepare your response. "You've said a lot and I need time to digest it. Let's talk again after lunch." "Wait a second, let me think about that." "Slow down, I really want to understand everything you're saying." "I'd like to give you an honest answer, but it's going to take some time. I'll call you tonight." Refusing to respond under attack can prevent an angry escalation. You don't need to apologize or explain—just postpone.

4. Clouding. Clouding involves finding the grain of truth in the criticism while holding on to your own assessment of the situation. It requires careful listening to find the piece of the criticism with which you can honestly agree. There are three ways of agreeing with your critic.

Agreeing in part involves acknowledging the part of the criticism that you agree with while ignoring the rest. Without losing the essence of the criticism, you can modify gross overgeneralizations such as *never* or *always*.

> *Partner:* This place is a pigsty! And you don't give a damn what it looks like, do you?
>
> *You:*   You're right, the house is a mess.
>
> *Partner:* Your fees are way too low. I can't believe you're so financially irresponsible.
>
> *You:*   Yes, my fees are low.

Agreeing in probability acknowledges that there might be a chance—however minute—that the criticism is accurate. In the previous examples, your responses might be: "It's possible that I don't care enough about keeping the house clean" and "You might be right that my fees are too low."

Agreeing in principle means that you acknowledge that if the condition your partner describes exists, then the conclusion that he or she made is likely. But you neither confirm nor deny that the condition exists.

Partner: If you don't work harder, you're never going to get a raise.

You: It's true, you have to work hard to get a raise.

Partner: If you don't spend more time with Jenny, you'll never have a good relationship with her.

You: You're right. If I don't spend time with Jenny I won't have a good relationship with her.

Notice that in neither case are you agreeing with the premise that you aren't working hard enough or that you're not spending enough time with Jenny.

Limiting the Damage

This is the strategy of choice when you perceive little or no hope of defusing your spouse's anger and opening up channels for more effective communication. You simply need to focus on minimizing your exposure to the anger and on limiting the damage to your self-esteem.

No matter what you've done or how you feel, you don't deserve to be attacked or abused verbally. In the face of an angry attack, one way to limit the damage is to refuse to continue the discussion. Once blaming, name-calling, threatening, or sarcasm begins, disengage from the interaction. If you can, take a time out (see chapter 11) so that both of you can cool off. Even if you believe you're at fault, letting yourself be subjected to a verbal assault isn't the answer.

Remind yourself that what you're hearing is just one person's opinion, not the truth. Even if that person is someone you care about, it's still only one person with one opinion. You can simply choose to disagree. Remind yourself that you're only human, doing the best you can, and that everyone makes mistakes. Not living up to your own or your spouse's expectations doesn't make you a bad (or incompetent or selfish or stupid) person.

At the end of every month Cami juggled unpaid bills until the first came around and Dan brought home his next paycheck. Invariably they fought during this stressful period. Dan accused Cami of being incompetent in her role of managing the household. Cami responded by criticizing Dan's poor earning potential. The fights usually escalated until Cami was in tears. This time she decided to do something different.

> *Dan:*   Here's a second notice for the phone bill. Why isn't it paid?
>
> *Cami:*   Well, if I pay that, I can't pay the electric bill. I figured we could get by without the phone, but not without heat.
>
> *Dan:*   I can't believe you've spent our entire month's income again. It just blows my mind. Why can't you ever remember to put aside what we need for bills before you go gallivanting off on your shopping sprees?
>
> *Cami:*   I didn't "go off on any shopping sprees" as you put it. We simply don't have enough money to go around.
>
> *Dan:*   Don't start that bullshit again! All the other guys' wives manage just fine on the exact same income. You're hopelessly irresponsible with money and should just admit it.

Cami realized that the conversation was heading into old familiar territory. She reminded herself that Dan was just giving his opinion and took a deep breath before continuing.

> *Cami:*   Look, Dan, I don't want to talk about it right now. We're both upset and I don't think it helps us solve the problem. Let's take a time out and pick it up later when we've cooled down.
>
> *Dan:*   (*grumbling*) Fine. I want to go to the gym anyway.

Getting Practice

Use the following examples to practice developing each of the assertive responses to criticism. Sample answers follow each example.

Barbara always worried when she called Darron at work and got only his voice-mail. She didn't call deliberately to check up on him, but occasionally needed him to buy something at the supermarket on his way home. And although Darron had never given her any reason to suspect he was having an affair, Barbara had heard rumours about the big male-dominated computer engineering companies and their attractive secretaries. She tried to reassure herself, but usually ended up asking Darron a few questions about his whereabouts. Darron was invariably defensive and reluctant to answer. Barbara pursued.

> *Darron:*   You're so paranoid. No matter what I say you always question it. If you don't start trusting me more we'll never have a decent relationship.

Possible assertive responses for Barbara:

Probing response:

Acknowledging response:

Deflecting responses

1. Content-to-process shift:

2. Assertive preference:

3. Assertive delay:

4. Clouding

> *Agreeing in part:*

Agreeing in probability:

Agreeing in principle:

Possible answers:
Probing: What is it that bothers you about my questions?
Acknowledging: I guess I do question what you say a lot. I sometimes need reassurance of your commitment to me.
Deflecting responses
1. *Content-to-process shift:* You seem really angry that I'm asking you these questions.
2. *Assertive preference:* I hear that you don't want me to ask these questions. It's important to me to know the answers.
3. *Assertive delay:* Let me think about what you've said and let's talk about it later.
4. *Clouding:*
Agreeing in part: It's true, I do sometimes question what you say.
Agreeing in probability: It's possible that I'm a little suspicious.
Agreeing in principle: It's true that good relationships are based on trust.

Arlene and Rick had lived together four years before deciding to get married. Arlene had been wanting to formalize their commitment in this way for some time but Rick had been reluctant to change the status quo. In the year since their marriage, there had been a number of nasty confrontations over household responsibilities. Arlene believed that Rick had stopped pulling his weight once they'd wed; Rick believed that Arlene's standards had risen now that she was married. The confrontations would usually begin with Arlene expressing her frustration:

"Since we got married you never help around the house
anymore. You just sit around and let me do all the work.
I'm sick and tired of feeling like your slave."

Possible assertive responses for Rick:

Probing response:

Acknowledging response:

Deflecting responses

1. Content-to-process shift:

2. Assertive preference:

3. Assertive delay:

4. Clouding

   Agreeing in part:

   Agreeing in probability:

   Agreeing in principle:

   Possible answers:
   Probing: What is it that bothers you about my being less involved in the house than you?
   Acknowledging: I guess I have been enjoying feeling taken care of lately.
   Deflecting responses
   1. Content-to-process shift: I feel really attacked and don't think I can respond right now.

2. *Assertive preference:* I hear that you would like me to do more house cleaning. I think the house is fine just the way it is.

3. *Assertive delay:* Wait a minute, I need to think about what you've said—those are pretty strong statements.

4. *Clouding*

Agreeing in part: It's true that you do more around the house than I do.

Agreeing in probability: You could be right that I'm not helping around the house as much as I used to.

Agreeing in principle: It's true, when you do all the work you feel exploited.

Think about an interaction you had with your partner where he or she said something angry. The interaction should be typical of your relationship and something that happens repeatedly. Using the worksheet provided on the next page, write out a brief description of the situation, what led up to it, and what your partner said. Then create as many alternative responses as are appropriate for the situation.

The more you practice these skills, the less awkward you'll feel using them. And the more you use them, the more you'll be able to respond to an angry criticism with something other than further anger and escalation. With less anger in your relationship, you'll have more opportunity for really listening to and understanding each other's thoughts, feelings, needs and wants. The potential benefits to your relationship are enormous.

Special Considerations

When your partner's anger escalates to physical violence and abuse, the techniques described in this chapter will not suffice. At these times it's necessary to have more than communication skills at your disposal. An essential first step is a firm commitment from your partner that he acknowledges the problem and is prepared to find other means of dealing with his anger. (Statistically, more men than women pose threats of violence to their partners.) Once he begins to work on finding alternatives to violence (*When Anger Hurts* by McKay, Rogers, and McKay [1989] is a good resource), the two of you will then have to address your communication skills. Meanwhile, at the first sign of anger, call for a time out (see chapter 11). If this doesn't work and you still feel at risk, or if your partner refuses to take responsibility for the violence, then separation may be your only safe choice. In either case, this would be an appropriate time to seek the help of a trained couples therapist.

Responding to Criticism Worksheet

Description of situation:

What my partner said:

Probing response:

Acknowledging response:

Deflecting responses
1. Content-to-process shift:

2. Assertive preference:

3. Assertive delay:

4. Clouding:
   Agreeing in part:

   Agreeing in probability:

   Agreeing in principle:

11

Time Out

Time out is a vital skill for keeping fights from escalating into verbal or physical abuse. It's perhaps the single most useful strategy for stopping violence and the battering syndrome. Key to the effective use of time out is to evoke it before tempers flare out of control; before the fight reaches a point where each person is focused on hitting back and getting even.

History

One of the pioneers of the time out was Daniel Sonkin (Sonkin and Durphy 1985). Sonkin, a prosecuting attorney in San Francisco, recognized that many cases of marital violence that come before the courts might be prevented with some training in anger-control techniques. Jeanie Deschner, in her book, *The Hitting Habit* (1984), adapted Sonkin's work into the "Time Out Contract" that you will use later in this chapter.

Theoretical Background

Gerald Patterson (1982) has examined the way anger escalates. He found that couples engage in sequences of aversive behaviors that are designed to influence or control the other person. Patterns of reactions and counter-reactions can play out with incredible speed. It's like the steps of a well-learned dance. When an aversive sequence of attack and counterattack begins, time out is the most effective way to break the chain reaction and prevent emotional damage. To use time out you have to (1) recognize that an aversive chain reaction is in progress and (2) commit yourself to stopping it before your fight has too much momentum.

Time for Mastery

A Time Out Contract can be developed during an hour-long discussion. You will need to practice time out several times *when you're not angry* to get the hang of it and develop confidence in the technique. When you succeed in using time out during an actual escalation, you're well on your way to mastering this vital skill.

Arrange a Time Out Signal

Partners need to agree on the signal they will use when a time out is necessary. Some people simply say, "Time out." Others use a statement such as, "We're beginning to get upset and I need to take a time out." "We're getting upset" has the advantage of being nonblaming and suggests that the time out is being called for the good of both of you. The simplest strategy is to use the hand signal employed in basketball and other sports—the "T" sign. You really don't need to say a word. Things start to escalate, you make the "T" sign, and your partner either makes the "T" sign back or says, "Okay, time out."

Agree on the Early Warning Signals

Agree with your partner on the early warning signals that most typically lead to escalation for you. Any indication of rising anger can be a signal for time out. Loud voices, name-calling, attacking "you statements," finger-pointing, shoving, or any form of physical threat should result in immediate time out. The sudden introduction of sore subjects in a conflict can trigger rapid escalation. You're in the middle of discussing car repairs, and suddenly the discussion takes a left turn into one partner's spending habits. Sore subjects are fine to discuss, but when they're injected into a conflict the focus suddenly broadens to include old sins and violations.

Another warning signal you may wish to use is the presence of *over-generalization*. When sentences start with "You always . . . You never . . . Nobody around here . . . Every time I . . ." there's a good chance of escalation. Over-generalized statements have a very accusing flavor and trigger strong defensive reactions.

Follow the Rules for Time Out

The following six rules are absolutely essential for making the time out structure work.

1. No last words. When someone calls a time out, his or her partner has the option of returning the "T" sign or simply saying, "Okay, time out." Under no condition should there be any further discussion. No explanations, no last rebuttals, no finishing a thought. Everything stops.

2. Leave immediately. The person calling the time out should immediately leave the room or, ideally, the house. If you can't leave (because you're in a car or an airplane), you should stop talking for a set period of time. A time out should last for one hour, give or take five minutes. If it goes longer, people start to feel abandoned. Shorter and there's not enough time to cool off. Stay out of each other's presence for the entire time; don't return early.

3. Always return when the time is up. Failing to come back only makes things worse. Your partner feels left and rejected. Conversely, the partner who remains at home should still be there at the end of time out. Don't take off and leave the partner who called time out wondering what happened.

4. Don't use drugs or alcohol during time out. Drugs and alcohol can exacerbate angry feelings and reduce impulse control. This will sabotage everything you are trying to accomplish with the time out.

5. Don't rehearse what you'll say or should have said. Focusing on the sins and shortcomings of your partner only fans the angry flames. For this reason, it's inadvisable to visit friends during a time out. With friends, you'll tend to complain and build a case against your partner. You'll rehearse and refine the accusations made during your fight. Not only will the time out fail to cool you off, but you'll have collected new ammunition for continuing the hassle.

Probably the best thing to do during a time out is some form of physical exercise. Walk or run or bike. Do the dishes or vacuum the floor or start putting up the shelves you've been meaning to get to. Physical activity distracts you and helps discharge some of the tension built up during an angry exchange.

6. Check in when you get back. Ask if the other person is ready to talk about the conflict. If not, *set a specific time to re-explore the issue*.

It's important that you not use time out to sweep things under the rug. If an hour isn't enough to fully calm down, if you're still feeling raw and hurt, make sure you arrange a time for discussion when you expect to feel less vulnerable.

Jeanie Deschner has suggested this strategy for checking in when you get back. Start the conversation with the phrase, "I know that I was partly wrong and partly right." Then admit to one technical mistake that you made. A technical mistake means something you did or said during the fight, as opposed to admitting that your whole point or position is wrong. This structure softens the tone of the conflict and allows both parties to re-examine the issues without defensiveness.

Make a Time Out Contract

When partners make a commitment to change, it's helpful to underscore that commitment with a written contract. If things are in writing, you're likely to take them much more seriously. The following Time Out Contract (adapted from Deschner 1984) offers a framework for making a change that will benefit both of you.

Time Out Contract

When I realize that my (or my partner's) anger is rising, I will give a "T" signal for time out and leave at once. I will not hit or kick anything, and I will not slam the door.

I will return no later than one hour. I will take a walk or use up the anger energy and will not drink or use drugs when I am away. I will try not to focus on resentments. When I return, I will check in to find out if my partner is ready to resume discussion. If not, we will agree on a specific time to reexamine the conflict.

[*Optional:* I'll start the conversation with, "I know that I was partly wrong and partly right." I will then admit to a technical mistake I made.]

If my partner gives a "T" signal and leaves, I will return the sign and let my partner go without a hassle, no matter what is going on. I will not drink or use drugs while my partner is away, and I will avoid focusing on resentments. When my partner returns, we will set a specific time for reexamining the conflict.

[*Optional:* I will start the conversation with, "I know that I was partly wrong and partly right."]

Name: _____

Date: _____

Name: _____

Date: _____

Practice Time Outs

The best way to build your confidence in the time out process is to practice when you're not angry. You might take a practice time out at the first sign of irritation, or just out of the blue, when nothing remotely anger-provoking is occurring. A practice time out has exactly the same structure as a regular one, except that you say, "Practice time out!" and you spend only fifteen minutes apart. Follow all the rules during the time out, including making the check-in when you return. Using two or three practice time outs will make it far more likely that you'll rely on the time out structure when real anger is occurring.

Monica and Oliver tended to escalate any time one of them raised his or her voice or made accusing "you statements." They agreed to use these as signals for time out.

In their written contract, either partner could verbally declare time out. The other partner could only say in return, "OK, time out." They had all the standard rules. But, in addition, they agreed not to call or visit anyone during time out. They both had a tendency to complain about each other to friends, and this only served to fuel their conflicts.

When returning from a time out, they agreed to check in and establish a time to finish the discussion.

Monica and Oliver never got around to a practice time out, so the next time a conflict arose, they completely ignored the time out structure. Monica admitted later that she thought briefly of calling a time out, but was so angry at Oliver that she wanted to stay on the attack.

Two more fights occurred, and no one called a time out. Finally, they agreed to go back to square one and immediately use practice time outs. They had two practice time outs on Sunday and one on Monday. On Wednesday, they were able to stop a "real" fight with time out.

Both Monica and Oliver felt good about the success. But on Saturday, Oliver called a time out after making a particularly mutilating attack on Monica. Rather than leave his remark unrebutted, Monica counterattacked and then called her own time out. Oliver started arguing that she wasn't honoring their agreement, and they fought for two hours about time outs!

Monica and Oliver decided to revise their original contract to handle "last words." Here's what they wrote:

> If one of us calls a time out right after an attack, the
> other partner can say, "Okay, time out. But you had the
> last word, and when we come back, I'll have the first
> word. And the one who calls time out has to say, 'Okay.'"

Over the next four weeks, Monica and Oliver used time out on three separate occasions. After eight weeks, they'd only used it one more time. Just having the structure in place seemed to reduce their tendency to escalate.

Special Considerations

Don't use time out to block communications. It's not appropriate to invoke time out merely because a subject has been raised that you'd prefer not to talk about. Wait until there are actual symptoms of anger (loud voices, name-calling, "you statements") before calling a time out. Remember that calling a time out doesn't mean an end to the discussion. It merely means that you *postpone* the discussion until a time when you are both less angry.

Some people are reluctant to call time outs because they don't want to leave their home. It's okay to stay at home if you can really separate yourself by going to another room and closing the door. If that's not feasible, or if a partner follows you from room to room after you've called time out, the only alternative is to physically leave the environment. If your partner is following you and won't let it rest, get in your car and take a drive. Remember to return no later than one hour after the time out.

Try not to call time out right after you've said something attacking. If possible, call the time out after your partner's last remark. That way your partner won't feel tempted to make parting shots. If you feel the need to say something conciliatory prior to calling time out, tell your partner that you're aware that you are both in a lot of pain, and that the pain is making you both upset. Say, "We need a time out, and we can finish this when we both feel cooler." If your partner doesn't listen, just repeat the words, "time out," and walk out the door. You may wish to remind your partner that you'll be back in one hour.

Some people have great difficulty with time out because their anger makes them want to strike out emotionally at a partner. Quite simply, they want revenge. This is a normal, understandable reaction when you're angry, but it has very destructive consequences. If your desire for revenge is so strong that you cannot bring yourself to call or honor a time out, then you need to work on your anger in different ways. Read chapters 4 and 9 on clean communication and coping with anger as a way to begin making fundamental changes in how you think about and relate to your partner.

Understanding
and Changing
What Goes Wrong

12

Identifying Schemas About Your Partner

Your partner exists in your mind. The real person is locked inside a psyche that you can never enter, never directly know. So you watch from the outside. You listen, you observe behavior, you remember. And over time you develop a set of summary conclusions called *schemas* that make up a psychological portrait of the person you're with.

Many schemas are simply the names of traits that you use to explain your partner's behavior and describe his or her personal qualities. A schema can be based on hundreds of small events and helps you to organize many different experiences into categories which are labeled. Arthur is frequently late getting home from work, spends at least half the day on Saturday golfing, neglects the dishes at times, and spends a lot of money on his hobby of collecting first edition books. Sylvia labels this behavior as "selfish," which is one of the negative schemas she's developed about Arthur. Notice that Sylvia's schema functions as both an explanation and a way of grouping many different things that Arthur does.

Bill observes that his wife is usually the first to pull away from a hug, that she speaks at times in a clipped and hurried style, that she frequently withdraws into crossword puzzles or a computer game at night, and that she rarely initiates sexual contact. He has put these behaviors into a category labeled "cold." And the schema of his wife as a cold person now influences him in many ways—from the amount he spends on her birthday present to his recent temptation to have an affair.

Negative schemas such as *lazy, stupid, pigheaded, cruel, hard, vain, incompetent, flakey, dangerous, crazy,* and the like have enormous power. Schemas are your only reality. What you *believe* to be true is the only truth you can ever have. The schemas you use to explain and interpret what your partner does, the labels that describe and fix a partner's identity for you, influence every dimension of the relationship. What you feel, what you give, what you ask for, and how you communicate are tremendously affected by how you've labeled your partner.

The more events there are supporting a particular schema, the stronger its influence becomes. On three or four occasions Jill observed Andy getting angry and shouting at the kids. She began to suspect that he had a hard time understanding and empathizing with them. Some years and many angry episodes later, Jill saw Andy as an unempathic man. With each angry episode, the schema got stronger and more malignant. These days, Jill's picture of Andy as unempathic has begun to include a sense that he's uncaring as well. Her own anger is increasing. She feels less generous toward Andy and less desire to be with him at all.

In addition to schemas about personality traits, you can also form schemas about your partner's motivations and intentions ("She's trying to control me . . . It's all ego; trying to build himself up by tearing me down . . . She's trying to shut me off from my friends . . . He's only nice when he wants to get laid"), feelings toward you ("She's tired of me . . . Underneath it all, he's angry") and judgments about you ("She thinks I'm unstable . . . He's decided I'm incompetent").

Negative schemas about your partner's motivations, intentions, feelings, and judgments about you can be enormously destructive. They are usually formed and supported by a great deal of mind reading. It begins with some ambiguous behavior that you interpret negatively. Once you've made the interpretation ("She thinks I'm boring"), all future related behavior tends to get labeled in the same way ("She's looking away . . . She's spent the whole evening talking to Simone . . . She's always buried in a book . . . She's changed the subject—I guess I'm boring her"). Over time a schema develops. And it becomes every bit as real and believable as your knowledge that the sky is blue. The schema grows into a painful thorn; more and more of your partner's behavior is explained by it. And more and more of *your* behavior is determined by it.

Perhaps the most destructive of all schemas is the belief that your partner doesn't love you. "If he loved me, he'd make time to be alone together." "If she loved me, she'd wear something that turned me on." "If there was any love at all, I'd see a little sacrifice." These beliefs hurt. But that's true of all negative schemas. They account for a tremendous amount of the pain in intimate relationships. Yet they are so often built on conjecture, on assumptions and fantasies that are no more real than the Wicked Witch of Oz.

The purpose of this chapter is to help identify some of your most influential schemas. Then, with a greater conscious understanding of these pictures you have formed, you can see more clearly how they affect your feelings and behavior. Later, there will be an exercise to determine the accuracy of some of your more potent schemas. You can literally "check out" many of the beliefs you've formed. Finally, there will be an exercise to develop *alternative explanations* for behavior you've labeled with your schemas. Through a process called *accurate empathy,* you can take a softer, more accepting view of some of your partner's habits. You can begin to explore how your partner's behavior is truly his or her best effort to cope.

History

George Kelly first introduced the concept of *personal constructs* (Kelly 1955). He recognized that all people develop a set of organizing beliefs about themselves and the world. These beliefs form a core personal identity. Taken individually, they are like pieces of a stained glass window: each has its own particular color and shape. But taken together, in the context of the whole mosaic, they form a complete picture. Constructs about others work the same way—each individual schema contributes its colors to a large and complex portrait.

Aaron Beck (Beck, Rush, Shaw and Emery 1979; Beck and Emery 1985; Beck, Freeman and Associates 1990) and Donald Meichenbaum (1988) have described how personal schemas lead to a variety of psychological problems. Anxiety, phobias, depression, and symptoms of chronic anger have all been related to the effects of negative schemas.

Jeffrey Young (1990) has developed a questionnaire to assess the strength of fifteen personal schemas. He's also shown how schemas affect relationships, often through the expectation that you will be hurt or mistreated. Many negative schemas are so paralyzing that they make you fearful of the slightest openness or vulnerability. Other schemas make you feel abused and angry. The net result is a disruption of intimacy.

Matthew McKay and Patrick Fanning (1991), building on the work of Young, Beck, and Meichenbaum, have developed a self-help program for changing personal schemas. The program provides a framework for testing a schema's accuracy and rewriting core negative beliefs.

Theoretical Background

Before exploring schemas about your partner, there are some basic things you need to know about how they work.

Why Schemas Are Enduring

Once you've established a schema about your partner's personality or intentions, there are two processes that tend to perpetuate it. The first is called *confirmatory bias* (Meichenbaum 1988). This is the tendency to pay attention only to events that support the schema. There is a natural propensity to ignore and filter out anything that doesn't fit with your preconceptions.

Remember Bill's belief about his wife's coldness? He kept track of anything that even remotely could be interpreted as cold behavior. But he conveniently forgot her backrubs, how she took his hand when they walked, the "I love you" note in his suitcase on the last business trip, and the very sweet kisses when they were in line at the ballet. Because these events were ignored, they never had a chance to soften Bill's "coldness" schema.

There's a reason for this. There's just no room in a negative schema for any positive data. The favorable facts don't fit. Therefore, they aren't remembered with the same clarity as the negative events. Remember how Sylvia labeled Arthur as selfish? Arthur took Sylvia skiing even though he hated to be cold. He edited a long paper she wrote in a comparative religion class. He walked the dog every night, even though it was her pet and he found poodles "entirely too bouncy." Sylvia never included these sacrifices and favors in her "selfish" schema because she paid attention only to behavior that confirmed her preset picture of Arthur. She could remember everything that "proved" her belief, but little that might prove a different view.

Mental grooving (McKay & Fanning 1991) is the second reason why schemas are so enduring. The mind often plays the same thoughts over and over—like a closed-loop tape. These psychological ruts are particularly seductive when you are under stress or facing an ambiguous situation. If you can't figure out what's going on, you tend to become anxious. Then you start the natural process of searching for memories or assumptions that will help you understand what's happening and respond appropriately. Your schemas are the assumptions that you most often use to explain ambiguous behavior from your partner.

When Bill's wife folded her arms and grimaced slightly during a conversation about his mother, Bill struggled for a moment to interpret the signals. But the moment of uncertainty passed quickly when he found his old mental groove—the "coldness" schema. In truth, his wife had an upset stomach, but Bill's schema never gave him a chance to find out. He "knew" what the reason was already.

Sylvia was puzzled when Arthur sold some of his prized first editions. But the "selfishness" schema helped her to explain it. He probably wanted the money for some expensive new hobby. The truth was that Arthur wanted money to build a new family room, but mental grooving kept Sylvia from imagining the slightest altruism.

The Vacuum Effect

Because people tend to use schemas to explain ambiguous situations and behavior, schemas have a vacuum effect. Negative schemas about your partner are often used to explain a lot of behavior that you just plain don't understand. And because much of what anyone does is ambiguous when viewed from the outside, a lot of your partner's innocent or irrelevant behavior may get sucked into a negative schema.

And the stronger a negative schema, the more memories it contains, the greater will be its suction power. After a while, Sylvia could explain nearly everything, even Arthur's fondness for suspenders, as some form of selfishness.

Schemas and Calibrated Communication

Negative schemas generate something really deadly to intimacy—calibrated communication (Bandler, Grinder, and Satir 1976). Here's how it works: Your partner does or says something that you falsely interpret with a negative schema. This assumption leads you to respond in inappropriate (often angry) ways. In turn, your partner has a defensive, angry reaction. By calibrated increments, your exchange moves further and further from the real facts of the situation. A great deal of hostility and hurt may get built on that first false assumption.

One of Manny's schemas about Cheryl is that she uses people. Here's a transcript of their conversation during a therapy session.

Cheryl:	I forgot to tell you. I got this class and I need you to baby-sit the kids on Wednesdays.
Manny:	*(influenced by the schema that he is being used)* What's the big deal about the class? Why do you have to take it?
Cheryl:	*(defensive)* Cause that's the time it's offered.
Manny:	*(getting loud)* The time doesn't matter. Why are you taking it in the first place? Just to take some time off?
Cheryl:	Fuck you.
Manny:	No, fuck *you*. You're a big drain. You know that? You just expect everybody to make life a big party for you. You know that?
Cheryl:	Stop pointing at me or I'll break your fuckin' finger off.
Manny:	There you go with the threats again. Always threats. My macho girl. A real gunslinger.
Cheryl:	Who's talking about threats? You were throwing my stuff in a bag and going to kick me out last week.
Manny:	*(shouting)* That's because of the name you called me. I won't even say it. I can't accept that. You say it once more and you're gone.

The fact is that Cheryl wanted to take a bookkeeping class so she could get a better job. Manny relied on his negative schema (she's a user) and misread the situation. Each counterattack pushed them further from Cheryl's original request until they were arguing about past threats and name-calling. It sounds almost funny, but a lot of partners fight in just this way—starting with a schema-based, false assumption and launching, step-by-step, into all-out war.

Time for Mastery

It will take a two-week assessment period to identify your more important schemas. The process of testing your schemas and developing alternative explanations could take as little as one or as much as sixteen weeks. It depends on the number and strength of the schemas you decide to test.

Identifying Your Schemas

The easiest way to identify important negative schemas about your partner is to keep a *thoughts log*. Over the next two weeks this log will be an invaluable tool in learning some things about your relationship. The next page shows an example of how to structure the log. Notice there are three columns labeled *Situation*, *Thoughts*, and *Consequences*. In the situation column, write down the circumstances surrounding any conflict or any point in time where you felt angry, sad, anxious, guilty, or hurt in relation to your partner. Some of the things you write down will focus on actual hassles, while others will be internal experiences that were never verbalized.

For each of the items in the situation column, write down in the thoughts column what you were thinking while the conflict or the emotion was going on. Specifically, what were you saying to yourself about your partner? How did you interpret or explain your partner's behavior? Were you labeling your partner in any way? Were you making any assumptions about your partner's feelings or judgments about you? It's important to write down *any* of these labels, interpretations, or assumptions. This information will later help you to identify some of your important schemas.

In the consequences column, write down what happened as a result of the conflict. Or if the initial situation was a feeling, note if the feeling and related thoughts influenced your later behavior. A sample from Julie's thoughts log (page 187) shows how this structure looks.

When Julie examined her thoughts log, she noticed certain repeated themes. The word "lazy" appeared often in the log. She frequently saw Jim as someone avoiding effort and shifting the burden of work to her. A second theme emerged from thoughts focusing on Jim's unwillingness to give. A third theme centered on the conviction that nothing would change, that Jim and the relationship would remain exactly as they were. Altogether, Julie's log confirmed three schemas about Jim: (1) lazy, (2) ungiving, and (3) cannot change.

Now it's time to use your thoughts log in the same way that Julie did. Do you find yourself describing the same personality traits over and over, using the same labels? Do you make the same or similar assumptions about your partner's motivations and intentions throughout the log? Do themes repeat regarding your partner's feelings or judgments about you? You'll find that schemas frequently can be described with a single word or short phrase. In the space provided, write the main schemas you've discovered from your thoughts log.

	Thought Log	
Situation	*Thoughts*	*Consequences*

Julie's Log		
Situation	*Thoughts*	*Consequences*
Angry at Jim.	He's leaving me with the work again.	I'm very cold. I don't speak to him.
Sad regarding Jim.	This is never going to get better. It'll always be the same problems.	Feel withdrawn, no interest in sex.
Fight over going to Mom's.	He's trying to get out of it even though I go with him to those boring soccer games.	Hostile, all night, very cold in the morning. Tell him to forget me going to soccer.
Angry at Jim.	He looks like shit. He's too lazy to find any clean clothes.	It turns into disgust. Very turned off by it all.
Fight over laundry.	He's got all the time in the world, but he won't even carry the laundry downstairs to the machine.	Very cold, not speaking. Go to Mom's and come home late.
Cold exchange over my car.	He won't even get off the couch for a minute to find out why it won't turn over. Lazy.	Stay cold all night. He decides to sleep on the floor in his sleeping bag.
Sad regarding Jim.	He's a blob. Mr. Sloth. That's the way it is.	Feel empty, don't want to talk.
Fight over bracelet.	He spends three hours looking for his agate bracelet, and he can't even help me with my car. He's selfish.	Feel resigned, tired, withdrawn.
Talked about the vacation.	He wants that music festival again, won't even consider going to Yosemite.	Feel angry, told him I wasn't going. He's upset.
Angry at Jim.	He won't fix the tape player so I can listen to my exercise tape. Lazy. Lazy. Lazy.	Feel cold, won't give him his haircut.

1._____

2._____

3._____

4._____

5._____

6._____

If you've identified some of your schemas, you're ready now for the next question: What are they costing you?

Paying for Your Schemas

It's time to take a look at the consequences column of your thoughts log. When Julie looked at her log, she could see a clear relationship between her schemas in the thoughts column and the consequences. When she thought of Jim as lazy or ungiving, she acted cold and angry. She looked for avenues of revenge (not going with him to soccer or to the music festival). She withdrew to the point where the relationship was nearly completely shut down and unrewarding for both of them. Jim's behavior may have been a problem, but Julie's schema-driven response was pulling them further apart.

Look at your own record of consequences. What happens when you focus on a strongly held schema? What do you say? How do you act? What do you feel? Pay attention to your nonverbal behavior. How do you convey the feelings that your schema brings to your partner? Are the long-term consequences a growing distrust or emotional gulf between you?

Now comes the most important question: If you weren't explaining and interpreting your partner's behavior with the schema, how would you respond differently? If Julie hadn't felt so much schema-triggered anger, for example, she might have figured out a way to reward Jim for being helpful. Julie realized that she was too angry at Jim to thank him when he did help and that she wasn't giving him much reason to make an effort. Julie began to suspect that her schemas were limiting her by shutting off options and possibilities. She sensed that a lot of things could change in the relationship if she thought and responded differently.

In the space provided below, list the main consequences that grow out of your schema-based behavior.

1._____

2._____

3._____

4._____

5._____

6._____

It takes courage to look at yourself and the responsibility you bear for what happens in a relationship. But recognizing how your schemas and responses impact the partnership is a major first step toward healthy change.

Softening Your Schemas

Notice that many of your schemas are generalizations or global labels implying that your partner always acts a certain way. Global labels like "lazy" and generalizations like "always ungiving" are often exaggerated. They ignore all the exceptions to the rule. Just as Bill's wife wasn't always cold and Arthur wasn't always selfish, Julie's Jim wasn't always lazy. He often shopped with her and cooked meals, did occasionally help her with her car, and had recently fixed her exercycle. There was no room in Julie's global schema to recognize Jim's efforts or moments of giving.

Right now, for each of the schemas that you listed, identify at least three exceptions from your partner's past.

Schema 1: _____

Schema 2: _____

Schema 3: _____

Schema 4: _____

Schema 5: _____

Schema 6: _____

In your relationship it's important to stop globalizing and generalizing. Schemas are helpful ways of organizing data. But they undermine your relationship when you think of your partner one dimensionally, ignoring all the exceptions to the rule you've identified.

Now it's time to make a commitment. When you catch yourself using schemas, make an effort to identify at least one exception. If you cut down on generalizing, you'll greatly reduce the reflexive tendency toward angry and aggressive responses.

Checking It Out

One of the best ways to beat the schema trap is to verbalize your assumption, to put your schema into words. The goal is to find out if the schema's true.

The key to checking it out is to ask questions using neutral, non-attacking language. Begin with a stock phrase such as "Sometimes I wonder ... Recently I had the thought ... There have been moments when I found myself suspecting ... Somehow I wondered if ... " These opening lines aren't accusatory. They don't imply that you already know the truth. The message is that you genuinely want to know and understand your partner and what's happening between you.

After the opening phrase, you need to describe your schema in a way that doesn't make your partner wrong or bad. The task is a little easier when you're checking out your partner's intentions, motivations, feelings, and judgments about you. "Sometimes I have the feeling that you see me as somewhat bumbling and helpless, like when I couldn't find the file on our house taxes." "I sense sometimes that you want to pull away, be less close, maybe avoid spending time together. Is there any truth in that?" "I've been imagining that you've been frustrated and angry at me of late. Like when you cancelled skiing and it felt like you were wanting to take things away from me, or maybe punish me. Have you had any feelings like that?"

Checking out is a much harder task when your schemas involve negative traits in your partner. The question you ask will have to be phrased delicately, using words that are as neutral and nonperjorative as possible. Write your question down in advance so you can edit out any phrases that would hurt your partner or increase defensiveness.

"Sometimes," Julie said to Jim, "I wonder about your ability to do things like the laundry and the dishes. Or jobs like fixing my car or the tape player. It seems very hard for you to do things like that, to find any energy for tasks. Does that seem true to you?" Julie had to write the whole thing out and change it several times to make sure there was nothing stinging and hurtful. The key was to describe the schema *behaviorally* ("hard to find the energy for tasks") rather than use labels like "lazy." Julie was able to describe her schema without kicking Jim in the teeth.

Jim had a very interesting response. He pointed out to her some of the many things he did do, such as shopping and cooking and fixing her exercycle. But he also told her that he felt pressured by her anger, by the very obvious snits she withdrew into. He found himself rebelling by dragging his feet on tasks that she wanted him to do. What Julie had once labeled as lazy and ungiving now seemed more like resistance in a power struggle. Jim's feedback was disturbing, but it had a corrective impact on Julie's schema.

Exercise. It's time for you to check things out. Go back to your list of schemas. Start by selecting the one that's least threatening. Script your questions in advance by choosing a neutral opening phrase: "Somehow I've wondered if . . ." Next, find a nonattacking way to describe your schema. Try to define it by using factual descriptions of events rather than global labels. You should conclude with a direct question about whether your understanding of things is true. Hone and polish your script until the tone is as supportive as possible while still expressing your basic question.

Now commit yourself to a time and place when you'll do your first checking out. This commitment is important because this is an anxiety-provoking process. There's a part of you that will want to avoid it like a case of mumps. Making a strong commitment will help push you past this very natural resistance. When you've done your first checking out and you're starting to get a feel for the process, go back to your schemas and write additional scripts for other assumptions you've made about your partner. You may find, just as Julie did, that checking it out will change how you view your partner and the relationship. It may also have an impact on some of the old, angry response patterns that were keeping you stuck.

It's strongly suggested that you keep a journal after each checking-out experience. Write down what you learned from your partner as well as any thoughts you have about how it changed your schema.

Building Accurate Empathy

This is an exercise to develop alternative explanations for behavior that you've labeled with a schema. The idea is to rework some of your negative assumptions by viewing your partner's behavior from an entirely different perspective. Accurate empathy is built on a basic conviction: everyone is doing the very best he or she can. If you consider your partner's needs, fears, assumptions, history, skills, and perceived choices, if you add all of these factors together, you'll find that your partner is coping in absolutely the only way he or she can.

Accurate empathy is a process by which you try to prove this new assumption. The six factors just described combine to form a person's *total awareness* as he or she makes any particular choice. These six elements influence and limit what your partner can do.

Exercise. Think back to a recent situation where you labeled your partner's behavior with a negative schema. To soften your schema and feel less sense of judgment, you need to identify the needs, fears, assumptions, history, skills (or lack of skills), and perceived choices that were affecting how your partner acted. Using your knowledge of your partner's behavior and history, show how each of the six items below influenced his or her actions.

1. *Needs*

2. *Fears*

3. *Assumptions*

4. *History*

5. *Skills (or lack of skills)*

6. *Perceived choices*

Here's how Julie used this exercise to soften one of her schemas. Jim's desire to attend the music festival again and his refusal to consider a vacation to Yosemite seemed an example of his unwillingness to give. Julie chose this conflict as a place to begin accurate empathy. She explored how each of the six elements contributed to Jim's behavior.

1. *Needs.* Music and songwriting are his main interests. He has a strong need for the validation of being around other musicians; playing with them, sharing his songs, etc. Missing the festival would be a major loss.

2. *Fears.* I've learned he's afraid of my controlling him. He feels that if he gives in to me, I'll run his life. Or maybe that he'll have to give up many of the things that are important to him. I'm starting to realize this is tremendously scary to Jim.

3. *Assumptions.* He assumes that I'll be angry and that he has to take a hard line not to be bulldozed by me. I think he feels that if he gives an inch, I'll take a mile.

4. *History.* His mother battled him constantly about music, wouldn't let him practice with his band, wouldn't let him jam in the house, didn't like his songs. Big power struggle that Jim usually lost. It had to be her way or no way. And she'd get very cold (like me) when Jim tried to buck her.

5. *Skills.* Jim doesn't know how to negotiate. It was all or nothing with his mother. It wouldn't occur to him that maybe there are some compromise possibilities here.

6. *Perceived choices*. He only gets a week's vacation, and I guess he feels that there's no time for anything but the festival. But we could go to Yosemite for a long weekend. Or he could take a few days unpaid leave. We're not that poor. I don't think he sees the options.

Julie used the accurate empathy exercise to change some of her attitudes about the conflict. She realized that a lot of the problem had to do with Jim's history, his fear of being controlled, and his inability to recognize alternative solutions. Instead of using her schema to get angry, Julie decided to negotiate actively with Jim on the vacation issue. As it turned out, they decided to take a four-day weekend for the Yosemite camping trip. Problem solving was a lot easier without the schema.

Any significant conflict that seems schema-driven is a good candidate for the accurate empathy exercise. Choose another conflict or two from the thoughts log so that you can get more practice with the process and have a chance to develop more alternative explanations for old schemas. When new conflicts arise, this is also an excellent way to assess and reinterpret what's really happening.

13

Old Tapes:
Separating Your Partner
from Your Parents

You've probably had the experience of meeting someone for the first time and being inexplicably drawn to or repelled by them. They may smile in a particular way that reminds you of someone in your past, or their accent reminds you of someone else. Maybe the way they lower their eyes or comb their hair—or maybe something you can't quite put your finger on—triggers a strong sense of familiarity. Although the actual resemblance may be minimal, your feelings may be so strong that you find yourself reacting to this new person as if they were the old familiar one. You make assumptions about them that may have no basis in reality, you draw inferences that may not pertain to them at all.

History

Harry Stack Sullivan (1953) coined the term *parataxic distortion* to describe this process of reacting to someone new as if they were someone from your past. In other words, you superimpose on one person a set of assumptions and inferences that really belong to another. The more intense the feelings and reactions, the more likely the person to whom you're really responding is your *parent*.

Theoretical Background

Parataxic distortion can occur in intimate relationships as well as with complete strangers. You can treat your partner as if he or she were your parent or someone else from your past. For example, you say to yourself, "She's not offering to help, she must not care about me," or "He's looking away, he must be disappointed." "He's got that demanding tilt to his chin, why isn't he ever satisfied?" Or you say, "She's not answering me—why does she want to humiliate me?" When assumptions like these about your partner are based on experiences from parental relationships, they can have disastrous consequences.

David experienced parataxic distortion in his relationship with his new lover, Ron. Each time Ron talked about his accomplishments at work, David got depressed and defensive. He interpreted Ron's joy in his own success as criticism of him. Instead of responding supportively with enthusiasm, he felt put down and angry. Unconsciously, David had confused Ron with his father, a very critical man for whom he could never achieve enough. Ron had no such standards and felt more and more hurt and misunderstood as the relationship continued.

Recognizing the association between your partner and your parent is not enough to break the influence of that link. Only when the two people can be separated in your mind will you stop reacting to your partner as if he or she were your parent. This chapter will help you to recognize and break that association.

Conditions Triggering Parataxic Distortion

High-stress interactions or situations that provoke anxiety increase the likelihood of parataxic distortion. As your stress level increases, so too does your sense of vulnerability. It's as if all the hurts you experienced as a child are ready to be triggered at the slightest provocation. As a result, it becomes more difficult to perceive things objectively. Any behavior, even slightly reminiscent of the person responsible for the hurts, can reawaken a whole set of accompanying reactions.

Situations that involve a conflict of needs increase the chance of parataxic distortion. When you're afraid your needs won't be met or when your needs are invalidated, your anxiety increases. June and her partner Frank struggled for two years with the issue of how much time they spent together. June always wanted somewhat more time together than Frank, and Frank always felt just a little guilty that his work was so interesting and time-consuming. Frank was perfectly clear that June and his controlling, overinvolved father were two separate, distinct people. But recently he was unusually busy on a large project at work and wasn't around much. June was hurt and disappointed. When she remarked that she hadn't seen much of Frank and that she missed him, his anxiety about work provoked parataxic distortion, and he responded to June with the same fear, guilt, and withdrawal that had characterized his interactions with his father.

The high levels of anxiety that sometimes accompany sexual interactions can also provoke parataxic distortion. Michael was in bed with his new lover, Nora. He was excited and at the same time nervous. They had only recently become lovers, and Michael still wondered about the impression he was creating. He soon lost himself in the pleasure of their lovemaking and was enjoying touching Nora and seeing her arousal increase. "Yes" she moaned softly, "that's wonderful," and then added in a whisper, "Gently, not so hard." Instantly, Michael felt like the too-big, clumsy, lumbering oaf of his childhood. His mother had always criticized him for being too rough, too clumsy, not careful enough. Michael experienced the same rush of rejection and humiliation and withdrew from Nora as swiftly as if she'd slapped him. It was no longer Nora he was reacting to—it was his mother.

For many people, the presence of relatives provokes parataxic distortion. Childhood reactions are most easily stirred by those who contributed to the process of growing up: the family. These are the people whose very presence is likely to trigger old hurts and reopen old wounds—even if their current behavior is very different.

Joanne was used to Mark's distracted silences while he read the paper or was otherwise deeply engrossed in some activity. She could usually get his attention if she really needed to, and for the four years of their marriage his uncommunicative moments hadn't been a problem for her. When her parents announced their impending visit, Joanne had mixed feelings. She hadn't seen them in a couple of years, and they hadn't come and stayed with her and Mark before. Yet she knew they triggered in her a deep sense of insecurity whenever she spent more than an afternoon with them. Deciding to put aside her misgivings, Joanne met their morning flight and welcomed them enthusiastically. Later, while Joanne was preparing lunch, her mother wandered into the kitchen carrying a magazine, sat down at the table, and offered to help. Joanne was surprised and pleased and suggested that her mother make the salad. She continued working on the souffle, occasionally glancing over at her mother who was still sitting at the table slowly leafing through the magazine. With a small sigh, Joanne realized that her mother hadn't changed at all. She still ignored everyone's needs but her own, despite insincere offers to help. That evening, Joanne related the incident to Mark as they were getting ready for bed. Mark was doing some minor repairs to the bedside clock radio as she talked. He responded with his familiar distracted grunts. Suddenly Joanne was furious. She felt ignored and rejected. Mark's silence no longer seemed benign but more like the sign of a selfish, uncaring person. The incident with her mother had triggered in Joanne the potential for parataxic distortion. Joanne was responding to Mark as if he were her mother.

Other high-stress interactions that increase parataxic distortion include any that require specific problem-solving skills, those that trigger competition, or situations that elicit feelings of depression or low self-esteem.

Parataxic Distortion Versus Making Use of Your Past

Your ability to recognize the similarity between a current situation and a past one means that you do not have to face each new situation totally unprepared. You say to yourself, "This is like that other situation. When that happened, I did such-and-such and it worked, so I'd better do that again now." Making generalizations in this way saves you time and energy. And when you're wrong, you get immediate feedback that helps you correct your assumption and recognize that the new situation is different from the old.

During occasions of parataxic distortion, you're trying to do the same thing. But the strong emotional reaction you have blocks the feedback you need to judge the accuracy of your assumptions. Your perception becomes a self-fulfilling prophecy. When you falsely assume that someone is angry at you, you're likely to respond defensively and perhaps get angry yourself. The other person, feeling unaccountably attacked, is also likely to respond defensively. The resulting escalation serves only to confirm your original (false) assumption: "See, he *is* angry."

Throughout Linda's childhood, she experienced her mother's expressions of sadness as disappointment in Linda's accomplishments. Her mother, frustrated by conditions of single parenthood and poverty, strove to reap satisfaction vicariously through Linda's activities and achievements. Linda felt pressured to succeed, but she also experienced the hollowness of her achievements, since they could never make up for the real unhappiness that her mother felt. Now, in her relationship with her husband Raul, she felt the same pressure whenever Raul expressed sadness. Linda falsely interpreted his sadness as disappointment in her and felt frustrated and pressured to somehow perform better. Her reaction was to pull back and distance herself. In the absence of any support or empathy from Linda, Raul would become even sadder and express disappointment in her reaction. Linda in turn would hear his disappointment and feel even more pressured, confirming her original assumption.

How to Recognize Parataxic Distortion

1. A sudden rush of intense negative emotion in response to something your partner says or does is one of the most distinct indicators of parataxic distortion. Perhaps you feel angry, sad, hurt, scared, ashamed, or controlled. The feeling makes you want to protect yourself in some way—withdraw, get reassurance, act aggressively.

2. A sense that your feeling is old and familiar is a second clue that you are experiencing parataxic distortion. You've experienced the feeling countless times. If you trace back far enough, you can recall feeling similarly when you were a child.

It's not the feeling itself, but the *familiar* nature of the feeling that's important. Lynn and her partner, Carol, were trying to discuss holiday plans. The discussion was not going smoothly. Carol was tired and cranky from a bad day at work, though Lynn could see that only in hindsight. At the time, she was confused and frustrated. Carol was usually such a reasonable person. Now no matter what Lynn said it seemed to be the wrong thing. The fight escalated quickly until Lynn left the room feeling ridiculed and humiliated. Although she'd never had such an interaction with Carol in the eight years of their relationship, the feelings were painfully familiar. As a child, her interactions with her alcoholic father had always been confusing at best and humiliating at worst. The intensity and familiarity of her reactions were a clue that parataxic distortion was occurring.

For Sandy, the sign that parataxic distortion was present in her relationship with Dean was a familiar feeling of resentment mixed with guilt that she experienced at meal times. Sandy's mother had been a closet binge-eater and had dealt with her own anxiety by rigidly controlling her daughters' food intake. Sandy never manifested the same problems. In fact, she ate healthily, exercised regularly, and was rarely sick. Nonetheless, she often felt as though Dean were scrutinizing or monitoring her eating habits. A glance or two across the table and she'd respond with all the old familiar guilt and resentment that she had felt as a child.

3. Recurring feelings—particularly anger—is a third sign to the presence of parataxic distortion. This is especially likely if the anger is accompanied by a "here we go again" sense of familiarity. And if you have the suspicion that the intensity of your angry responses regularly (or even sometimes) exceeds the provocation, parataxic distortion is even more likely.

4. Mind reading is another indicator of parataxic distortion. Mind reading occurs whenever you make assumptions about what your partner is thinking or feeling. No matter how long you've lived with a person or how intimate you are, you can never really know for sure what he or she is thinking or feeling at any particular time. When you make such assumptions, they're likely to be colored by childhood experience with one or both parents and may bear little resemblance to the present reality.

5. Fearing abuse and rejection from your partner (when no real danger of either is present) may also be an indication of parataxic distortion. There's nothing inherently frightening about a disagreement between two adults. But if you find it very scary, you may be reacting to your partner as if he or she were your parent and you were the frightened child. This is parataxic distortion.

Sophie experienced that fear in her relationship with Garrett. Whenever a conflict threatened, she felt terrified. She would visibly shrink in response to Garrett's raised voice. And though physical violence was never a part of their relationship, Sophie flinched when Garrett approached her at these times. Sophie was reacting to Garrett as if he were her abusive father.

Time for Mastery

The assessment phase takes one week. The process of challenging parataxic distortions may take from one-to-four weeks. Developing alternative coping behaviors will be an ongoing challenge. The first step can be accomplished in just a few days.

Do You Experience Parataxic Distortion?

This exercise will enable you to determine whether or not you experience parataxic distortion. Using a recent incident with your partner, find your way down the following decision tree.

Decision Tree

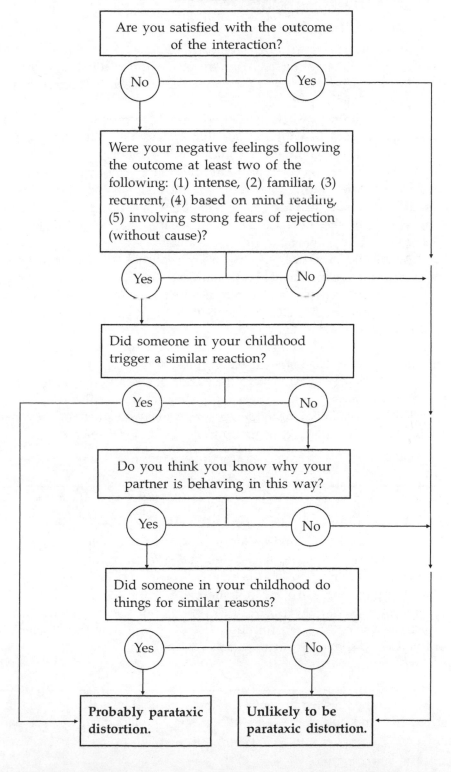

What Is the Nature of Your Parataxic Distortion?

Prepare a journal by turning a piece of typing paper sideways and dividing the left half of the page into three columns. Title these: *Description of incident, Feelings,* and *Self-statements about partner's behavior.* Leave the right half of the page blank.

During the next week, pay attention to the interactions or situations that occur with your partner that leave you feeling bad or unhappy. In the first column enter your brief description of the interaction or situation. In the next column write the feelings you experienced immediately before, during, and after the incident. In the third column describe what you said to yourself about what your partner said or did, why he or she did it, and what it meant. Enter each incident on a new page, and leaving the right side blank.

At the end of a week, return to your journal and put an asterisk by each of the feelings that felt old and familiar. Add another asterisk if the feeling was intense, and a third asterisk if the feeling is a recurrent one. Now consider the self-statements in column three. Put an asterisk next to each statement that could also describe how you felt treated by a significant person in your childhood. Add a second asterisk if that significant person was either a parent or sibling.

The asterisks indicate where the parataxic distortion is occurring—the more asterisks, the more serious the nature of the distortion.

Here's how Janine described a recent incident when she and her husband, Tim, entertained some mutual friends for dinner.

Janine's Journal

Description of incident	Feelings	Self-statements about partner's behavior
Darryl and Gaye were over for dinner. Tim insisted on telling them the story of our disastrous attempt to build a toolshed last weekend.	Anxiety when he said he was going to tell the story. Then humiliated, trapped, ridiculed and furious.	I can't believe he's really going to embarrass me like this. He's just doing it to put me down, show them how incompetent I am.

When she finished the entry, Janine evaluated her feelings and self-statements and added asterisks. When she counted them up, she had six in column two and two in column three—enough to suggest that parataxic distortion was clearly at work.

Challenging Parataxic Distortion

After recording incidents of parataxic distortion in your journal for a week, you will probably have developed an understanding of the characteristic nature of your distortions. The next step is to begin to challenge those distortions. Divide the previously blank right half of the pages of your journal into three columns. Label the first column *Who's in the room?* Title the second column *How is my partner similar?* and the third column *My response.* For each incident, fill out the relevant information in each of the columns, being as specific as possible. Here's how:

Who's in the Room?

In this column, identify which figure from the past is triggering the reaction. With whom did you feel this way before? Identifying the person will enable you to recognize what he or she did that was so painful. Perhaps your mother regularly humiliated you in front of your peers. Or your father was harshly critical whenever you didn't measure up to his excessive expectations. It's also important to identify how you felt at those times (controlled, humiliated, ridiculed, rejected, ignored, angry, afraid, helpless). Go ahead and write the person's name, and a one sentence summary of how you felt with that person.

Tom felt guarded with his girlfriend, Gail, particularly in sexual situations. If Gail suggested that Tom touch her more gently or more vigorously or if she asked him to move a little differently or suggested that they experiment with something new, he assumed that Gail's suggestions were veiled criticisms and lost all sexual interest. Tom identified his father as the person in the room with him. His father, a retired military man, had been extremely critical. When he'd catch Tom in the middle of some activity, homework or play, he'd criticize Tom's style and performance. Sometimes he'd make Tom repeat the activity many times before retiring in frustration at his "hopeless excuse for a son." He'd had excessive, unrealistic expectations of Tom, and Tom had inevitably failed to measure up to those standards. Tom felt constantly hurt and criticized. Tom answered the question *Who's in the room?* by writing down: "Dad. Hurt, unworthy."

How Is My Partner Similar?

Something your partner does is triggering the parataxic distortion response in you. It's essential that you identify as specifically as possible the ways your partner is similar to your parent (or other significant childhood figure). What does he or she actually do that triggers your response?

But you also need to do something more. Look for any evidence indicating that your partner is different from your parent, that he or she has different motives or feelings toward you. How does your partner explain his or her behavior? What has your partner told you about his or her feelings and needs? How has he or she behaved differently from your parent in the past? Since your assumptions about your partner's behavior and the intention behind that behavior aren't likely to be completely accurate, it's essential to explore alternative explanations.

Go ahead and write down the ways your partner reminds you of your parent. And also put down any information you have that shows your partner to be different.

Tom recognized that Gail wasn't really much like his overcritical father. But sometimes when she asked him to do something, her request would sound a little like an order. And in the area where he felt the most vulnerable, lovemaking, those requests were the most painful to hear. "Touch me harder," she'd say, or "No, don't stop." And Gail wasn't good at giving verbal compliments either, although physically she was very affectionate. Since he didn't hear much that was positive about his behavior, it was easy for Tom to interpret what he did hear as negative. He didn't have to ask Gail about her intentions since she had told him that she wasn't criticizing what he was doing, especially his lovemaking. She was simply letting him know how to help her enjoy herself even more.

Tom answered the question *How is my partner similar?* this way: "Sounds as if she's giving orders, like Dad. Doesn't praise. But she's very affectionate and she says, and I believe it, that she's not critical and disgusted with me."

My Response

In this column write a short sentence that describes your coping strategy. What did you do when your partner behaved in ways that triggered parataxic distortion?

Now think about the outcome: Was your response effective? What happened in your relationship when you used this coping strategy? Did your response have any long-term effects? What usually happens between you when you use this response? Was this example typical?

Tom described his response in the last column: "Withdraw, resist, and shut down. Outcome: Gail gets hurt and rarely initiates sex."

Alternative Coping Strategies

At this point, you've been able to identify which parent is in the room with you, what they did, and how you felt. You've identified what your partner is currently doing that's similar to your parent, and how he or she may actually be different. You've identified your current coping strategies and how they're affecting your relationship.

You probably use some of the same coping responses now that you used as a child. Chances are that the coping strategies you used then didn't work to solve the problem. You withdrew or rebelled or sulked—but nothing changed. Now, when your partner behaves in ways that trigger your parataxic response and you engage in the same old coping strategies, they most likely still don't work.

The strategies didn't work in the past because the way your parents behaved towards you was mostly due to who they were—rather than to what you were doing. Your responses couldn't change who they were then, and these same responses are even less workable now, since the assumptions they make about your partner are more accurately applicable to your parent.

Remember the difficult times David had when his lover Ron talked about his accomplishments at work? He experienced Ron's joy in his own success as criticism. David responded with the same depression and defensiveness that had characterized his relationship with his critical father. It was no more successful now than it had been then. Ron felt hurt and misunderstood and withdrew more and more from David.

Lisa's mother had begun drinking heavily after her marriage ended. She hung out at bars after work and came home drunk, sometimes with men who rarely stayed till morning. Lisa, who had been eight when her parents divorced, had spent a lot of her childhood alone, fending for herself. She frequently felt a similar loneliness in her relationship with Jeremy. She knew that Jeremy wasn't really avoiding her; he was the new partner at his law firm and working almost sixty hours a week. Still, Lisa never felt satisfied with the amount of time they spent together or the depth of their interactions when they were together. But the more she pursued—demanding more time, complaining, even threatening—the more Jeremy withdrew. Her coping strategies were as unsuccessful with Jeremy as they had been with her mother.

It's time to develop some alternative coping strategies. There are four useful strategies:

1. Change how you express feelings and needs (see chapter 2).

2. Check out your assumptions about your partner (see chapter 12).

3. Learn how to negotiate (see chapter 6).

4. Learn problem-solving skills (see chapter 7).

Decide which strategy or combination of strategies you're going to use and read the appropriate chapters thoroughly. Then plan when and how you will initiate the new behaviors. Write out, as specifically as possible, what you plan to say to your partner. Practice your script until you feel confident—it's okay to take notes with you when you approach your partner.

David decided to check out his assumptions about the meaning behind Ron's pleasure in his work achievements. He carefully prepared a script and the next time they were together he began. "Ron, I know I haven't been very supportive when you've told me about your successes at work. I used to get criticized a whole lot when I was a kid, and I think I've been hearing your achievements as reflections on my own lack of success. I assume you're criticizing me and then I get depressed and defensive. I'd like to check out those assumptions with you. Do you feel disapproval or disdain for me at those times?" Ron was surprised and relieved to finally understand David's responses and was quick to reassure him that his assumptions were totally inaccurate. Ron explained that because this was his first job with major responsibilities, his successes were very exciting. He had no comparisons of any kind in mind. After further discussion, David, also very relieved, agreed to check out his assumptions with Ron whenever he felt that old familiar feeling.

Lisa decided to use a combination of strategies in approaching Jeremy. She developed her script and asked Jeremy if they could talk a little that night. He agreed. Lisa began by telling Jeremy how alone she frequently felt when he worked long hours and then brought even more work home to do in the evenings and on weekends. "I know you have to work hard in your new job," she continued, "but I need more time with you to feel connected. What I'd really like is for you not to work past eight o'clock during the week, and not at all on weekends. Would you be willing to try negotiating around this?" Jeremy agreed. He clarified his needs, and after further discussion, they came up with the following compromise: Jeremy would set aside two nights a week to spend with Lisa from seven o'clock onwards. In addition, he would clear one day each weekend for their activities. In six months, when he was more established, they would renegotiate for additional time.

After filling in all the columns of his journal, Tom was clear that his current coping strategies of withdrawal, resistance, and shutting down weren't successful in his relationship with Gail. He decided to try some problem-solving strategies with her and developed his script. He had to practice what he wanted to say over and over before he was ready to tell Gail in person. To reduce his anxiety, Tom decided that he would raise the issue before they got into bed. He asked Gail if she was willing to talk to him that evening, and she agreed. Taking a deep breath, Tom started: "Gail, you know I have a hard time when we're making love and you tell me to do something different. I feel really criticized and want to withdraw. But I don't think that simply asking you to stop making those suggestions will work for you, so maybe we can do some problem-solving about it."

Gail repeated that she didn't mean to be critical, and said that she enjoyed their lovemaking. "Usually what we're doing feels fine, it's just that it would sometimes feel even better if it were a little harder or softer or whatever. How can I tell you without you feeling criticized?" After discussion of some options, they decided on two things. First, they talked further about the kinds of things each liked to do during lovemaking, including things that they'd like to try. Tom agreed to take responsibility for suggesting they try something new occasionally, using the material generated by their discussion as a guide. He also agreed to remind himself that Gail loved him, and that asking him to do something didn't mean he was doing anything wrong. And Gail agreed to verbalize more her enjoyment of their lovemaking prior to suggesting changes, and her appreciation of Tom in general.

During the lovemaking that followed, Tom started out somewhat anxious. But because they'd talked about the issue, they were able to introduce a little humor into the situation. Tom suggested they try something new (that Gail had already expressed an interest in), and her response was a definite Yes! She giggled, he smiled. At one point Gail murmured "That's perfect. Now just a little harder." Tom experienced the pull toward old feelings of being criticized, but held onto the "that's perfect" part of her statement and tried to touch her a little harder. Gail responded appreciatively, and Tom felt not only the immediate pleasure of being able to satisfy her, but also the realization that the outcome of their lovemaking was going to be very different from their usual experience.

14

Coping with Your
Defenses

No partnership is without pain. And no matter how committed or
caring you are, there will always be moments when it hurts to be
together. Intimate relationships create a special openness—and with it,
a vulnerability. It's likely that no one else can nurture, or hurt you, as
much as your partner.

The vulnerability you feel may also include sensitivities and feelings from early relationships. Times when you felt controlled, abandoned, afraid, wrong, or ashamed with your parents may be evoked
by similar situations now with your partner. It's easy for a harsh word
or a critical look to open old wounds.

Each partner copes with the pain that intimacy brings in his or
her own way. On some level, everyone is a bit of a prizefighter—learning to bob and weave, to dodge and dance and counterpunch. Everyone
develops *defenses*.

Defenses do two things: (1) they help you avoid or cope with pain,
and (2) they undermine your relationship. When your partner says

something that makes you feel bad and unworthy, you want to stop the hurt. The usual reflex is to defend against it. *How* you defend is mostly a product of your individual style and what you learned from your family growing up. You might get mad and counterattack, or do something to distract from the issue, or turn off emotionally, or slip into a "please don't hit me because I'm hitting myself" type of self-blame. Whatever defense you choose, it's one that your experience has taught you will block or diminish how bad you feel.

There's nothing wrong with stopping pain. Protecting yourself from hurt or fear or shame is a good thing. The problem is that defenses damage the fiber of your relationship. They create distance, they deceive, they destroy trust. Whether you counterattack, distract, or turn off emotionally, the effect is a loss of intimacy. Defenses are psychological walls that keep you safe, but over time they also become barriers. The more you use defenses, the thicker and more impenetrable those barriers will be.

History

The concept of psychological defenses was first elaborated by Anna Freud in her book, *Ego and the Mechanisms of Defense* (1946). The defenses most typically used in intimate relationships are avoidance, denial, and acting out (turning the feeling into behavior).

Since Freud, object relations therapists such as James Masterson (1981), Otto Kernberg (1976), and others have looked at the role of defenses in undermining relationships. Cognitive therapists such as Jeffrey Young (1990) have shown how defenses help people to avoid the pain associated with deeply held beliefs (schemas) about self-worth, safety, competence, and many other core identity issues.

Theoretical Background

Anna Freud's idea was that certain feelings are so threatening or even intolerable to the ego that the ego develops special mechanisms to push them out of awareness. Here are some of the feelings triggered by intimate relationships that people often defend against:

Rejection or abandonment	Guilt
Hurt	Shame or humiliation
Feeling unworthy or unlovable	Failure
Loneliness	Jealousy
Emptiness	Numbness or deadness
Feeling drained	Feeling wrong or bad
Feeling controlled or engulfed	Sadness
Fear	Loss

Any of these feelings can have a powerful effect, strongly motivating you to *avoid* it, *deny* it, or *turn it into action*.

These three major defenses are like primary colors, of which there are many shades and hues. In this chapter, each major defense is broken into six subtypes that may help you recognize your own defensive maneuvers.

Time for Mastery

You can identify your major defenses in one or two days. The recovery plan can be implemented in one additional day, but it will take six weeks of focused effort to change the habit of using a particular defense.

Identify Your Defenses

Right now, review the following list of defenses and put a check mark by the ones that remind you of your own behavior.

Avoiding

☐ **Turning away.** You turn your focus to outside relationships instead of your partner. Rebecca had shifted most of her social energy away from James, whose inability to talk about his feelings left her feeling lonely and cut off. She spent hours with a women's group that collected children's clothes for refugees. Rebecca liked the group and it's work, but it's real importance to her was as a way of avoiding her feelings with James.

☐ **Turning off.** This defense uses coldness and emotional withdrawal to protect you from painful feelings. Jerry felt hurt when Enid questioned his remodeling plans for the kitchen. He avoided the feeling by getting very cold and shut down. He buried himself in the paper and gave monosyllabic answers about drawer depths and thicknesses of plywood. In an hour the hurt had passed and he wanted to reengage. But now Enid was hurt and acting very icy herself.

☐ **Triangulating.** Triangulating involves adding a third person to your partnership dyad. You begin to invest romantic or sexual energy in someone outside of your relationship. Al was a high-powered, critical guy. His wife, Sheila, was afraid of his anger. And she lived with a sense that he might some day abandon her. To protect herself from these feelings, she triangulated by developing a sexually-charged relationship with Al's attorney. They never slept together, but always seemed on the verge of doing so. Now Sheila was less concerned about Al leaving her, and she had little interest in dealing with Al directly about their problems. Her main concern was finding enough free time to visit the lawyer.

☐ **Addictions.** People can become addicted to food, alcohol, drugs, gambling, shopping, and virtually any form of excitement as a way of coping with painful feelings in a relationship. Arthur had strong feelings of unworthiness after Bob complained that his part-time job wasn't bringing in enough money. He suppressed those feelings with a six-pack of beer per night. And when Bob complained about that, he began to drink vodka as well.

☐ **Compulsive activity.** Perhaps the most common form of this defense is workaholism, but compulsive activities can include projects, hobbies, and virtually any enterprise that siphons time away from your relationship. Andy felt empty when sitting in the living room with Laura. As she talked about the children and minor events from the day, he'd begin to feel a sharp, unnameable yearning. Andy solved the problem by taking on three new work projects that required so much of him that he rarely got home before 9:30 at night.

☐ **Giving up.** This defense involves stopping all efforts, going on strike, or waving the white flag of surrender. Leanne felt ashamed after Larry criticized her for "being a turtle with its head in the shell." She'd been trying to talk more about current events (like Larry wanted) and be more involved in conversations. But that remark ended the campaign. Leanne gave up and, as a result, Larry grew increasingly withdrawn.

Denial

☐ **Showing nothing.** There are two versions of this defense. In the first, you fear rejection and carefully avoid revealing anything about yourself. You're afraid that if you show much, you'll be negatively judged. Ralph experienced himself as flawed. He was afraid that anyone who really knew him would reject him. So his defense was to be unbearably bland and agreeable. Eventually his girlfriend did reject him, wondering "if there was anyone home behind that pleasant smile?"

The second version involves situations where you feel hurt and angry. You show nothing, so you don't give your partner the satisfaction of knowing that he or she got to you. Julie was hurt by Lenny's comments about her shade of lipstick. She showed nothing, refusing to "give him the satisfaction of thinking that he got to me." But saying nothing meant that Lenny was never alerted to Julie's vulnerability about her appearance, and he kept on making inadvertent hurtful remarks.

☐ **Compliance.** The effort here is to be perfect, pleasing, placating. To be whatever a partner wants. At the bottom of this defense is a hope that if you can just be perfect, no one will hurt you. At root Howard felt unlovable, so he coped with the feeling by being incredibly accommodating. He hated crafts fairs, but he went to them with his woman friend. He hated cooking elaborate three-hour dinners together, but he did it anyway. He hated "working on problems," which meant saying he was sorry for his failures "to be more sensitive." But he did this too. Howard's extreme compliance left him feeling like he had no self in the relationship. He felt suffocated and eventually began looking for an excuse to break things off.

☐ **Competing.** This defense requires you to be better than your partner: a better parent, more creative, more generous, and so on. Bill carried deep feelings of unworthiness for most of his adult life. He coped by competing, trying to be better than his wife. He worked hard at trying to be closer to his stepdaughter than his wife was and got more involved than his wife in a civic fundraising project. He also focused on (and often mentioned) his slightly higher monthly salary. The net effect was to create distance and resentment.

☐ **Boasting.** This defense is closely associated with competing, but it's slightly more brazen. The effort is to block feelings of unworthiness by constantly pointing to evidence of one's value. Miranda felt like a failure because she'd recently been laid off. She pushed the feeling away by boasting about her hot tennis game, her "amazing work in sculpture class," her new powers of speed reading, etc. Her style put her boyfriend off. One day he asked when she ever let up on the "self-hype."

☐ **Distracting.** In this defense, you derail attention from any situation or issue that triggers painful feelings. Whenever Simone would ask Shawn about his relationship to his mom, he felt a rush of shame. His mother, who'd been hospitalized several times for manic-depression, had been alternately loving and rejecting as her symptoms had waxed and waned. Rather than experience his feelings, Shawn kept changing the subject. He derailed the discussion of his mother and his childhood so consistently that Simone wondered if he was capable of any real intimacy.

☐ **Forgetting.** You let important, but disturbing things, slip out of your mind. Andrea told Guy a million times that she needed him to listen more when she was telling about problems at work. These admonitions always made Guy feel bad about himself, and he'd apologize profusely. He handled the painful feelings by promptly forgetting everything Andrea had said.

Acting Out

☐ **Attacking.** This defense turns the pain into an angry fight—either verbal or physical. Every time Leah felt really helpless or inadequate with her lawyer husband, Ralph, she'd start to attack him verbally. He was so good at arguing a point that she always felt defeated by his superior skill with words. She reacted by pushing the painful feelings away with an angry broadside. Leah paid for the defense later when she had to apologize and felt even worse about herself.

☐ **Passive aggression.** This defense acts out your anger indirectly. The idea is to hurt your partner in a way that won't trigger blame or a backlash. Noel always neglected to start the coffee maker for her husband on mornings after fights. She still felt hurt, and she acted out her hurt and angry feelings by "forgetting" something he counted on.

☐ **Fault finding.** In this defense you act out hurt or angry feelings by criticizing, ridiculing, or sarcastically belittling your partner. Fault finding is passionless anger; there's no affect. Your own feelings of hurt and inadequacy are covered by calmly exposing your partner's flaws. When Paula felt guilty or ashamed about her own behavior, she'd launch into a dispassionate discussion of Sigorny's failures. She'd ridicule Sigorny's cooking, her hair, the way she walked, her perfectionism with school work—anything to shield herself from her own feelings. Unfortunately, Paula's defense created emotional distance from Sigorny. Their sexual relationship declined in frequency and feelings of closeness. And Paula felt hurt and rejected about that, which only triggered a whole new round of fault finding.

☐ **Revenge.** Revenge is a consciously planned strategy to hurt your partner at some future time. By contrast, attacking, passive aggression, and fault finding are far more spontaneous forms of acting out. Rachel took revenge on Dan for his belittling remarks. She'd deliberately wear something alluring and act subtly provocative. When Dan responded with a sexual overture, Rachel would appear disgusted. "Dan, if you want me to feel any interest in that, then you'd better start acting as if you like me. Otherwise you can forget it."

☐ **Demanding.** People who are fearful of rejection, abandonment, or hurt often cope by demanding. They act out the fear by requiring that a partner provide a high degree of support, help, or attention. Another version of the demanding defense is *overcontrol*. This strategy is frequently used when jealousy is a factor between partners. The jealous partner seeks to diminish his or her fear by monitoring and controlling the relationships of a lover or a spouse. Eugene felt increasing distance in his relationship with Trudy. It frightened him. He handled the fear by demanding back rubs, special favors, and a lot of attention from Trudy. His defense, however, left Trudy feeling drained, which in turn triggered *her* defense of turning off and turning away. It was a vicious cycle that spiraled into a less and less satisfying relationship.

☐ **Self-blame.** This defense can be summarized as "You're right, I'm awful, please don't hit me." You cope with your fear of rejection by rejecting yourself first. Larry was always the first to admit it when he screwed up. He'd point out his mistake in some detail and sound extremely disgusted with himself. But after a while, his wife wasn't buying it. She noticed that over and over he'd excoriate himself for screwing up, but never seemed to change his behavior. She found herself increasingly angry with Larry's self-blame because it felt more like manipulation than an honest apology.

Find Examples of Your Defenses

In the previous section you placed a check mark by each defense that you're aware of using. Now in the space provided below, identify at least one example of each defense you marked. Be sure the example relates to your behavior with your partner. If there are several prime examples of a particular defense, you may need a separate piece of paper for this exercise.

Examples of Avoiding

Turning away: _____

_____

Turning off: _____

_____

Triangulating: _____

_____

Addictions: _____

_____

Compulsive activity: _____

_____

Giving up: _____

_____

Examples of Denial

Showing nothing: _____

_____

Compliance: _____

_____

Competing: _____

_____

Boasting: _____

_____

Distracting: _____

_____

Forgetting: _____

_____

Examples of Acting Out

Attacking: _____

_____

Passive Aggression: _____

_____

Fault Finding: _____

_____

Revenge: _____

_____

Demanding: _____

_____

Self-blame: _____

_____

Identify the Pain

As you've learned, the purpose of every defense is to protect you from feeling emotional pain. It always works to some extent, otherwise you wouldn't use it. Being able to identify the pain you're trying to block is a crucial step to overcoming the use of any destructive defense.

On the following worksheet, write down in the column marked *Defense* each defense you checked. Under the column marked *Pain,* write down the emotion that your defense protects you from feeling, or at least helps you diminish. Use the list of emotions in the "Theoretical Background" section of this chapter to give you ideas. Think of your example for each defense, and ask yourself this question: "If I couldn't use the defense, what would I have to feel?" Imagine it. See the scene and try to visualize what would happen if you didn't engage in defensive behavior. What would you experience inside? What pain would you have to face?

Leave the *Cost* column blank for the moment.

Jillian was a master of "showing nothing." She wrote that down under the *Defense* column. To identify the underlying pain, she turned to her example: "Art says he doesn't feel like going out to dinner and the movies. I say fine, we can save some money, and go in to do the dishes." Jillian immediately realized that she didn't want Art to see how hurt she was. She assumed he wasn't going out as a revenge for a previous fight. And she wasn't going to give him the satisfaction of knowing he had really disappointed her.

Next Jillian explored another example to make sure that hurt was always the pain she defended against. The previous night, Art had declined her sexual overture. It felt to Jillian that he was punishing her for having herself declined the night before. Jillian showed nothing because she didn't want her hurt to be obvious.

Jillian had initially marked other defenses, including turning off, compulsive activity, competing, passive aggression, and fault finding. She eventually crossed off "compulsive activity" because it seemed related to pain (emptiness) that wasn't really associated with Art. "Competing," she realized, was something she did at work rather than at home. For her remaining defenses, Jillian kept going over the examples. She reviewed the situations and her emotional reactions. Sometimes she tried to imagine what she would have felt *without* using her defenses. These underlying feelings were listed in the pain column.

Knowing Your Defenses		
Defense	*Pain*	*Cost*

Jillian's Defenses Worksheet

Defense	Pain	Cost
Showing nothing	Hurt	
Turning off	Hurt/fear of rejection	
Passive aggression	Hurt/anger	
Fault finding	Unworthy/shame	

Identify the Cost

Now it's time to ask yourself what your defense costs—for you, your partner, and your relationship. Think through as many examples as you can of each defense, and try to determine the emotional outcome. How did you feel afterward? Were you depressed, angry, frightened, guilty, ashamed? How did the defense impact your partner emotionally? What's the outcome for your relationship? Do you feel farther apart? Are you physically less intimate? Is your partner now engaging in his or her own defense?

Harry used two main defenses—giving up and demanding. When his wife, Tina, asked for things that triggered feelings of failure or a sense of being controlled, Harry would declare defeat and put an end to the whole discussion. He tried to analyze the cost by looking at emotional outcomes. He usually felt wrong and guilty after using his defense, his wife was angry and distant, and the relationship's temperature could turn subzero for days.

After these periods of alienation had gone on for a while, Harry began to fear abandonment. To cover that fear, Harry demanded favors, sex, time together—anything to feel closer. But when Harry explored the emotional outcomes from his demands, he saw that Tina grudgingly acquiesced, but seemed more and more involved with the dog, the neighbors, her friend in the next town—anything but him! Harry's worksheet looked like this:

Harry's Defenses Worksheet

Defense	Pain	Cost
Giving up	Failure/being controlled	Feeling guilty, wrong. Tina angry and distant. Deep coldness between us.
Demanding	Afraid of abandonment	Tina turns away from me. It seems

like she doesn't
come back; it
keeps getting
worse.

Choose a Place To Start

Now it's time to decide where you want to make changes. Work on only one defense at a time. If you try to work on more, you're likely to feel overwhelmed and give up.

Choose a defense that has a significant cost for you and your partner. Make sure it's one that occurs often enough so you'll have opportunities to practice new behavior. When you've identified the defense you want to work on first, you're ready for the next step: recovery.

Recovery

Defenses are addicting. Because they temporarily reduce pain each time you use them, you use them more and more. They become reflexive; so automatic that they appear with hardly any conscious choice at all. But you are aware now that each defense has a cost. Each time you defend yourself from pain you further damage your relationship.

This form of addiction is precisely what the alcoholic feels. A drink can temporarily stop feelings of loneliness, unworthiness, loss, or fear. But the drink also makes him dysfunctional, which in the end only makes matters worse. Ending an addiction, whether to drugs and alcohol or to certain defensive behaviors, requires that you commit to a recovery program. The recovery from a defense has five steps:

1. Acknowledging the defense to your partner.

2. Identifying and acknowledging times you've used it.

3. Admitting the pain that underlies your defense.

4. Acknowledging how much using the defense costs you, your partner, and the relationship.

5. Asking your partner's help and support in developing an alternative to your defense.

The steps aren't easy to do. Each will take preparation, perhaps even writing out what you'll say in the form of a script. And it will take courage. You'll have to admit to things that may temporarily leave you feeling very bad about yourself and very vulnerable to your partner. There is no other way.

The fifth step is critical. It requires a real plan worked out by you and your partner. When you feel the familiar pain, and with it the impulse to use the old defense, you need to make a commitment that you'll acknowledge the pain instead of slipping automatically into defensive behavior. And your partner needs to make a commitment that he or she will listen to your pain openly, supportively and without engaging in counterdefense. Your partner may wish to reread the listening chapter to be more prepared for the challenge of hearing your pain without feeling guilty and wrong and mounting some counterattack.

Here are two examples of the five-step process at work.

Henry's Process

Step 1

Henry: I've been doing a lot of fault finding, Irene. I've done some thinking about it, and I can see how much it goes on.

Step 2

Like when I criticized you for those baggy pants, or when I was kind of putting you down about things you were buying at the grocery store. I also remember doing that about your arrangements for the kids' summer camp. It happens a fair amount.

Step 3

When I'm fault finding, I realize that underneath I feel guilty and wrong. I feel like something's wrong with me. I'm not helping enough or supportive enough or caring enough. It's just this bad feeling I get that I push away by getting on your case.

Step 4

And I'm starting to realize how that fault finding affects us. After a while I feel even more guilty. And I can see I'm hurting you and kind of pushing you away from me.

Step 5

Irene, I need your help to stop this. I want to stop. Whenever I'm about to find fault, I'm going to try to tell you about what I feel underneath. I guess about the guilt I feel. It's going to be hard. I just need you to listen. You don't have to fix anything.

Irene: Is there something I can do to help you feel less guilty?

Henry: If I'm kicking myself for something I shouldn't be, tell me. Otherwise, just let me know that you love me and you're glad we're together.

Irene: What happens if you start fault finding without stopping yourself?

Henry: Just see if you can gently remind me and ask me what the pain is that I'm feeling underneath.

Henry had to write out the basic concept of each step so that he could remember it. He used his "Knowing Your Defenses" worksheet and his list of examples to get the information he needed.

The fifth step, where you ask for support and help, always involves promising to tell the underlying pain instead of using your defense. In exchange, you ask your partner to listen openly and nondefensively. Other optional requests include reminding you if you're lapsing back into your defense, and asking what your pain is. You may ask your partner for still other kinds of help. When you script what you're going to say in Step 5, you should write each request down in advance.

Henry prepared for Step 5 by listing these requests he would make of Irene:

1. Listen openly.

2. Give him feedback if he was being too hard on himself.

3. Acknowledge that Irene loves and wants to be with him (this is most important for coping with the pain of guilt).

4. Remind him gently if he lapsed into fault finding.

5. Ask him what pain he was feeling underneath.

Regina's Process

Step 1

Regina: I notice I'm trying to be perfect, to do everything flawlessly or at least the way you like it so you'll feel satisfied with things.

Step 2

Like going to the basketball games when I'm not really crazy about the sport. Or obsessing over how to juggle the bills. Or just kind of going along with things, like when you wanted to have Mr. Shilf and all his family over for dinner.

Step 3

I know why I do it, because underneath I'm afraid you'll be angry if I say no to anything, and then I'll worry that we're falling apart or something. I can't stand that feeling of distance or that something's wrong, so I just go along with things.

Step 4

But I realize it's affecting me and us. I end up feeling kind of angry and—I don't know—like there's a lid on my feelings. Just shut down. And then even though I fear us being distant, I *feel* distant. And I have to pretend I'm not. I'm not really being myself with you.

Step 5

Jim, I need your help with this. I need to stop just going along with things I don't want to do. It's costing me too much. I'm going to tell you when I want to say no and why. And also tell you when that scares me. From you, I need a good listener, someone who won't get angry at me. I need you just to say to me that you still love me and everything's okay—even if you're really disappointed that I don't want to do something. Even if I don't go along with everything, tell me that things are okay.

Jim: You're asking me to remind you that I love you even when you say no to me and I'm disappointed.

Regina: Yes, 'cause I have all these bad feelings otherwise, and I don't think we're as close as we could be.

Jim: It's a tall order, but I'll try.

To prepare her statement, Regina took material from her Knowing Your Defenses worksheet. In preparing Step 5, Regina realized that the thing she needed more than anything from Jim was some reassurance that the relationship would still be solid even if she stopped being perfect. As Jim remarked at the end, the work on defenses is "a tall order." But it's extremely important for you and your partnership that you both try.

15

Identifying Your Couple System

A system is a pattern of interaction that develops over time in any group of people: couples, families, organizations, communities. The behavior of any person in the system influences and at the same time is influenced by the behaviors of all the other members. A system is like a circle of dominoes. A change in any person's behavior usually triggers changes in other members' behaviors. Systems are predictable. The patterns of interaction are repeated. And the more that response patterns are repeated and familiar, the more certainty everyone has about what will happen next.

Madeline hated the way David left his clothes lying about the bedroom. It felt disrespectful to her and she regularly asked him to pick them up. The more Madeline nagged, the more David's reassurances appeared to be simply lip service. He felt criticized and unaccepted. Every now and then Madeline exploded with frustration. "I can't stand it anymore! Why do you have to be such a slob? This house is a pigsty!"

"If you hate it so much why don't you just leave?" David responded.

"If you can't stop living like a pig, I might."

"Well, if you weren't such a damn controlling bitch, I might be more willing to pick up occasionally."

After a period of coolness between them, David usually did a more thorough cleanup than usual, Madeline warmed up, and once more calm prevailed. However, each cycle exacerbated and reinforced David's fears of not being accepted and Madeline's fears of not being respected. Trust between them decreased and the overall level of intimacy in their relationship suffered.

The only way to prevent deadly spirals like this is to learn to identify your particular system, recognize the patterns of behavior that aren't working, and develop strategies for intervening.

It's important to note that if a system is severely dysfunctional, it may be necessary to seek the help of a qualified therapist in creating healthy change.

History

Until the 1950s, therapy rarely included anyone other than the "symptomatic" person. The "patient" was the alcoholic, the depressed person, the person contemplating divorce, the acting-out child. Strange, inexplicable interactional patterns that were later related to family systems theory were first noticed in psychiatric hospitals. When the families of hospitalized schizophrenics came to visit, it was observed that if the patient got better, someone else in the family usually got worse. Moreover, it was noted that in general, change was stubbornly resisted in families, even when that change meant the improvement of a loved one.

Noting the stubborn resistance to change shown by the families with which he worked, Don Jackson (1957) coined the term "family homeostasis." He saw how the homeostatic pull towards stability and away from change existed even when change meant the improvement of a loved one.

As early as 1965, Jackson used the concept of *roles* to explain the repetitive interactional patterns between spouses in a marriage. Each partner has characteristic behaviors that support and enact his or her particular role of pursuer, distancer, caretaker, victim, and so on.

Over the next couple of decades research made it more and more clear that a person's behavior doesn't exist in a vacuum, but is affected by the responses of others. Gregory Bateson (1979) was one of the earliest system's theorists to define the concept of *circularity*. Circularity assumes that each action is determined in part by the preceding action and determines in part the subsequent action. Couple systems were seen as a circular chain of stimulus and response in which each person's behavior is a response to the other's and every action is also a reaction.

Theoretical Background

Characteristics of Systems

Circularity. When linear thinking is applied to couple interactions, a common perception of each person is "If you didn't _____, then I wouldn't _____". The concept of circularity is essential in defusing the search for the cause of the problem. Circularity defines every action as a reaction and thus sees each person's behavior as dependent on the other's. According to this concept there is no beginning and no ending to the couple's interactions, just an ongoing circle of actions and reactions.

Suzanne was reading the paper in the living room; her husband Tom was downstairs, engrossed in a new program for his computer. It seemed to Suzanne that all Tom did these days when he got home from work was play with that damn computer. She suddenly remembered she wanted to ask Tom about the party Saturday night. "Tom!" she called. And again, this time somewhat angrily, "Tom!" Still no answer. Tom was totally engrossed. He never felt as if he had enough time to relax and just amuse himself. Suzanne was always bugging him about something and he found it suffocating. When he got the opportunity, he tuned her and everything else out. Suzanne stomped down the stairs. "Jesus, can't you stop fiddling long enough to even answer me? You'd think you were married to that computer." Tom, hurt, didn't respond. Suzanne was furious. "Well since you'd rather spend time with that machine than with me, maybe I'll find someone who wants me."

"All I want is a little peace and quiet. You don't need to get neurotic," muttered Tom. Suzanne exploded and a big confrontation ensued.

After a few minutes, Suzanne stormed upstairs and started getting ready for bed. Tom stayed downstairs. He planned to stay as far away from Suzanne as possible for a while. He concentrated on his computer. Fifteen minutes later, Suzanne reappeared with two cups of cocoa. She gave one to Tom, saying "Peace?" and raised her eyebrows in a questioning look.

"Thanks," mumbled Tom, and took a sip.

Both were silent for a minute, and then Suzanne said brightly, "Well, I'll see you in bed. Goodnight." Several hours later Tom finally climbed the stairs to bed.

Using a diagram, the circular nature of Suzanne's and Tom's interactions become clearly visible.

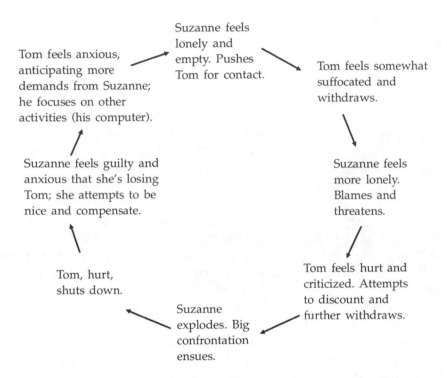

If you look at the interaction solely from Suzanne's perspective, it's clear that Tom began this fight. If he'd merely answered "Yes" when she called, she would have just asked him about the party and that would have been that. His passivity with her, his tendency to withdraw and tune her out, made her feel alone and empty.

From Tom's perspective, Suzanne was clearly to blame. She was so critical. Hell, he couldn't even spend an hour on the computer without her finding fault. If she didn't criticize so much he might feel more like spending time with her.

From a circular perspective, it's easier to see how Tom and Suzanne's behaviors are in fact reactions to each other's behavior—with neither to blame for the resulting interaction. Tom's withdrawal triggers Suzanne's criticisms, while Suzanne's criticisms trigger Tom's withdrawal. This is particularly clear if you know that half an hour earlier Suzanne had sharply criticized Tom for not helping her fold the laundry.

This particular interaction between Suzanne and Tom was dependent on their last interaction and will to some extent determine the tone of their next interaction. Neither began this cycle and there is no end.

Homeostasis.   Once a system develops, it can feel as if the more you try to change, the more things stay the same. This is the tendency towards homeostasis, the pull to keep the system stable and consistent. It doesn't mean change is impossible, only that it's difficult. To change, you must resist the pull to homeostasis.

One factor that maintains homeostasis is reinforcement. This refers to the way each partner overtly or covertly supports the behavior patterns of the other so that they tend to continue. Remember Madeline and David? David felt unaccepted, and one way to cope with that feeling was to rebel and go back to "slob" behavior. Rebellion made him feel less hurt by Madeline's judgments. So rebellion was negatively rein-forced because it *reduced pain*. Madeline's angry, blaming behavior helped her temporarily feel less hurt by David's lack of respect for her needs. It too was negatively reinforced because it stopped pain. Home-ostasis keeps the system going because each time someone tries to change it (Madeline demanding that David clean up) she or he often uses strategies (put-downs and blame) that reinforce the same old be-havior (rebellious slobbiness).

Sandy and George were having a characteristically difficult time deciding where to spend the holidays. George wanted to go to his parents' again, arguing that his parents were old and wouldn't be around much longer. Sandy, who always felt criticized by George's mother, wanted them to begin establishing their own holiday traditions, especially given their recent discussions about starting a family soon. They'd been arguing for a long time and were holding rigidly to their positions. The real issue beneath their interaction was different. George often felt as if Sandy were trying to control him. He felt he would be losing control if the holiday weren't structured the way he wanted. Sandy often felt unloved and uncared for. She wanted George to dem-onstrate his love by protecting her from his critical mother. The more she pushed for George to demonstrate caring behavior the more George felt out of control and responded with angry determination. The more determined George was, the less cared for Sandy felt. The situation be-came more and more heated.

"Since you obviously care more about what your mother wants than what I want, you should have married her!" yelled Sandy.

"Well, I shouldn't have married you, that's for sure!" retorted George.

"Then why did you?" demanded Sandy.

"Christ if I know," said George.

"Oh yeah? Well I don't know why I married you either—certainly not for your prowess in bed!" sneered Sandy.

George paled slightly and without another word walked into the bedroom, pulled a suitcase from on top of the armoire, and began throwing his clothes into it.

Sandy felt like biting her tongue. Her reference to George's problem of premature ejaculation felt like a step too far, and she was scared. She followed George into the bedroom.

"I didn't mean that" she began rapidly. "Look, it's okay, we'll go to your parents' this year, we can always start our own traditions later."

Her apologies were profuse. Five minutes later, George grudgingly accepted them.

When Sandy referred to George's sexual problem, she was using a new strategy (sexual put-downs) in an attempt to change the system. She was in effect saying to George, "Get more flexible or I'm not going to be so accepting anymore (of your sexual behavior)." George felt threatened and his fears of loss of control increased. So he fought even harder for control by threatening abandonment. Sandy's attempts to change the system were met by strong attempts by George to reestablish homeostasis. The pull for homeostasis (threatened abandonment) was too strong, and Sandy relented, apologizing.

But what if she hadn't? That single statement might have led to a variety of changes in the system. True, the relationship might have ended there. But stating the problem aloud could also have opened the way for George and Sandy eventually to talk honestly about their relationship and decide to seek treatment together. It's impossible to predict in what direction a system will change in response to stimulus, but if the pull to homeostasis is resisted, the system will change and adapt.

Roles. People take different roles in relationships. Often these roles reflect what they enjoy doing, what they do best, and what their expectations are of the relationship. In healthy relationships, these roles are flexible and often are exchanged between partners. But sometimes the roles that are held reflect what the person feels he or she "should" be doing. A person can feel stuck in a role that offers little reward or opportunity for getting his or her own needs met. The more rigidly held the role, the more likely this is to be the case. Common roles in relationships include those of *caretaker, child, blamer, martyr, pursuer, distancer*, and *parent*.

Patty was the *caretaker* in her relationship with Jay. She massaged his shoulders while he watched TV, prepared meals that he enjoyed, and rarely wondered whether in focusing on Jay's needs her own needs got met. In fact, Patty rarely even thought about what her own needs might be.

On the other hand, while Daniel took a helpless *child* role with Marion, Marion took a *martyr* role. Like Patty in her relationship with Jay, Marion also put her partner's needs before her own. However, Marion was not only very clear about her own needs, but communicated to Daniel in indirect ways that she was in fact sacrificing those needs for him. The message was that he should therefore be grateful or feel indebted to her—which he did.

Marion and Daniel had additional roles involving Daniel's drinking: Daniel was the alcoholic, Marion the enabler or coalcoholic. Marion reluctantly provided the excuses to Daniel's boss when he was too hung over to go to work; she hunted till she found Daniel's hidden stash of whiskey bottles and poured them down the sink; she kept the household running and took care of the kids.

Typical Couple Systems

Although there are as many different systems as there are couples, there are also a few common systems that are seen over and over again.

Pursuer-distancer. Jason and Ashley are a typical pursuer-distancer couple. Jason, the *pursuer*, consistently wants to spend more time with Ashley sharing activities, talking about feelings and the relationship, and having sex. Ashley, the *distancer*, wants more privacy, more autonomy, and more time for the pursuit of independent activities. The more Jason pursues, feeling somewhat deprived and abandoned, the more Ashley distances, feeling somewhat suffocated and overwhelmed. And the more she distances, the more he pursues. Meanwhile the degree of intimacy between them remains at a fairly constant level.

Blamer-placater. Cassie and Rachel have been together for two years. Cassie, the *blamer*, regularly criticizes Rachel for her appearance, her behavior, her opinions. Rachel, the *placater*, wants to avoid conflict at all costs and so always makes the necessary accommodations. She is quick to accept responsibility for Cassie's displeasure and tries hard to "fix" her appearance, her behavior, and her opinions. Because Rachel accommodates to Cassie's criticisms, she positively reinforces Cassie's blaming style. And because Cassie temporarily stops blaming when Rachel accommodates, the accommodation is negatively reinforced. Thus the pattern is reinforced and homeostasis is maintained.

Overfunctioner-underfunctioner. There are myriad variations of this system. Katie and Paul are a typical example. Paul, 47, is a well-established attorney, while Katie is 29 and has never worked. Throughout the ten years of their marriage, Paul has lavishly provided Katie with everything she wanted, trying to keep her happy and occupied while his work demanded so much from him. Yet even after a long day at the office or in court, it's Paul more often than Katie who fixes dinner and he who briefly straightens the house before bed. Katie is too often tired out from some activity or other. More disturbing to Paul is Katie's behavior when they attend one of his many business functions. Katie flirts outrageously with everyone from city officials to retired judges to law clerks. She always apologizes profusely when Paul expresses his hurt, but somehow her behavior has never changed. One reason why this behavior has never changed is that it is subtly reinforced by Paul. Katie's relative youth and sexiness has always indirectly increased Paul's self-esteem. Although overtly upset and hurt by her flirting, Paul also experiences pride that Katie is his wife and has chosen to remain with him despite many younger potential suitors. In exchange, Paul is willing to work to take care of Katie and insure her happiness within the marriage. The more she flirts, the more his "manhood" is rewarded, and thus the more he indirectly rewards the flirting.

The following categories can be seen as specific subsets of the over-functioning-underfunctioning system.

1. *Child-parent.* Barbara is stable, responsible, perhaps a little martyred, while her husband, Larry, frequently acts like an irresponsible or irrepressible child. Larry "tries hard" but he just doesn't seem to understand. He doesn't remember to call when he and a colleague decide to have a few drinks after work and he is going to be home late for dinner. He forgets that they are invited to lunch at Barbara's parents' and instead spends the day playing golf with a friend. He invariably forgets Barbara's birthday and their anniversary. Barbara would never think of treating Larry with the lack of respect that she feels from him. Important dates are marked clearly in her calendar well in advance, and she does a great deal of caretaking to compensate for things Larry forgets or plain never thinks of doing.

By "picking up the slack" for Larry and treating him like a child, Barbara reinforces Larry's childish irresponsibility. Her attempts to model more responsible behavior by taking care of everything in fact maintain the behavior. At the same time, the feelings of moral righteousness that Barbara experiences, coupled with the occasional childlike spontaneity and gaiety that Larry brings to the relationship, positively reinforce Barbara's caretaking behavior.

2. *Alcoholic-enabler.* Couple systems are often built around the use of alcohol or some other substance. In Marion and Daniel's relationship,

there were cycles of well-defined drinking periods and nondrinking periods. Certain behaviors (fighting, having sex) only occurred during drinking periods, while others (talking about the children and their needs) only occurred while sober. Even though Marion earnestly wanted Daniel to stop drinking, she frequently behaved in ways that in fact helped maintain the drinking, such as making excuses to his boss when he was incapable of working.

3. *Sick person-caretaker.* Many couple systems are organized around one partner's physical illness or psychiatric disorder. Bruce had known about Deborah's headaches from the beginning of their relationship. He saw himself as a nurturing person and didn't wholeheartedly dislike the idea of his partner having a minor disability. Within a short time, their whole relationship seemed to become focused on Deborah's headaches. Certain behaviors triggered them and had to be avoided at all costs, others were risky but occasionally worth it. Fights usually had to stop when Deborah felt a headache coming on, often when she was in a losing position. Sometimes their lovemaking also fell prey to Deborah's headaches.

Despite his discomfort with these limitations, Bruce's view of himself as a nurturing person was bolstered and reinforced by her disability. Thus he continued to take care of her whenever necessary. Bruce's solicitous behavior in turn reinforced Deborah's headaches. Deborah's ability to avoid uncomfortable situations such as fights when plagued by a headache was also reinforcing. Though painful, this disability had great utility.

Time for Mastery
The assessment of your system will probably take one to two weeks.

Identifying Your System
To begin to identify your particular system, it's important to look for the areas in your relationship that seem characteristic. Look for areas that are not necessarily pleasant or enjoyable, but familiar. A "here we go again" feeling, as if you could substitute a tape or video for the real interaction, is a good indication that you're on the right track.

Circularity
Think about the last fight or frustrating interaction you had with your spouse or partner. Or think about the last time you said to yourself, "If only he or she would (or would not) _____" or "He or she is doing it again," and what the occasion was that prompted you to

think that. Write out what each of you said and did, trying to be as accurate and detailed as possible. Go back to the point in the interaction when things were just starting to be problematic and continue through the good time or recovery time until things are right back to the same problematic feelings or situation.

Now look over your description. Is it possible from what you've written to assign blame for starting the fight? If so, go back to the beginning of the interaction you've described and think about what could have preceded that "first" step. If this is difficult, see if your partner is willing to help by doing the exercise himself or herself and comparing notes with you. Once you can no longer assign blame, you should be able to draw an arrow from the end of your interaction to the beginning. Any familiarity you feel about the interaction you've just described is an indication of the repetitive, stable nature of your system. It is also the reason why your description should demonstrate a complete circle, ending at its starting point.

Now go over your description step-by-step and fill in how you and your partner were reacting emotionally at each point. What were the feelings that corresponded to each behavior? Again, get your partner's help if you need it.

You may find it difficult to identify the steps that lead from the end of one fight when things are feeling resolved and okay to the beginning of another conflict or problematic situation. The often invisible (and nonproblematic) steps in between are usually marked by changes in feelings linked to small, nondramatic behaviors. Remember Jason and Ashley? Imagine that, like Jason, you'd felt deprived and abandoned by your partner and you'd finally convinced her to spend more time with you. You agreed to see a movie the next night, and while sitting together in the dark, you noticed that she didn't take your hand. It wasn't a big deal and wasn't a problem, but it did register and leave a slightly sour taste in your mouth. You made love that night and it was very pleasurable, and when you got up in the morning you suggested a shower together. Your partner said no thanks. Again it wasn't a problem, but it added to the sour taste and predisposed you to react to other small signs of perceived rejection. Eventually you felt deprived and abandoned again.

Or remember Katie and Paul? Imagine that like Paul, you felt threatened by your partner's behavior and scared that she might leave you. After a big argument where you expressed your dismay at her behavior and she apologized and professed her love, you felt reassured and relaxed. Later that night, your old buddy called and before your partner handed you the phone she exchanged a quiet joke with him.

It wasn't a big deal, but your stomach did a little jump. In bed, the two of you assumed your "spoon" positions for a cuddle, and your partner was the first to move away. Not a problem, not even worth noticing really, but you did, and your anxiety quietly began to grow again. These are the tiny steps that contribute to the movement from one conflictual situation to another.

Using the information you gathered above, break down each step into the following format:

You

Behavior:
Feelings:

Your Partner

Behavior:
Feelings:

Repeat this format for each step until you reach the point where the cycle is just about to start over. Draw an arrow from that point on the chart right up to the beginning again. If that end point doesn't lead back to the beginning, then something's been left out. You need to look for the missing steps and fill them in.

Marcel and Louise had been living together for almost a year. Marcel, a successful salesman, was friendly and gregarious on the job. At home, he wanted nothing more than to spend his time with Louise, talking, watching TV, making love—or just hanging out together. Louise worked alone in her office, and after five she wanted to get out and socialize, to mix and to be with people. She felt somewhat suffocated by Marcel's desires, which were often voiced as demands, and filled many of her evening and weekend hours at the gym or with visits to friends and family. Marcel frequently felt abandoned and alone, waiting around for Louise to come home. Sometimes he wondered if this were the right relationship for him, but when he and Louise did get time together it was usually enjoyable. More often he wondered why Louise stayed with him since she wanted so little contact and intimacy. They went round and round trying to resolve this dilemma, but nothing ever seemed to change. Marcel described their interaction in this way:

Marcel's Example

Me

Behavior: I overhear Louise telling someone on the phone that she would see him (?) in half an hour—her third night out so far this week. "You're going out again?"

Feelings: A little bereft already—I haven't seen Louise other than in bed or at the breakfast table in days.

Louise

Behavior: "Yeah, I'm meeting Janice for a quick drink. Won't be long."

Feelings: Probably happy to be going.

Me

Behavior: In a somewhat complaining tone: "I never see you these days—you've got time for everyone but me."

Feelings: Hurt and a little pissed off.

Louise

Behavior: "Oh, come off it—don't start with me. I'm just meeting Janice for a drink, not going away for a week."

Feelings: Frustrated. Probably thinks I'm a demanding bastard.

Me

Behavior: "Well, for all I see you, you might as well be going for a week."

Feelings: More pissed off.

Louise

Behavior: "Look, if you're not happy with our relationship, why don't you just say so. You're always implying that what I'm doing is wrong, that I shouldn't see my friends or family or workout or anything. Jesus, what are you looking for—a Siamese twin?"

Feelings: Defensive and angry.

Me

Behavior: Muttering: "Not you, that's for sure." Louder: "Why don't you just go and leave me alone."

Feelings: I don't know—angry, scared, lonely.

Louise

Behavior: "Fine!" And she storms off.

Feelings: Who knows.

We didn't see each other that night; I went to bed early, feeling frustrated and angry, and was already asleep when Louise got in. The next morning we took our coffee to the table in silence.

Me

Behavior: I try to sound normal. "So how's Janice doing?"
Feelings: Wanting to smooth things out between us.

Louise

Behavior: She sounds cool. "She's fine."
Feelings: I guess still upset with me, keeping her distance.

Me

Behavior: "Look I'm sorry for overreacting last night. I was really a jerk."
Feelings: A little anxious, wanting things to be okay between us.

Louise

Behavior: "I know, but it's okay. Forget it." She smiles, somewhat warmly.
Feelings: Forgiving.

We both left for work, and that night Louise seemed to make a point of staying home and just hanging out. We lay on the couch in the living room, reading, separate but connected.

Me

Behavior: Stroking her hair.
Feelings: Excited, thinking about making love later.

Louise

Behavior: Keeps reading.
Feelings: I don't know. She seems pretty relaxed.

Me

Behavior: "What's say we fool around for a while?"
Feelings: Hopeful, cautious.

Louise

Behavior: "Not tonight. Let's just read."
Feelings: A little irritated.

Me

Behavior: "How about just some cuddling?"
Feelings: Deprived and alone. Hurt.

Louise

Behavior: "I'm tired. I just want to space out."

Feelings: I guess tired. Certainly irritated.

Me

Behavior: "I thought that was the point of staying home tonight. I can't even remember the last time we made love."
Feelings: Disappointed and hurt.

Louise

Behavior: "Give it a rest, Marcel."
Feelings: Frustrated.

Me

Behavior: "Okay, okay." Deciding to button my lip and try to enjoy the time together.
Feelings: Determined not to bug Louise again. But feeling a growing desperation.

Here Marcel drew an arrow to the beginning of his description—a cycle.

Homeostasis

It's essential to determine how your behaviors are reinforcing your partner's behaviors in the service of maintaining homeostasis. Look over your description of behaviors and feelings. Find and mark the points in the sequence where your behavior either validates your partner's fears or anxieties, making those responses more likely, or reinforces your partner's behavior either positively (by giving a direct reward such as forgiveness and intimacy after a fight) or negatively (your partner's response blocks pain triggered by your behavior).

Validation. Marcel looked over his description. He recognized that each time he complained about not seeing Louise enough or making love enough, he validated the perception that he assumed Louise had of him as demanding and never satisfied. And each time Louise went out or seemed to withdraw from intimacy, Marcel's fears of being unloved and abandoned were validated.

Reinforcement. Marcel knew that his demanding behavior was painful for Louise and made her feel suffocated and engulfed. Staying away or going out was negatively reinforced because it helped her escape the pain. He also knew that Louise's withdrawal was extremely painful for him and that his angry responses to the withdrawal were also negatively reinforced because they temporarily made him feel less helpless and hurt. As a result of these patterns of reinforcement, the homeostasis of the system was maintained.

Roles

Think about the roles you play consistently in your relationship. Look at the following checklist. Go down the list and mark with an X those roles that apply to you in your relationship. Have your partner mark with a Y those roles that apply to him or her. Remember that you may each play more than one role in your relationship.

Pursuer: wants more closeness and intimacy.

Distancer: wants more space and separateness.

Blamer: finds fault, criticizes.

Placater: accepts responsibility, placates.

Overfunctioner: takes excessive responsibility for the relationship and all its related tasks.

1. Parent: overresponsible, parental.

2. Martyr: overresponsible, guilt-inducing.

3. Enabler: overresponsible, allows alcoholic behavior.

4. Caretaker: overresponsible, nurturing.

Underfunctioner: takes minimum responsibility for the relationship and all its related tasks.

Child: irresponsible, carefree.

Alcoholic: underfunctions due to alcohol consumption.

Sick person: underfunctions due to physical or psychiatric illness.

This next exercise will help you evaluate the consequences of living these roles. Answer the following questions.

1. What behaviors does your role prevent you from engaging in?

_____

_____

_____

_____

2. What feelings does your role prevent you from experiencing or expressing?

_____

_____

_____

3. What needs does your role prevent you from meeting or expressing?

_____

_____

_____

_____

Marcel identified himself as primarily playing the pursuer role in his relationship with Louise. He made the following list:

1. What behaviors does the pursuer role prevent me from engaging in?

    Making plans for myself or with my own friends. I'm too busy waiting around for Louise to come home in case she has time for me.

    Withdrawing. Developing personal interests.

    Relaxing. I'm always on edge, waiting and wondering.

2. What feelings does the pursuer role prevent me from experiencing or expressing:?

    Comfort. I'm always uptight about when I'm going to see Louise next, or when I'm with her, how long we're going to have before she goes off.

    Anticipation. I can't let her know how much I'm hoping to see her and therefore how disappointed I get when she goes out.

3. What needs does the pursuer role prevent me from meeting or expressing?

    To have my own privacy. I'm always making myself available in case Louise has time for me.

    To develop myself personally. I don't even know in what ways, but I know all I do is hang around waiting.

    To develop my own relationships with friends or family.

Remember Marion and Daniel? Daniel was an alcoholic, clearly an underfunctioner. Marion took responsibility for the relationship, put Daniel's needs before her own, and highlighted the sacrifices she was making. It was difficult and embarrassing for her to acknowledge even to herself that her roles were those of martyr and enabler, both examples of overfunctioning. Marion's list included the following:

1. What behaviors do the martyr and enabler roles prevent me from engaging in because of my martyr and enabler roles?

Relaxing. There's too much to do.

Going to friends' houses for dinner with Daniel. I always worry about Daniel drinking too much.

Having big holiday dinners (at Christmas, Thanksgiving). I always worry about Daniel's drinking.

Going out dancing with Daniel. I worry about his drinking.

In fact going out anywhere or doing anything with Daniel where there might be alcohol.

2. What feelings do the martyr and enabler roles prevent me from experiencing or expressing?

Sadness. I feel weak and uncomfortable.

Anger. I'm afraid he'll use that as an excuse to go off and drink more.

Happiness. I don't really ever feel happy, I'm always anxious or preoccupied.

3. What needs do the martyr and enabler roles prevent me from meeting or expressing?

To not have to worry about Daniel for a change and focus on me.

To enjoy Daniel's company without anxiety or judgment.

To have more contact with my family. I'm too focused on the day-to-day problems to focus on planning a vacation to see them.

To further my education. To go back to school for my Masters degree. I'm too afraid that the household would fall apart if I were away at classes.

If you've been stuck in your role(s) for a long time, you may have difficulty with this exercise. It may be hard to identify what you want to do or what you need. Imagine the ideal relationship, where you're relieved of your role(s). What could you do then that you can't do now? What could you express that you can't express now? What needs might you consider meeting that you wouldn't consider now? Go back to the list above and complete the exercise.

Special Considerations

It's understandable that the fastest and easiest changes in a relationship occur when both partners participate in the work. But given the nature of systems, if you make changes in your behaviors, the relationship will inevitably change. There are situations, however, when it's essential that rather than attempt to do the work alone, you seek professional help from a trained couples therapist. If your relationship contains any physical violence or abuse, trying to change the system on your own can be dangerous.

Now that you've identified the particular patterns that characterize your relationship, you need to focus on changing those patterns. Knowing how your behavior affects your partner doesn't mean you can simply stop behaving in those ways. Recognizing the limitations of the role(s) you hold, doesn't mean you can simply take on a different role. Realizing the pull toward homeostasis doesn't mean you can automatically resist it. The next chapter will provide you with the tools you need to intervene in your system and make the desired changes in your relationship.

16

Intervening in Your System

Identifying your system doesn't necessarily help you change that system. There is nothing automatic about the step from identification to intervention. It will take a committed effort at doing the exercises in this chapter for real systemic change to occur.

Each partner is 100 percent responsible for the couple system. You are behaving in ways that keep it running and keep your interactions going in circles. If you don't take *full* responsibility for your part in maintaining the system, nothing will change. Waiting to see if your partner is going to change before committing yourself to change won't work. Forget what your partner does or should do. You have no control over that. All you can control is your own behavior; all you can change is yourself.

You are personally responsible for changing your responses that keep the system spinning, that keep the same painful pattern coming around again and again. Unless you take full responsibility for changing your behavior, the outcome of your patterns won't change. If you don't like the way an interaction is heading, it's entirely up to you to do something different that will alter the outcome.

Time for Mastery

It will take you less than a week to develop your strategy for intervening in your system. How long it takes for changes to occur depends on how consistently you stick to your strategy. A committed approach should bring some noticeable changes within two-to-eight weeks.

Breaking the Circle

As you learned in the previous chapter, your system is an endless circle of interactions with no defined beginning or end. Changes made at any point in the cycle affect the path of the circle from there on and lead to a different outcome. However, there are certain places in any interaction where it's easier to intervene than others. These places are the "weak links" in the system. They usually occur (1) early in the cycle before much pressure has built toward the next problematic interaction, (2) at a point where your behavior isn't yet highly defensive or aggressive, and (3) where your behavior is clearly reinforcing an unwanted response from your partner.

When you've identified a weak link in your system, here are the guidelines for intervening:

1. Stop doing what you're doing. A different behavioral response at this point has the potential for changing the entire outcome of the interaction. Although there's no guarantee that new behavior will succeed in producing the change you'd like, it's certain that the same old behavior won't alter anything.

2. Describe your feelings and needs using *whole messages* (see chapter 4). Talk about what hurts and what you want directly, without blaming, attacking, or shutting down. Identify any aversive strategies you are using at this point in the cycle (see chapter 8). Then script out, in advance, *whole messages* to replace aversive behavior.

3. Reinforce *new* **behavior.** You want your partner to change—but your current strategy isn't working. That's because what you're doing right now *reinforces* the unwanted behavior. Your job at this point is to think of ways to reinforce the behavior you want, rather than the old cycle. Positive reinforcement includes praise, affection, expressions of appreciation, help, and encouragement—anything that feels rewarding to your partner.

4. Describe your couple system (optional). Tell your partner about your cycle of response, how you both keep ending up back at the beginning. Explain that no one is at fault, that each of you copes in ways that trigger unwanted behavior in the other. Neither of you is bad or wrong; you're just trapped. Note: if this gets a negative response from your partner, drop it. Try negotiation instead.

5. Negotiate new solutions (optional). Each of you has different and sometimes conflicting needs. These needs are at the root of repeated behavior that keeps your cycle going. You and your partner have *equally valid needs*. No one's needs are better or bigger—just different. The principle of equally valid needs is the key to successful negotiation. When you accept that your partner has a right to his or her needs, then you can work toward solutions that feel comfortable to both of you. Chapter 6 on negotiation will help you develop specific strategies.

Let's look at how these guidelines apply to some couple systems.

Remember Barbara and Larry? They had an overfunctioner-underfunctioner relationship. Barbara was the overfunctioner. She made all the social arrangements for the two of them (often without consulting Larry), marked the dates clearly in her calendar, and took care of any planning that had to be done. She never forgot her appointments and called in the unlikely event that she was late or her plans changed. Barbara felt hurt and unsupported and very alone in the relationship. Larry, the underfunctioner, had a "bad memory": he forgot arrangements he made with Barbara, he forgot her birthday and their anniversary, he forgot to call when he was going to be late for dinner. He forgot to call his parents on their birthdays too. He spontaneously suggested activities and was disappointed when Barbara pointed out the conflict with already scheduled events. He felt stifled and powerless in the face of Barbara's tendency to make plans without consulting him.

The more irresponsibly Larry behaved, the more hurt and alone Barbara felt, and the more she attempted to fix things by reminding and nagging him about his responsibilities. The more Barbara nagged and reminded Larry, the more he felt belittled and infantilized, and the less he seemed to remember. Barbara felt more and more hurt and alone; Larry felt more and more powerless and infantilized.

Eventually, a big confrontation followed. Barbara decided to make plans for herself that didn't require Larry's participation. She felt even more alone and angry. Larry felt guilty and compensated by becoming more focussed on the relationship and less forgetful. With the extra attention, Barbara's hopes and expectations rose and she again took on her role as social director, making plans for the two of them without consulting Larry. Larry felt powerless again and promptly developed a poor memory—and the cycle continued.

Barbara and Larry's system looked like this:

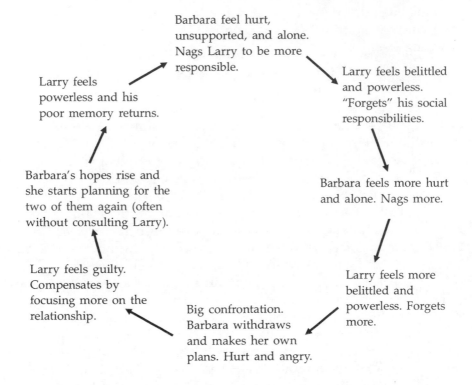

Larry identified his weak link as occurring when he first became aware that Barbara had planned something without consulting him. At this point, little pressure had built up for him, his behavior wasn't highly defensive or aggressive (or in his case, passive-aggressive), and his "forgetting" tended to reinforce Barbara's nagging response.

Barbara identified her weak link as occurring the first time Larry forgot something important to her. At this point, it was early enough in the cycle before she was too frustrated and angry, her behavior wasn't yet highly aggressive, and her nagging reminders reinforced Larry to escape by rebelling and forgetting her plans.

Larry decided to use the five guidelines to intervene in the system.

1. He made a commitment to himself to recognize and stop the old behavior of saying nothing but forgetting the event.

2. He developed a script in advance in which he told Barbara his feelings and needs in a whole message: "Barbara, you made this dinner

date for us with Gary and Linda without checking with me first. When you make plans for the two of us without consulting me, I feel left out. And I feel belittled by your constant reminders about those plans. I want to be a full partner in this relationship and participate in all the planning. So I'd like you to make only tentative plans until you can talk to me. I have no objection to your making your own plans without expecting me to join you."

3. Larry decided to reinforce Barbara's new behavior by listening attentively, thanking her for checking with him, and by honestly considering whether he wanted to participate in the activity. If he agreed to attend, he would write a note in his calendar, and then he would attend (he never missed work appointments when he'd written them in his calendar). If he decided he didn't want to do something, he would say so clearly. Then Barbara would have the opportunity to make plans of her own, independent of Larry.

4. Larry and Barbara had agreed to work together on intervening in their system so there wasn't a need for him to describe the system to her.

5. Larry told Barbara that he was willing to negotiate for new solutions.

Barbara settled on her own approach to the five guidelines.

1. She made a commitment to stop reminding and nagging Larry about plans they had or responsibilities of his.

2. She developed a script of her feelings and needs to tell Larry. "Larry, we had plans to visit my sister tonight at 6:30, and it's now 8:00. You're only just getting home—I guess you forgot. I feel really hurt and alone when you forget the plans we have, especially when they're important to me. I need you to follow through with any plans we make, otherwise I'll make plans for myself that won't include you."

3. Barbara had difficulty deciding how to reinforce Larry's new behavior. Just saying thank you when he behaved more responsibly and showed up to an event or remembered a special occasion didn't seem like enough. But she worried that promising Larry something positive at those times felt like more of the same pattern of her being in charge. So she also decided to negotiate with him.

4. Because Barbara and Larry were working together on their system, neither felt the need to describe that system to the other.

5. Barbara initiated a negotiation session after identifying some conflicting needs: Larry wanted to be consulted whenever Barbara made joint plans, but sometimes a decision had to be made immediately, before she had time to check with him. As a secondary issue, Barbara wanted to address her concern that trying to reinforce respon-

sible behavior might conflict with her desire to help Larry feel more powerful in the relationship.

Each wrote out their needs and some possible solutions. After some discussion, the following agreements were made:

a. Barbara would consult with Larry before making plans, and if a decision had to be made on short notice, she would simply say no (or accept for herself only).

b. An exception to this could occur if Barbara had previously talked to Larry about the possibility of some event and he had expressed enthusiasm.

c. If Barbara made a plan without consulting Larry, he would politely decline to attend that event.

d. When Larry remembered and followed through with his responsibilities, Barbara would reinforce Larry with a sincere "thank you" and a hug.

e. If Larry hadn't initiated plans for her birthday or their anniversary (or other special holidays) at least two days before the date, Barbara would make plans for herself with her own friends or family.

Bob and Amanda had a blamer-placater system. Bob, the blamer, regularly criticized Amanda's appearance, her behavior, her opinions. He particularly disliked the way Amanda behaved when they were with friends and didn't hesitate to tell her. He felt disappointed and frustrated that Amanda didn't seem to learn from his advice and interpreted her behavior as reflecting a lack of respect for his feelings and desires. This in turn triggered feelings of unworthiness.

Amanda, the placater, wanted to avoid conflict at all costs and was quick to accept responsibility for Bob's displeasure. She apologized frequently, promised to try harder, and reassured Bob that she'd improve. But she felt hurt and rejected in response to his criticism, and, though her intentions were good, she forgot from one time to the next what Bob wanted from her. Or she'd promise compliance but not really intend to change. Sometimes she would even deliberately ignore him until he was really upset.

When Bob saw Amanda doing or saying the exact same thing that he'd told her not to, his feelings of frustration and unworthiness mounted and he escalated his blaming and criticism ("I just told you that I hate it when you talk about Astrology, and there you go asking people's signs again"). Amanda's placating increased, as did her feelings of hurt and rejection—but very little of her behavior changed. Eventually Bob would blow up, and a big confrontation would ensue ("I can't believe I've told you a million times and you're still spouting these inane astrological interpretations of our friends' lives!"). Amanda cried, promised to stop, and told Bob that maybe she wasn't the right woman for him. Bob, feeling guilty, attempted to compensate by being nice and complimentary to Amanda. Feeling only a little mollified, Amanda withdrew and paid less attention to Bob. And the cycle began again.

Using a diagram, Bob and Amanda's system looked like this:

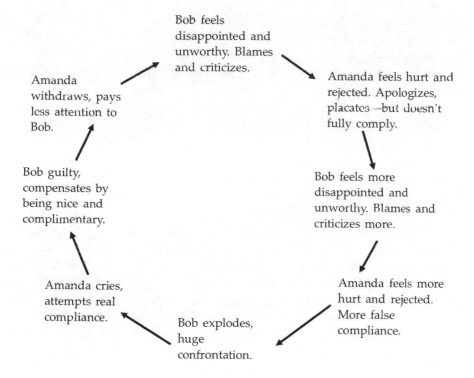

Amanda identified her weak link early in the cycle, when Bob first criticized or blamed her and she felt hurt and rejected. At this early stage, little pressure had built for Amanda, her behavior hadn't become highly defensive, and her placating behavior positively reinforced Bob's blaming and criticizing.

Bob's weak link also occurred very early in the cycle. This was when he first felt disappointed and frustrated that Amanda's behavior wasn't appropriate and interpreted her continued behavior as reflecting a lack of respect. This is the point at which there was little explosive pressure built up for him, his behavior wasn't yet highly aggressive, and Amanda's placating behavior was negatively reinforced by Bob's response of temporarily stopping the blaming and criticizing.

Bob and Amanda decided to use the five guidelines for intervening in their system. Amanda used the guidelines in the following way:

1. She made a commitment to herself to recognize and stop her old placating behavior.

2. She wrote out a script in which she told Bob her feelings and needs in a whole message. It went like this: "Bob, you sound angry and blaming. I guess you're unhappy about my behavior. But when you criticize me I feel hurt and rejected. I would like you to tell me what you want from me in less blaming ways. If the blaming doesn't stop, I'll politely withdraw from the conversation until it does."

3. Amanda decided that if Bob were willing to tell her what he wanted without blaming she would reinforce him by listening attentively, thanking him, and giving his request serious consideration rather than lip service.

4. She described their system in the following way: "When you don't like what I'm doing and begin blaming, I feel hurt and rejected. Because I want to avoid conflict, I'm willing to agree with whatever you say, take the blame, reassure you that I'll change, whatever. But really I resist you because of how the blaming makes me feel. You get frustrated when I don't do what I've promised to do, and so you start blaming again. We seem stuck in that cycle. Neither of us is at fault, we just cope with our feelings in ways that don't seem to work for us. You cope with feelings of frustration, lack of respect and unworthiness by blaming; I cope with feeling hurt and rejected by making promises I don't keep. Neither of us is bad or wrong, we're just trapped."

5. Amanda wasn't willing to negotiate around the blaming, critical behavior. But she was willing to negotiate for new solutions if Bob's nonattacking requests seemed reasonable.

Bob used the guidelines also.

1. He made a commitment to himself to recognize and stop his blaming, critical behavior.

2. The process of scripting a whole message was painful for Bob because he suspected that many of the things he said to or asked of Amanda were not appropriate. How she dressed and the opinions she expressed were reflections of her taste, and he really didn't have the right to criticize them. He looked for ways to say what he felt without blaming and making her wrong. "When you wear tie-dyed jeans to a

dinner party, I think it doesn't really fit the occasion. Then I feel embarrassed, like people must think we have no sense of what's appropriate. It's terribly uncomfortable for me, and I wish you'd agree to change even if you think I'm being silly ... To be really honest, I'd rather skip the party than feel this uncomfortable."

3. Bob decided to reinforce Amanda's agreement by commenting positively on any outfit that seemed remotely appropriate and thanking her for going along with him. Amanda was always responsive to neck rubs, so he also decided to try that too.

4. Bob and Amanda had already discussed their system together.

5. Bob was willing to negotiate new solutions if it seemed necessary.

Now it's time to return to the diagram you drew of your own couple system in the previous chapter. The first step is to identify your weak links. Find the point that's early in the cycle where you are first aware of painful feelings but feel little pressure to explode, where you're not behaving in a highly defensive or aggressive way and your behavior is reinforcing an unwanted response from your partner. Put an asterisk at that point on the diagram.

Intervention Plan

Using the five guidelines described above, develop your intervention plan.

1. *Stopping.* Write here the behavior you plan to stop and the situations where you'll have to watch for it.

_____

_____

_____

_____

2. *Whole messages.* Develop your whole message using the four components:

Your observations (objective facts):_____

_____

_____

Your thoughts and opinions: _____

_____

Your feelings ("I" messages): _____

_____

Your needs (specific behavioral changes): _____

_____

_____

_____

_____

3. *Reinforce new behavior.* Write your strategy for reinforcing new behaviors for your partner. _____

_____

_____

_____

_____

4. *Describe system.* Describe your system in nonblaming ways. _____

_____

_____

_____

_____

5. Negotiate equally valid needs.

His/her need: _____

_____

My need: _____

_____

Possible solution: _____

_____

Fighting Homeostasis

Homeostasis refers to the tendency for systems to remain stable and to resist change. This is what gives rise to the feeling of "here we go again." You will already be experimenting with new and different behaviors as a result of the previous section. These different behaviors will on their own begin to alter the usual interactional patterns which you and your partner have established. At the same time, you may be experiencing a pull to return to the old familiar patterns, or you may find your partner "upping the ante" in an attempt to retain the old system. It's tremendously important now to consistently resist this pull.

When you try to change your system, and it isn't working, the force of homeostasis is getting in the way. Perhaps you are somehow validating your partner's negative expectations about you, your new strategy to change the system is still reinforcing your partner's old behavior, or something else you're doing is still reinforcing your partner's old responses.

Validation

Your system got established at the beginning of your relationship. It's been around awhile. There have been dozens, perhaps even hundreds of experiences that have led your partner to expect certain things of you. Those negative expectations won't change overnight. Even though you've started to intervene in the system, it will take your partner time to recognize that you have changed. Meanwhile, your partner may react as if nothing is different. He or she may present you with the same painful responses.

There are two things you should do while your partner is still reacting to old expectations:

1. Be consistent. Stick with the new strategies you've developed to change the cycle. Try not to let your partner's expectations and reactions discourage you. It may take weeks, maybe even several months, for your new behavior to finally sink in and be noticed by your partner. Pointing out your new behavior might also help, but the impact will be far more significant if your partner figures it out him or herself.

2. Surprise your partner. Plan to do something different from what your partner expects. Say yes when your partner expects you to say no (and vice versa), suggest an outing when your partner expects to have to initiate activities, offer to help when your partner expects you to avoid effort, and so on.

Patrick recognized his tendency to react negatively when reminded of his and Allie's social obligations. He realized that this tendency validated Allie's ongoing fears of him backing out of these obligations at the last minute, leaving her to attend alone. He decided to try expressing himself differently next time the opportunity arose. Sure enough, the following week Allie reminded him of a fundraising dinner they'd promised to attend. Patrick was immediately aware of his disappointment and irritation, but he also noticed Allie's face go tight with expectation and knew that this was his opportunity.

"Well, I'm really tired and would prefer to just hang out this evening, but I know how important it is to you, so of course I'll go," he started.

"Look, if it's such a sacrifice for you, don't bother," retorted Allie.

Patrick realized that Allie had been so caught up in her own expectations that she didn't really hear what he'd said and was responding in the same old way as if he'd also said the same old things. He was tempted to just say "Forget it," but instead persevered.

"Allie, look, I'm happy to go with you. In fact it's because I love you that I'm happy to go; I was just telling you how I'm feeling and I happen to be tired."

Although Allie was still a little suspicious, it was an excellent start, and their usual conflict was almost entirely avoided.

Reinforcement

Your new strategy, or some other old behavior, may still be reinforcing your partner to respond in traditional ways. Here's what you can do:

1. Check reinforcers. Reinforcement can take the form of rewards: an apology, an offer of compromise, a moment of closeness. Notice if you are doing anything, either immediately before or right after your partner's unwanted behavior, that may function as a reward.

It's also important to look for negative reinforcement. Are you still doing something that causes your partner pain? And has he or she learned to limit that pain with a response that you don't like?

Larry and Barbara were right in the middle of their familiar cycle. Larry was being his usual absentminded self, forgetting their social appointments; Barbara was frustrated after efforts to change the system by leaving reminder notes in Larry's appointment book. She had started consulting with Larry before making any joint plans and had stopped nagging at him, but she was anxious that he would still forget. Barbara began to realize that these reminders must somehow be reinforcing

Larry's behavior, because the more of them she stuck in Larry's appointment book, the worse he became. Almost invariably they fell out or he forgot to read them.

Pressuring Larry reinforced his passive avoidance response. If things were going to change, Barbara would have to either consult with Larry and then trust that he would remember and show up or make plans for herself and simply invite him along with no expectations. The following week, Barbara mentioned in passing that she was going to a work party that Friday, and if he'd care to join her she'd love his company. As it turned out, Larry didn't "remember" to join her for that event. But he did remember to show up for the dinner he'd agreed to have with their friends. And eventually, without pressure or negative expectations, Larry began remembering even the "optional" events better.

2. Ask your partner. Sometimes the direct methods are the best. Ask your partner how your new strategy works for him or her. If Barbara had asked Larry, she'd have learned that her reminder notes were extremely annoying. He felt like scraping them out of his appointment book as soon as they appeared. He had to keep lifting them up to read his "real" appointments. And they still made him feel controlled, like a kid getting a thousand cautionary instructions from his mom before he left for school.

Another question you might try is this: "I know you're doing ___ _____ because of something I'm doing and how that makes you feel. Can you tell me what I'm doing that triggers your response?" The answer could be very enlightening. If not, try this follow-up question: "How do you feel just before you _____ _____?" If the feeling is a negative one, find out if your behavior in any way triggers it.

3. Negotiate a new solution. Here you go back to step five in the intervention guidelines. Identify your conflicting needs in the situation, then negotiate a solution that incorporates aspects of those needs.

Jon and Claudia were caught in their respective pursuer-distancer roles. Jon had identified his weak link as occurring early in the cycle when he was beginning to feel abandoned. This was the point where he started making requests-that-sounded-like-demands of Claudia that they spend more time together. He had decided instead to tell Claudia that he missed her and ask her when she thought they might have some time together. Claudia had identified her weak link as the moment before she responded to Jon's demands by becoming distant and evasive. She had decided instead to tell Jon that she felt resentful of his demands, but to try anyway to suggest a time they could spend together. Jon had his own business as a consultant and could make his own schedule, usually working between 30 and 35 hours a week. He had plenty of leisure time and went to the gym, to the library, and watched a lot of videos. Because Claudia was taking classes two nights a week, her leisure time was limited. And she was actively engaged in several social pursuits in which Jon had little interest. But she worked at containing her frustration with Jon's demands, and tried to come up with some reasonable suggestions. The problem arose when Claudia's suggestions were consistently met by disappointment from Jon. His disappointment felt like pressure to Claudia, who felt more resentful and resistant.

Finally Jon suggested they try to negotiate a new solution. They clarified their conflicting needs—Jon wanted more time with Claudia; Claudia wanted more time to pursue independent interests. Each validated the other's needs as important, and compared possible solutions. Jon's optimal solution was that Claudia set aside three evenings and both weekend days each week to spend with him. Claudia suggested that they plan on one evening during the week, one full weekend day and that Jon accompany Claudia to one of her social events. Their compromise solution was to spend two evenings during the week as well as one full weekend day. In addition, Jon could accompany Claudia to her reading group on Thursday evenings if he chose. They agreed to talk briefly on Sunday nights to schedule the upcoming week. Once Jon knew exactly when he was going to see Claudia he was able to relax and plan how to fill the rest of his leisure time. He did occasionally feel lonely, but he knew when he would see Claudia and knew also that he could always go to her reading group if he needed a dose of her before their next scheduled date. Claudia felt some stress trying to fit all her activities into her now more limited free time. But she felt much less pressure from Jon; in fact, now that he'd stopped bugging her about more time together, she was able to enjoy their time together more than she had in a long time. She even began thinking that perhaps on her summer break they could spend a week camping in the mountains together.

Roles

When the circularity of your system isn't clear, but you can identify your role, you can experiment with changing it. The first step is to think of what a new role would be: not simply the opposite of where you are now, but somewhere along a continuum of responses. It will help to look at the three lists you developed in the previous chapter describing the behaviors, feelings, and needs that are being suppressed by the old role. Look at what you would be doing and expressing more of if you gave up this role for the new one. Think of a phrase that describes this new role. For example, if you've been the "caretaker" in your relationship, a new role might involve being "selectively selfish" (as opposed to being totally selfish). An alternative to "pursuer" might be "somewhat self-sufficient" (not "distancer"); "overfunctioner" might change to "selectively self-focused" or "selectively dependent" (not "underfunctioner"); a "placater" might try to become "assertive." Look again at the lists you created in the previous chapter. Cross out the questions at the top of each list and replace them with these new headings. Replace "What behaviors does my role prevent me from engaging in?" with "What behaviors will my new role allow me to engage in?" Replace "What feelings does my role prevent me from experiencing or expressing?" with "What feelings will my new role allow me to express?" And replace "What needs does my role prevent me from meeting and expressing" with "What needs will my new role allow me to express or meet?" Notice that each of the items involves action—doing something, expressing your feelings, or asking for what you want. If any of the items on your list aren't in action form, rewrite them now so they require you to say or do something differently. For example, under the needs list, you might have noted, "Want help with house maintenance tasks." To convert that to an action statement, write specifically what you're going to *do*: "Ask Bill to help me with the shopping and the vacuuming." "Don't get to feel vulnerable" might be rewritten as "Tell John I'm lonely when he goes on business trips." "Want to be more spontaneous" could be converted into "Suggest to Carol that we go out to dinner tonight instead of cooking."

Wanting something from your partner isn't enough to change your old role. You have to ask your partner for what you want. And you have to be specific enough so he or she knows exactly what you need.

Patty, a caretaker in her relationship with Jay, chose the alternative role of "selectively selfish." She realized that the items in her three lists would change dramatically in this new role. She wrote:

1. I would occasionally take time for myself, to have a bath, to read a book. I would occasionally order takeout instead of cooking (or maybe I would even ask Jay to cook once in a while?). I would ask Jay about getting a housecleaner in once a week to reduce my load.

2. I would admit to being tired—even if Jay were tired too. I could express anger or hurt or disappointment or anxiety when ap-

propriate, and if Jay had a hard time with those feelings, then
we'd have to work it out together.

3. I would be able to ask Jay to help more often. Specifically I'd
   ask him to help me fold the laundry and empty the dishwasher
   (which of course is no guarantee that he would).

She rewrote part of her list of feelings into action statements. "Express anger or hurt or disappointment or anxiety when appropriate"
became "tell Jay that I'm angry about the graffiti on our wall," "Tell
Jay that when he doesn't ask me how my day was, I feel hurt," "Tell
Jay that I'm disappointed about his decision not to visit my parents'
with me," and "Tell Jay that I'm scared sometimes when his business
meetings run so late."

Barbara chose "selectively self-focused" as her alternative to her
overfunctioning role with Larry. She noted the following changes in her
three lists.

1. I would make plans for attending certain events alone. I would
   plan to celebrate holidays and special occasions with my family
   or good friends if I hadn't heard from Larry ahead of time. I'd
   order takeout for myself rather than cooking. I might put a
   calendar on the fridge and mark important engagements on it—
   a good substitute for nagging.

2. I would be able to be happy when Larry chooses to participate
   with me, while knowing I'm going to have a good time anyway
   in his absence. I would be more serene when I have no plans,
   because I'm not dependent on Larry to have a good time when
   I do have plans.

3. I would take care of my need to celebrate important days the
   way I want to—with friends or family.

Barbara had to work on rewriting many of her items so that they
required direct action. Her rewritten list looked like this:

1. I would go to the ballet with Joan and the symphony with
   Pauline. I'd plan to celebrate my birthday and other special occasions with my friends or family if I hadn't heard from Larry
   at least two days before. I'd tell Larry that unless I hear from
   him each day that he'll be home for dinner, I probably won't
   cook an elaborate dinner, and may even order takeout. I'll put
   a calendar on the fridge and mark important engagements on
   it—but won't say anything verbally to Larry.

2. I'd tell Larry how happy I am when he chooses to participate with me, and zip my lip when he chooses not to. I'd tell him what a good time I've had when I've attended something in his absence. I'd tell Larry my desire not to be dependent on him for having a good time, and tell him when I've had fun just hanging out at home alone.

3. I would tell Larry my decision about spending special occasions with family and friends unless he tells me at least two days ahead that he wants to celebrate with me.

Ben, the placater in his relationship with Michele, chose "assertive" as his alternative role. His three revised lists included the following items:

1. I would give Michele an honest opinion of her reports when she asks me to review them. I would tell her that I disagree with her parents' political position—and express my own. I would absolutely stop apologizing whenever things don't work out the way Michele wants. I would leave my clothes exactly where I want to when I take them off.

2. I would tell Michele that I don't like it when she blames and criticizes me—that it hurts my feelings and pisses me off. I would tell her when I'm frustrated at work (and if she criticizes, tell her again that I don't like it).

3. I would ask Michele what she likes about me and why she's with me. I would tell her that I'm going to politely withdraw from the conversation whenever she starts blaming or criticizing—and then do it.

Before launching into these changes, it's essential that you recognize that you might meet with resistance from your partner. The nature of homeostasis, as described previously, implies that there will be a pull to revert to the same old behaviors. The pull may be in the form of an escalation of your partner's old behaviors or subtle suggestions that you should feel guilty for "abandoning" your partner. Although changes are uncomfortable, the short-term discomfort will be far outweighed by the long-term benefits of a healthier, more intimate relationship. You might consider talking with your partner about your decisions with respect to changing your role and letting him or her know ahead of time what kinds of changes might be expected. Use your skills for clean communication so that your partner doesn't feel criticized by your decision to make changes. Try problem-solving techniques on any potential issues that either of you think might arise.

One day at a time. Now, after identifying the new behaviors that go with your new role, it's time to put them into effect. Each day, choose one item from your three lists to actually carry out. Start with what feels easiest, then work up from there. Try to have implemented at least one item from *each* of your lists by the end of the first week. And from now on, each morning make a deliberate plan to act—at least once that day—based on your *new* role. This should be an ongoing commitment.

Patty felt very anxious the first time she told Jay she was tired and asked him to help out with dinner. She was hyperalert for signs of his disapproval and was enormously relieved when, after a surprised pause, he agreed—and helped! The following evening, she prepared dinner and got the kids off to bed. But this time, instead of keeping Jay company while he relaxed in front of the TV, she relaxed in a hot bath with a book and a recording of Beethoven's sixth symphony. Although he didn't overtly complain, Patty could almost see Jay's raised eyebrows when she acted "out of character." She explained as best she could her decisions about taking better care of herself rather than focusing solely on him. Although he truly loved Patty and wanted to be supportive, Jay had to struggle with his discomfort over the diminished attention he received from her. Patty, on her part, had to struggle not to give up her stance when Jay whined a little or was clearly disappointed in her lessened accessibility. On occasion she did give up her needs, and that was okay too.

Barbara told Larry that she wasn't going to bother cooking unless he informed her ahead of time that he was going to be home for dinner. She was anxious that day when she realized that she was going to have to follow through with her decision. When Larry got home from work that night at nine o'clock Barbara was in her pyjamas watching a video. She said a quick hi and resumed watching. When Larry asked about dinner, Barbara took a deep breath and calmly stated, "There are leftovers from last night, or salad fixings if you'd prefer. I really wasn't hungry." Larry's disappointed expression was a little painful, but Barbara was proud of herself for resisting. And she enjoyed watching the movie—even alone!

Ben decided to tell Michele that he didn't like it when she blamed or criticized him, that he felt hurt and pissed off, and that it didn't seem helpful either to him or to them as a couple. It didn't seem like the easiest task on his lists, but it seemed like one of the most important. That evening he had his opportunity. Michele was paying some household bills and reconciling the checkbook from the joint account. There were some entries missing. She turned to Ben and complained, "I wish you'd take more responsibility with entering the checks you write. I can't believe you managed to stay solvent all those years on your own if this is any indication of your financial skills."

Ben caught himself preparing to apologize and stopped. He knew he hadn't written any checks from the joint account since Michele had last reconciled it. He took a breath and said, "I really don't like it when you automatically blame me for the missing checks. It hurts my feelings and pisses me off. Especially since I haven't written any checks."

Michele stared at him for a long time, said "Fine," got up and walked into the bedroom. Ben sat down on the couch and leafed through a magazine, trying to concentrate on slowing his breathing and calming his racing pulse. When he finally went to bed, Michele was already asleep.

Next morning they sat down to breakfast together as usual. Michele glanced at Ben and commented, "You should wear the other blue tie with that shirt; that one's kind of wimpy-looking."

Once again Ben had to struggle with his impulse to agree and change ties. He repeated his message from the previous night: "Michele, I really don't like it when you criticize my choice of clothes or anything else. It hurts my feelings and pisses me off."

Once again Michele stared at Ben a long while. Finally she said, "Bye," grabbed her bag, and rushed out the door. It wasn't his dream response, but silence was an improvement over criticism.

Special Considerations

Intervening effectively in your system isn't going to happen overnight. Some attempts at new responses won't change anything. Or they'll work some times but not others. Keep experimenting with new behaviors till you have several possible choices. Practice them over and over again until you become skilled. Sometimes you'll catch yourself falling into the old patterns—take time out to think about what's happening and try again. These are all simply challenges. If you're struggling to find a new behavior or a point in the pattern at which to intervene, consult with your partner. He or she is probably as much an expert on the problems of the relationship as you are. You can use your partner as a resource in making a design for change.

17

Expectations, Rules, and Acceptance

This chapter is about waking up from the dysfunctional dream of the ideal relationship. It explains how your dream of the ideal relationship was formed in childhood. It explores the way your assumptions about how people should act in the ideal relationship get codified into rules and how you expect your partner to share and obey these rules. This chapter also shows what happens when the dream becomes a nightmare—when you and your partner have conflicting expectations and therefore conflicting rules about such things as the division of labor, how to raise children, how to spend money, and so on. In this chapter you'll do exercises designed to help you identify the dysfunctional dream, examine the implications of your unspoken rules, and learn to make your expectations and needs known more directly and effectively.

When you are clear and reasonable about your expectations, you can more frequently get the caring, respect, and fairness you desire in your relationship. And when you don't get what you want, you can learn to accept your partner's occasional shortcomings.

History

Long-term relationships usually follow a progression from a honeymoon stage of infatuation and high expectations, through a period of disillusionment and mutual adaptation, to a calmer era of acceptance and mature love. Much of this chapter is based on a common sense analysis of this progression and does not evolve from an identifiable body of research or clinical practice.

However, many writers have noted that couples tend to enter into relationships with differing expectations. Cognitive therapists in particular have repeatedly pointed out that your dream of the ideal relationship creates expectations that you bring to your real relationship (Jacobson and Margolin 1979). These expectations become codified in unspoken rules, which McKay, Rogers and McKay (1989) call "conditional assumptions." Aaron Beck (1988) makes much of the symbolic meaning that gives unspoken rules their power.

The section on acceptance departs in two directions from the usual western therapist's determination to fix what doesn't work. First, it is based more on observation of successful couples than on clinical experience with couples in crisis. Second, the notion of acceptance in this chapter flows from the Buddhist idea of freeing yourself from the desire for change in the future so that you may embrace reality and achieve serenity in the present.

Theoretical Background

John Bradshaw and the "inner child" movement have in recent years refined our ideas of how family of origin issues persist into adulthood. When you were a child, you started dreaming your dream of the perfect family. If your childhood was marked by abuse and neglect, you probably rejected your parents' failings and dreamed about a very different relationship: one in which you were safe and nurtured, where your partner could be counted on to be present, to respect your boundaries, and to care for you.

If your childhood was marked by good, consistent care, you probably introjected more of your parents' values and modeled your ideal relationship on aspects of theirs. You dreamed of a more similar relationship—one in which you matched or surpassed your parents' successes.

Most people's ideal relationship is actually a combination of these twin influences: "When I was a kid I swore I'd never put my job first, ahead of my family the way my dad did." "I've always appreciated how my mom stood up for her kids, and I try to do the same."

Movies and your earliest dating experiences also influenced your vision of the perfect romance, as you idealized the tough guy, the suave gentleman, the alluring heroine, the self-less caregiver, and so on (Dattilio and Padesky 1990).

At first these expectations tend to be met. In the romantic stage of a new relationship, both of you are eager to please, willing to cater to each other's whims, and able to easily overlook "minor" annoyances and disagreements. Love smooths over the bumps and stones, and the honeymoon rolls along on a smooth highway for a while.

Some of your expectations continue to be met, and that is wonderful. Other of your expectations are not met, but you adjust and accept that life isn't always what you hope for. The trouble arrives when your partner doesn't meet some of your most cherished expectations and you can't adjust. When this happens, your expectations become *rules* that dictate how a relationship ought to be, how loving partners ought to behave.

The rules that flow from these frustrated expectations have some interesting characteristics.

1. They tend to be covert, unspoken rules, because you consider them to be self-evident and universal. "Good wives don't contradict their husbands in public." "A real man puts his family first."

2. The covert nature of the rules is often written into the rules themselves. "She should realize that I need time to unwind when I get home." "He should do what needs to be done around here without me having to ask." Your partner is supposed to read your mind. If you have to tell your partner about the rule, then compliance doesn't count.

3. If they were openly expressed, these rules would often be in the form of "should" statements. "He should help me when I'm tired." "She shouldn't yell so much at the kids." Psychoanalyst Karen Horney refers to such rules as the "Tyranny of the Shoulds."

4. These rules often have conditional or implied meanings. "If he cared, he would get home on time." "If she respected me, she wouldn't try to reorganize my desk." These implied meanings take on great symbolic value, way out of proportion to the actual rightness or wrongness of the behavior involved. Aaron Beck (1988) places strong emphasis on looking for the symbolic meaning behind big fights over what appear on the surface to be minor irritations.

5. These rules tend to be such "hot buttons" because they center around core self-esteem issues: personal worth, feeling cared for, and being treated fairly. Respect, caring, and fairness are the themes that show up repeatedly when people uncover their most important expectations in a relationship.

6. Covert rules are most likely to be found in these areas of your relationship: division of labor, finances, leisure time, in-laws and friends, children, and sex.

7. The most damaging situations occur when each partner has an opposing rule with opposite meanings. For example, Betty had a rule that her husband Jack "should always be here when I need him." Jack had a rule that Betty "shouldn't bother me at work." When the water heater died and Betty called Jack at work to come home and deal with the emergency, he got irritated and told her to just call a plumber herself. This precipitated a big fight that lasted two weeks. The underlying opposed meanings kept the fight hot. To Betty, Jack's not coming home meant that he didn't care about her; to Jack, Betty's interrupting him at work meant that she didn't respect the importance of his role as a breadwinner. These kinds of opposed meanings polarize a couple and entrench them deeper and deeper into their positions.

8. The rules take on the nature of absolute laws or moral imperatives. Breaking a rule is a sin or a felony and deserves punishment. So when one partner breaks a rule, the other partner metes out punishment by withdrawing, yelling, sulking, name calling, or some other aversive strategy. Since the offending partner usually has no idea of the rule that has been broken, the punishment seems unjustified, so he or she retaliates. A Kafkaesque cycle of retribution ensues in which both partners feel unjustly punished for unknown crimes. Both feel that they are right and the other is wrong.

The way out of the cycle is to rigorously examine the situations that chronically lead to trouble and identify your unspoken rules. Then you figure out the symbolic meaning of the rule for you. This allows you to restate the rule in the form of an assertive request that is appropriate to each situation. Issues of worth, caring, and fairness can be dealt with separately, in the open. The ultimate goal is to seek mutual acceptance of the reality of each other's traits and ability to meet your mutual expectations.

Time for Mastery

It only takes a few days to start identifying your rules. But it can take several months to develop the skill of separating self-esteem issues from rules and restating them as assertive requests. It takes time because your expectations of the ideal relationship are deeply rooted in your past and you have already spent a long time associating certain behaviors with caring, fairness, and respect.

Identifying Your Rules

The first step is to identify your unspoken rules that underlie areas of conflict in your relationship. In each of the areas listed down the left side of the form that follows, try to think of a recurring conflict or a common situation that bothers you. In the first column, write a brief description of what your partner does or doesn't do that bothers you. Then in the second column, write out the rule you think your partner should follow.

Identifying Your Rules		
	What my partner does or doesn't do that bothers me	*The rule I'd like my partner to follow*
Division of labor		
Finances		
Leisure time		
Relatives and friends		
Children		
Sex		

Here is an example of how Regina filled out her form. She is a speech therapist, married to Todd, an electrical engineer.

Identifying Your Rules

	What Todd does or doesn't do that bothers me	The rule I'd like Todd to follow
Division of labor	Doesn't take trash piles to dump, yard's a mess.	The man should take out the trash.
Finances	Buys and builds electronic kits for stereo and computer components that steal time from the family and end up costing more than the finished products at the discount store.	He should put his family first and stop wasting time and money.
Leisure time	When we bike together, he always rides way ahead because he can go faster.	He should stay close to make sure I'm all right.
Relatives and friends	Never wants to visit my mom, is rude to her.	He should love my family.
Children	Never helps Buddy with his homework.	He should show an interest in his son's school work, spend quality time together.
Sex	Goes weeks without even looking at me, then suddenly wants sex right this minute.	He should be romantic, it's up to him to set the mood.

Identifying the Meaning Behind Your Rules

Behind important rules there are symbolic meanings or implications that give the rules their power. To discover these meanings, ask yourself "What does it *mean* when my partner disobeys this rule?"

To uncover meanings, look for how each rule relates to these areas.

1. Fairness. Jackie did all the laundry and cleaned the house by herself. Her husband Harris took care of their cars and mowed the lawn. As Harris grew older, he lost his interest in cars and started putting off maintenance or paying to have car work done and the lawn mowed. Jackie became more and more irritated because the division of labor no longer seemed fair to her.

2. Caring. Eugene loved to have his back rubbed. His wife Carol often rubbed his back for a minute when he climbed into bed. When she didn't rub his back, he lay there in silent yearning, thinking, "She knows how much I love her back rubs. If she really cared for me, she'd do it without my asking." Sometimes he gave her back a few rubs to kind of give her the message. (Carol, by the way, sometimes refrained from rubbing Eugene's back, thinking, "Why should I rub his back? He hardly ever rubs mine. It's not fair.")

3. Respect. Craig signed up for an expensive time-share vacation arrangement without consulting his wife Mindy. She was furious because he "didn't respect" her mind. She felt he didn't think she was capable of helping make a complex decision. She resented being treated "like a little dog that will trot after its master wherever he wants to go."

In the space below, write out the rules you have identified and their meanings. Put the meanings in an "If _____, then _____ _____" format. For example, "If my partner respected me, then my partner would consult me about important decisions."

Rule	Meaning
_____	If _____ , then _____ .
_____	If _____ , then _____ .
_____	If _____ , then _____ .

Here is how Regina phrased the meanings of some of her rules for Todd:

Rule	Meaning
The husband should take out the trash.	

	If Todd was doing his fair share, then he would take out the trash.
He should love my family.	If he cared for me, then he would be gracious and interested in my mother.
He should be romantic, he has to set the mood.	If he respected me, then he wouldn't ignore me or take sex for granted.

Analyze Your Rules

You analyze your rules by asking five questions:

1. Is the rule secret?

2. What is the history behind the rule?

3. How does the rule serve your self-interest?

4. Does breaking the rule really mean what you think it means?

5. Does your partner have a corresponding, opposite rule?

You may not have an answer to all five questions for each rule you consider. But at least one of the questions will give you a new insight into how your rule works, how it came to be, and why it causes you so much trouble in your relationship.

Pick the rule that gives you the most trouble, and ask yourself:

1. Is the rule secret?   Have you communicated this rule to your partner? The legal system says that ignorance of the law is no excuse. But that doesn't apply to relationships. The laws of the land are published and public, so citizens are expected to be aware of them. The laws of relationships are all too often a secret known only to one of the partners. In relationships, ignorance of the rules *is* an excuse.

It's tempting to think, "I don't have to spell this rule out. It's self-evident. Everybody knows that you shouldn't contradict your spouse in public." Private rules remain unstated not only because they are based on unconscious assumptions, but because they are seen as obvious moral principles that everyone should know and act on. This self-evident quality becomes a part of the rule itself: "She should know I'm having a bad day without me having to tell her." "He should see that I need help and volunteer without me asking." "She should know how I feel."

2. What is the history behind the rule? Rules often get their power and meaning from your personal history. What old fear or anger or loss from your past is powering your current rule? For example, May hated it when her husband Sam went out in his dune buggy instead of helping her with house chores. She worried that if she had to do all the dirty work, she would become a drudge like her own mother. She might get so worn and unattractive that her husband would leave her just like her father left her and her mother.

Think about the situation you're in. How does it remind you of things that happened in your childhood? How does it remind you of past relationships? What happened then that you are afraid might happen now? What did you swear you would never let happen to you?

3. How does the rule serve your self-interest? Although rules usually seem to be self-evident matters of right and wrong, there is usually an advantage to you lurking behind the high moral principles. In other words, your rule is usually set up so that you benefit when your partner obeys the rule.

For example, Miranda's rule for Paul was that he should never correct her or make critical remarks about her when they were out in public. This seemed like basic human courtesy to her. It involved real issues of caring, respect, loyalty, and so on. But this rule also served her self-interest—it saved her from being called to account for any silly or outrageous behavior at parties. In therapy, Miranda admitted, "This rule about no public criticism allows me to drink and carry on with my friends, and if he complains, it's *his* fault."

4. Does breaking the rule really mean what you think it means? If your partner complains about your expenditures, does it really mean that she doesn't respect you? Look in other areas of your relationship to see if she shows respect. Perhaps she defers to your political judgment, considers you an expert on tools, respects your privacy when you're on the phone, or doesn't mess around with your things. This evidence that she actually does respect you suggests that her criticism of your expenditures must have another meaning.

Look for evidence that your partner does care for you, does respect you, does treat you fairly, does have loyalty to the relationship. If you find such evidence, then consider that your partner breaks your rules for some reason other than lack of respect, fairness, and so on.

5. Does your partner have a corresponding, opposite rule? If your partner is not breaking your rule out of pure meanness, why is the rule being broken? Consider the possibility that your partner has an unspoken rule that is in conflict with yours.

For example, Sabrina was worn out by her two-year-old and four-year-old by the end of the day when Harold got home. Her unspoken rule was that "Harold should offer to take over the kids when I'm tired." She wanted him to jump in and start playing games with the kids, get them into the bathtub, put them to bed, and so on. But Harold very rarely volunteered to help, which to Sabrina meant that he didn't care. Actually, Harold cared a lot, but he had his own unspoken rule: "Don't intrude on Sabrina's territory." He often noticed that Sabrina was getting crabby with the kids, but he had learned since the kids were babies that Sabrina considered herself the expert on child rearing and resented any interference with her methods. So he stifled any impulse to jump in and take over.

Sabrina and Harold were stuck because their mutually exclusive rules were hidden and unstated. The rules remained unclear for a long time because they each had related rules about asking for what you want. Sabrina thought, "I shouldn't have to ask for help—he should volunteer," while Harold thought, "I can't read minds—if she wants me to help, she should ask."

Rewrite Your Rule as an Assertive Request

When rules are restated as assertive requests and shared with your partner, real compromise and change become possible.

The formula is simple:

1. Put your rule in the form of a *request* for a specific behavior.

2. Explain the meaning behind your rule in the form of feeling statements, without blame or anger.

3. Include some of the history behind your rule, if appropriate.

Remember Todd and Regina? Here is how Regina rewrote her rule about quality family time.

> *Request:* I would like you to not work on electronic kits between dinner and Buddy's bedtime. I'd like you to spend that time helping me with the dishes and helping Buddy with his homework.

> *Feeling:* When you leave us right after dinner, I feel like you don't care, like we're not important. I also resent having to do what feels like more than my fair share.

> *History:* It reminds me of how I felt abandoned when my father spent hours away from home at ball games and car races.

Take a moment right now to rewrite your most important rule as an assertive request, with clear feeling and history statements.

Request:

Feeling:

History:

Acceptance

If you both practice identifying your rules, analyzing them, and then sharing them in the form of assertive requests, you have the greatest chance possible of getting what you want out of your relationship.

But nobody gets everything they want, every time.

When you don't get what you want, despite your best, persistent efforts over time, is it time to move out? Must you get a divorce? Maybe not. Maybe you need to cultivate acceptance.

Acceptance is not just giving up. It's a mature, appropriate response to many situations. There are three exercises that can increase your ability to accept what cannot be changed.

1. Good news, bad news. As the old jokes go, there is good news and bad news. For everything about your partner that you don't like, there is probably something that you do like. Nobody is all bad news. In the left column below, write down what your partner does or doesn't do that you really dislike. For each item in the left column, make an entry in the right column of something that your partner does or doesn't do that you like.

Bad News   *Good News*

When you do this exercise, you can list apples and oranges. That is, your good news items may not necessarily relate logically to your bad news items. For example, Marsha hated the way her partner Grace left dirty dishes lying around and liked Grace's mechanical ability. Messiness and mechanical ability are not logically related.

On the other hand, you can compare apples to apples and oranges to oranges. That is, you can look for the good news aspects of your bad news items. It's like looking for the silver lining in a cloud. For example, Marsha realized that Grace often left dirty dishes lying around because she was a very spontaneous, easily distracted person. And Marsha loved Grace's spontaneity and enthusiasm. Marsha realized that if Grace were neater and more organized, she might be less spontaneous and fun.

Another example of the silver lining effect is Pat and Nancy. Nancy's insistence on staying till the last minute of every party irritated and bored Pat, but her incessant sociability meant that he never had to concern himself about organizing their social calendar. Nancy did all the telephoning, planning, and arranging that Pat hated to do.

2. Compassion. Compassion means understanding your partner's faults and loving him or her anyway. The basis of compassion is the realization that people always do what seems best at the time. At any given time, you can be sure that your partner is doing his or her best to survive: seeking pleasure, avoiding pain or loss or danger, meeting needs, compensating for past painful experiences, and so on. Your partner's actions may not always be the most effective or reasonable solutions to the problem of survival, but that proves rather than denies your partner's essential humanity.

Pick one of the "bad news" items from the previous exercise—something that your partner consistently does or fails to do that bothers you and is not likely to change. Enter it in the space below, then answer each of the subsequent questions.

Behavior that bothers me:

How does this behavior help my partner seek pleasure?

How does this behavior help my partner avoid pain?

What need is my partner trying to meet?

How can I help my partner meet this need?

What past experience makes my partner likely to do this?

How can I minimize the effect of this behavior on me?

How could this behavior be worse?

Here is how Jeanie completed this exercise:

Behavior that bothers me:
Jerry tells dirty jokes at parties.

How does this behavior help my partner seek pleasure?
He likes to make people laugh.

How does this behavior help my partner avoid pain?
It keeps him from being bored.

What need is my partner trying to meet?
The need to be liked.

How can I help my partner meet this need?
Smile instead of frown when he tells a joke.

What past experience makes my partner likely to do this?
His Dad and brothers are the same way. It's their family style.

How can I minimize the effect of this behavior on me?
Go into another room when the jokes start.

How could this behavior be worse?
He could be chasing other women instead of just joking about sex.

3. Pick your battles. Fight for the biggies and let the little stuff slide. You may never have a house that is as neat and tidy as you want, but that's okay as long as the kids get a good education. Your partner may never fully participate in your hobby, but that's tolerable because your partner supports you in your career. You may never have deep intellectual discussions with your partner, but you can be satisfied in knowing that you can trust your partner to stand by you when the going gets tough.

Use the space below to identify the bottom line issues that you must be assured of to stay in a relationship. Think in terms of the biggies like trust, honesty, loyalty, and so on. In the other column list the little stuff that you can afford to let slide.

Biggies   *Little stuff*

Remember that the perfect, ideal relationship doesn't exist. It's a mirage, a dysfunctional dream that can blind you to the real work and real joy of a long-term relationship. Between every couple there are real and significant differences, some of which cannot be smoothed or fixed. Sometimes you must accept the differences as unreconcilable and simply overlook much of what you don't like about your partner.

When you stop concentrating on your partner's negative traits that can't be changed, you are freed to notice, enjoy, and build on the positive qualities that attracted you in the first place.

Bibliography

Alberti, Robert E., and Michael Emmons. 1986. *Your Perfect Right.* Fifth rev. ed. San Luis Obispo, California: Impact Publisher.

Azrin, N. H., B. J. Naster, and R. Jones. 1973. A rapid learning based procedure for marital counseling. *Behavior Research & Therapy,* 11, 365-382.

Bandler, R., J. Grinder, and V. Satir. 1976. *Changing With Families.* Palo Alto, Calif.: Science and Behavior Books.

Bateson, G. 1979. *Mind and Nature.* New York: E. P. Dutton. In Hoffman, (1981).

Beck, A. T. 1979. *Cognitive Therapy and the Emotional Disorders.* New York: New American Library.

Beck, Aaron T. 1988. *Love Is Never Enough.* New York: Harper & Row.

Beck, A. T., A. J. Rush, B. F. Shaw, and G. Emery. 1979. *Cognitive Therapy of Depression.* New York: Guilford Press.

Beck, A. T., and G. Emery. 1985. *Anxiety Disorders and Phobias: A Cognitive Perspective.* New York: Guilford Press.

Beck, A. T., A. Freeman, and Associates. 1990. *Cognitive Therapy of Personality Disorders.* New York: Guilford Press.

Bradshaw, John. 1988a. *Bradshaw On The Family.* Deerfield Beach, Florida: Health Communications.

——. 1988b. *Healing the Shame That Binds You.* Deerfield Beach, Florida: Health Communications.

——. 1990. *Homecoming.* New York: Bantam.

Bry, A. 1976. *How To Get Angry Without Feeling Guilty.* New York: New American Library.

Dattilio, Frank M., and Christine A. Padesky. 1990. *Cognitive Therapy with Couples.* Sarasota, Florida: Professional Resource Exchange.

Deschner, J. P. 1984. *The Hitting Habit: Anger Control for Battering Couples.* New York: Macmillan.

D'Zurilla, T. J. and M. R. Goldfried. 1971. "Problem Solving and Behavior Modification." *Journal of Abnormal Psychology* 78:107-26.

Ellis, A. 1962. *Reason and Emotion in Psychotherapy.* New York: Lyle Stuart.

——. 1975 *A New Guide to Rational Living.* North Hollywood, Calif.: Wilshire Books.

Fisher, Roger, and William Ury. 1981. *Getting to Yes: Negotiating Agreements Without Giving In.* Boston: Houghton Mifflin.

Freud, Anna. 1946. *Ego and the Mechanisms of Defense.* New York: International Universities Press.

Haley, Jay. 1976. *Problem Solving Therapy.* San Francisco: Jossey-Bass.

Harper, R. A. 1961. *A Guide to a Successful Marriage.* North Hollywood: Wilshire Books.

Hazaleus, S., and J. Deffenbacher. 1986. "Relaxation and Cognitive Treatments of Anger." *Journal of Consulting and Clinical Psychology* 54:222-226.

Hoffman, L. 1981. *Foundations of Family Therapy.* New York: Basic Books.

Jackson, D. D. 1957. In Hoffman 1981.

Jackson, D. D. 1965. In Walsh, N. (ed). 1987. *Normal Family Processes.* New York: The Guilford Press.

Jacobson, Neil S., and Gayla Margolin. 1979. *Marital Therapy.* New York: Brunner Mazel.

Jourard, Sidney M. 1971. *The Transparent Self.* Revised ed. New York: Van Nostrand Reinhold.

Kelly, G. A. 1955. *The Psychology of Personal Constructions.* New York: W. W. Norton.

Kernberg, Otto. 1976. *Object Relations Theory and Clinical Psychoanalysis.* New York: Jason Aronson.

Lange, Arthur, J., and Patricia Jakubowski. 1976. *Responsible Assertive Behavior.* Champaign, Illinois: Research Press.

McKay, Matthew, Martha Davis, and Patrick Fanning. 1983. *Messages: The Communication Skills Book.* Oakland, California: New Harbinger Publications.

McKay, Matthew, Peter D. Rogers, and Judith McKay. 1989. *When Anger Hurts: Quieting the Storm Within.* Oakland, California: New Harbinger Publications.

McKay, Matthew, and Patrick Fanning. 1991. *Prisoners of Belief.* Oakland, California: New Harbinger Publications.

Madel, S. F. 1957. In Brown, R. 1965. *Social Psychology.* New York: The Free Press.

Mahoney, M. 1974. *Cognitive Behavior Modification.* Cambridge, Massachusetts: Ballinger Publishing.

Masterson, J. 1981. *The Narcissistic and Borderline Disorders.* New York: Brunner/Mazel.

Meichenbaum, D. 1977. *Cognitive Behavior Modification.* New York: Plenum Press.

Meichenbaum, D. 1988. "Cognitive Behavior Modification with Adults." San Francisco: Workshop for Advances in Cognitive Therapies: Helping People Change.

Novaco, R. 1975. *Anger Control: The Development and Evaluation of an Experimental Treatment.* Mass.: C. D. Health.

Osborn, A. F. 1963. *Applied Imagination: Principles and Procedures of Creative Problem Solving.* Third ed. New York: Scribner's.

Patterson, G. R. 1982. *Coercive Family Process.* Eugene, Oregon: Castalia.

Rogers, Carl. 1951. *Client Centered Therapy.* New York: Houghton Mifflin.

Rubin, I. R. 1969. *The Angry Book.* New York: Collier Books.

Salter, Andrew. 1949. *Conditioned Reflex Therapy.* New York: Farrar, Straus and Giroux.

Smith, Manuel J. 1975. *When I Say No I Feel Guilty.* New York: Dial Press.

Sonkin, D. J., and M. Durphy. 1985. *Learning To Live Without Violence: A Handbook for Men.* San Francisco: Volcano Press.

Stuart, R. B. 1980. *Helping Couples Change: A Social Learning Approach to Marital Therapy.* New York: Guilford Press.

Stuart, R. B. 1969. "Operant-interpersonal Treatment for Marital Discord." *Journal of Consulting and Clinical Psychology* 33:675-682.

Sullivan, Harry Stack. 1953. *The Interpersonal Theory of Psychiatry.* New York: Norton.

Tavris, C. 1982. *Anger—the Misunderstood Emotion.* New York: Simon & Schuster.

Watzlawick, P., J. Weakland, and R. Fisch. 1974. *Change.* New York: W. W. Norton.

Wolpe, J. 1958. *Psychotherapy by Reciprocal Inhibition.* Stanford, California: Stanford University Press.

Wolpe, J., and A. A. Lazarus. 1966. *Behavior Therapy Techniques*. New York: Pergamon Press.

Wood, C. 1986. "The Hostile Heart." *Psychology Today* 20:9.

Young, J. 1990. *Cognitive Therapy for Personality Disorders*. Sarasota, Florida: Professional Resource Exchange.